Elements of Digital Transformation

Elements of Digital Transformation is a practitioner's guide to the digital transformation process. It is also a guide for managers in today's organizations that are accelerating digital transformation to modernize core technology capabilities and processes. The book discusses such key components of digital transformation as processes, principles and best practices, frameworks and proven methods. It also covers such novel concepts in digital transformation as the first time right framework, incident management transformation, digital factory, cloud migration, API-first approach and legacy modernization. Other highlights of the book include:

- A cloud migration framework along with a cloud migration methodology, rollout strategy and migration principles
- Principles and approaches for legacy modernization and process modernization
- Smart ticket management, smart problem management, proactive maintenance and ticket-avoidance architecture
- The novel digital factory approach to automate the software process Generative Artificial Intelligence use case for digital transformation

Detailed case studies, a sample digital transformation exercise and a consulting exercise for digital transformation provide readers with real-world digital transformation scenarios and best practices. The book also discusses DevOps, automation and agile delivery models that help in digital transformation.

Elements of Digital Transformation

Shailesh Kumar Shivakumar

CRC Press
Taylor & Francis Group
Boca Raton London New York

CRC Press is an imprint of the
Taylor & Francis Group, an **informa** business
AN AUERBACH BOOK

First edition published 2024
by CRC Press
2385 NW Executive Center Drive, Suite 320, Boca Raton FL 33431

and by CRC Press
4 Park Square, Milton Park, Abingdon, Oxon, OX14 4RN

CRC Press is an imprint of Taylor & Francis Group, LLC

© 2024 Shailesh Kumar Shivakumar

ISBN: 9781032488103 (hbk)
ISBN: 9781032482132 (pbk)
ISBN: 9781003390893 (ebk)

DOI: 10.1201/9781003390893

Typeset in Garamond
by Newgen Publishing UK

I would like to dedicate this book to:

*My parents, Shivakumara Setty V and Anasuya T M from whom
I loaned love and strength,
My wife, Chaitra Prabhudeva and my son Shishir from whom
I loaned time and support,
My in-laws Prabhudeva T M and Krishnaveni B from whom
I loaned help and courage.
And
To all my school teachers who bestowed lots of love and knowledge upon me.*

Contents

PART IV DIGITAL TRANSFORMATION OF PROCESS

PART V DIGITAL TRANSFORMATION OF OPERATIONS

PART VI DIGITAL TRANSFORMATION CASE STUDIES

Preface

Group Elements of Digital Transformation is a practitioner's guide for the digital transformation process. As modern enterprises are accelerating the digital transformation process to modernize their core, technology capabilities and processes, the book serves as a guide for the modern enterprises.

Key Differentiators of the Book

The book covers digital transformation from various dimensions and elaborates on the digital transformation process, methods, digital transformation framework, principles, best practices for digital transformation. As cloud migration is one of the main exercises of digital transformation journey, a dedicated book chapter defines cloud migration framework along with cloud migration methodology, cloud migration options, cloud migration stages, cloud migration roadmap and cloud migration principles. Readers will understand various legacy modernization strategies and modernization paths. The book also discuss the methods and best practices for user-experience transformation, digital platform performance optimization and modernization through microservices. The book also discusses the DevOps, automation and agile delivery models that help in digital transformation.

The book introduces novel concepts such as first time right framework and digital factory. The first time right framework provides the methods, tools and processes to cover all the Software Development Life Cycle phases to ensure the first time right delivery. The digital factory framework defines a standard set of processes and automation tools to develop high quality software reliably.

Readers will also understand various automation measures that can be used for efficiently managing the digital operations and optimizing the ticket management processes through smart ticket management, smart problem management, proactive maintenance, ticket-avoidance architecture and so on.

Readers also get to know the real-world digital transformation case studies with proven transformation methods and best practices. The book discusses the API-first design approach and principles for developing API-enabled businesses

The book also discusses the novel digital factory approach to automate the software process.

Book Organization

We have organized the book into six parts. The first part introduces the digital transformation concepts and proposes the digital transformation framework. The second part covers the migration and modernization by elaborating the legacy modernization and cloud migration methodologies. Next part deals with digital transformation of technology and discusses microservices, digital factory, first time right methodology, experience transformation, performance optimization and artificial intelligence (AI). We also discuss the recent digital transformation trends in AI and generative AI and its impact on the digital transformation. Fourth part discusses the digital transformation of the processes including the agile delivery and digital transformation of incident management. Fifth part discusses the digital transformation methods for optimizing the digital operations wherein we discuss DevSecOps-based automation and digital transformation of operations. The final part discusses the digital transformation case studies.

The book would be useful to CXOs, digital evangelists, IT architects and developers.

Acknowledgments

I would like to immensely thank my managers at Amazon—Ramanan Kannan for his committed mentorship and guidance, Vijay Srinivasan for his incredible care and support, Ekta Parashar for her wonderful encouragement and Anupam Mishra for outstanding leadership. My sincere thanks for supporting me wholeheartedly.

My sincere and heartfelt thanks to my colleagues and mentors at Amazon— Sudhanshu Ghai for his continuous and exceptional support, Satyajit Roy for his beautiful wishes and active support, Akshath Balachandra for his incredible mentorship and inspirational leadership, and Aamir Sait for his constant encouragement and for exceptional leadership. I am indebted by your help and support.

I would also like to sincerely thank my colleagues at Amazon—Gaurav Singh, Adhipranesh V, Kiran Viswanathan, Praveen Jayakumar, Deep Pai, Rajjat Kumar, Tapan Hoskeri, Reena M, Alok Singh, Abdul Waheed, Amit Kumar, Suresh Kaniappan, Lini Karanath, Sai Sriparasa, Binu Aiyappan, Prashant Singh, Pramod Kumar, Lalit Kumar, Ashish Patel, Ramanuj Vidyanta, Rahul Gupta, Abhishek Mandal, Ilica Chauhan, Samit Deb and Madhavi Watve. I am grateful for the continued support and guidance. My sincere thanks to Prof. P. V. Suresh, Director, SOCIS at IGNOU for his incredible encouragement and mentorship.

My special thanks to John Wyzalek, Stephanie Kiefer and Kara Roberts at Taylor & Francis/CRC Press for providing all necessary and timely support in terms of review, guidance and regular follow-ups.

About the Author

Shailesh Kumar Shivakumar, PhD, is working as solutions architect at Amazon Web Services India Private Limited (AWS India). with over 22 years of industry experience. His areas of expertise include cloud technologies, digital technologies, software engineering, Java Enterprise technologies and performance engineering.

He was involved in multiple large-scale and complex digital transformation programs for Fortune 500 clients. He has hands-on experience on a breadth of digital technologies and has worked on multiple domain areas such as retail, manufacturing, e-commerce, avionics etc. He was the chief architect of an online platform that won "Best Web Support Site" award among global competitors.

He is a published author of eight technical books published by world's top academic publishers such as Elsevier science, IEEE Press/Wiley, Chapman and Hall, Apress/Springer Books. He has authored 27 technical white papers, published 15+ research papers in peer-reviewed international journals and has received more than 240 citations and has written numerous technical blogs. He has authored 25 textbook chapters for undergraduate and postgraduate technical courses. He has delivered two talks at the Oracle JavaOne 2013 conference and has presented papers at multiple IEEE conferences.

He is a Guinness world record holder of participation for successfully developing a mobile application in a coding marathon. He has two granted US patents and six patent applications in the area of web and social technologies. Shailesh is listed in "Marquis who's who 2018" and he has been honored with the prestigious Albert Nelson Marquis Lifetime Achievement Award 2018 for his outstanding contribution to the profession and community. He is an India Book of Records record holder of "Maximum books on Digital Technologies published internationally by a single author" and is honored with Grandmaster certification from Asia Book of Records. Dr Shailesh is on the Editorial Review Board of International Journal of Project Management and Productivity Assessment (IJPMPA) and is a reviewer for International Journal of Cognitive Informatics and Natural Intelligence (IJCINI) and International Journal of Green Computing (IJGC). His books are cited in

Wikipedia articles and couple of Q&A interviews about his books are published in Infoq magazine.

He holds numerous professional certifications including, Deep Learning Nanodegree Program, AWS Certified Solutions Architect professional, AWS Certified Advanced Networking - Specialty, TOGAF 9 certification, Oracle Certified Master (OCM) Java Enterprise Edition 5, Sun-certified Java programmer, Sun-certified Business Component Developer, IBM-certified Solution Architect—Cloud computing, IBM Certified Solution Developer—IBM WebSphere Portal 6.1 and many others.

He holds a PhD in computer science along with two master degrees and has done executive management program from Indian Institute of Management, Calcutta. He lives in Bangalore, India and can be reached at Shailesh.shivakumar@gmail.com. and at https://drshailesh.in/

Abbreviations

ACID	Atomicity, consistency, isolation, and durability
AD	Active Directly
AI	Artificial Intelligence
AJAX	Asynchronous JavaScript and XML
API	Application Programming Interface
AWS	Amazon Web Services
BAU	Business as Usual
BCP	Business Continuity Process
CD	Continuous Deployment
CI	Continuous Integration
CORS	Cross Origin Resource Sharing
COTS	commercial-off-the-shelf
CPU	Central Processing Unit
CQRS	Command and Query Responsibility Segregation
CRM	Customer Relationship Management
CSS	Cascading Style Sheet
DR	Disaster Recovery
DRY	Don't Repeat Yourself
ERP	Enterprise Resource Planning
ESB	Enterprise Service Bus
FTP	File Transfer Protocol
FTR	First Time Right
HA	High Availability
HTML	Hyper Text Markup Language
HTTP	Hyper Text Transfer Protocol
IDE	Integrated Development Environment
IT	Information Technology
JNI	Java Native Interface
JS	JavaScript
JSON	JavaScript Object Notation
KYC	Know Your Customer
ML	Machine Learning
MVC	Model View Controller

MVP	Minimum Viable Product
NFR	Non-Functional Requirement
NLP	Natural Language Processing
OCR	Optical Character Recognition
OS	Operating System
OWASP	Open Web Application Security Project
POC	Proof of Concept
QA	Quality Assurance
RACI	responsible, accountable, consulted and informed
REST	Representational State Transfer
ROI	Return on Investment
RPA	Robotic Process Automation
RP	Recovery Point Objective
RT	Recovery Time Objective
RWD	Responsive Web Design
SDLC	Software Development Life Cycle
SIEM	Security Information and Event Management
SLA	Service Level Agreement
SMS	Simple Message Service
SMTP	Simple Mail Transfer Protocol
SOAP	Simple Object Access Protocol
SOC	Security Operations Center
SOP	Standard Operating Procedure
SQL	Structured Query Language
SRP	Single Responsibility Principle
TC	Total Cost of Ownership
UAT	User Acceptance Testing
UI	User Interface
WAF	Web Application Firewall
WOA	Web Oriented Architecture
XML	Extensible Markup Language

DIGITAL TRANSFORMATION INTRODUCTION

Chapter 1

An Introduction to Digital Transformation

Introduction

Digital transformation involves the application of digital technologies with the aim of a change of key business operations, products, processes, organizational structures and management concepts [10]. Digital transformation impacts enterprises, business models, processes, relationships and products to improve the performance and scale of the enterprise [11]. Digital transformation aims to enhance the value delivered to the customers through adaptation of new technologies and enhanced business processes. In the process, digital transformation also leverages the disruptive technologies to improve the organization efficiency, staff productivity and innovation speed. Digital transformation is all-pervasive across business functions and processes to redefine the way organization functions.

Digital transformation involves transforming the customer experience by understanding customers better and optimizing the touchpoints; improving the operational process through process digitization, worker enablement and performance management; and redefining the business model by digitizing the business and introducing new digital capabilities. Digital transformation transforms outdated legacy technologies and adopts new technologies. Digital transformation is an all-inclusive transformation of the processes, customer experience, operations, tools, technologies. Digital technologies enable the end-users by providing engaging user experience, employees through productivity improvement tools and the business through self-service features and analytics. Digital transformation synchronizes the IT strategy with the business strategy [47]. Many businesses transform their physical products into digital offerings and products as part of digital transformation [48].

Digital transformation is seldom a onetime activity. Digital transformation is an ongoing process where we continuously and iteratively refine the existing business processes, tools, products to improve the customer value and achieve the strategic objective.

A Gartner survey reveals that 42% of CEOs say that digital transformation is at the core of their business [1]. The main drivers of digital transformation are profitability, customer satisfaction, and faster time to market [2]. Organizations aim to redefine the customer experience, improve the revenues, reduce costs and improve the differentiation [2]. In the post pandemic era, 88% of business leaders are looking for a scalable and agile IT environment [3]. The main advantages of digital transformation are renewed customer experience, data-backed decision-making, easier collaboration and better market penetration [4]. Digital transformation has impacted infrastructure (from data center to hybrid cloud), applications (from monolith to microservices) and processes (from waterfall to DevOps) [5].

Definitions

As digital transformation covers a broad set of technologies and has a wide variety of impact, let us look at some of the definitions of digital transformation.

Digital transformation is the "use of new digital technologies, such as social media, mobile, analytics or embedded devices, in order to enable major business improvements like enhancing customer experience, streamlining operations or creating new business models" [23].

Digital transformation is "the application of technology to build new business models, processes, software and systems that result in more profitable revenue, greater competitive advantage, and higher efficiency" [21].

"Digital transformation is the investment in people and technology to drive a business that is prepared to grow, adapt, scale, and change into the foreseeable future" [41].

"As such, the Digital Transformation goes beyond merely digitizing resources and results in value and revenues being created from digital assets" [24]. Digital transformation is a combination of both procedures of digitization and digital innovation with an intention of improving existing products with advanced abilities [46].

Digital transformation is "the realignment of, or new investment in, technology and business models to more effectively engage digital customers at every touch point in the customer experience lifecycle" [25].

"Digital Transformation is now commonly interpreted as such usage of Information and Communication Technology, when not trivial automation is performed, but fundamentally new capabilities are created in business, public government, and in people's and society life" [26].

"Digital Transformation is defined as the use of technology to radically improve performance or reach of enterprises" [27].

"Digital Transformation is the changes that digital technology causes or influences in all aspects of human life" [28].

Broadly the definitions of digital transformation can be categorized into three main categories—*technological, social and organizational* [22]. Technological aspects include the disruptive technologies, digital frameworks and platforms; social aspects include the influence of the digital transformation on the overall society; and organizational aspects include the impact on people, culture, organizational processes and governance.

Drivers for Digital Transformation

Changing business environment, changing consumer expectations, accelerated connectivity of users and devices, competitive pressure and ambition for global presence are all forcing enterprises to redefine the business process through digital transformation.

The primary digital changes that organizations embark on using digital transformation can be categorized into three categories [13]; *substitution* wherein the existing tools or processes are replaced by digital technologies, *extension* wherein the existing processes or tools are improved by digital technology and *transformation* wherein the digital technologies transform the existing processes and tools. Rising customer expectations, speed of innovation, business transformation, unlocking data silos, intelligent work processes, cost optimization and increasing efficiency are also the drivers behind digital transformation [12].

The goals of digital transformation can be classified into two main categories; *social* and *economic* [16]. The social goals include fostering more innovative and collaboration culture in the organization, enabling upskilling and learning, ensuring efficient governance and quality of service, strengthening data protection, transparency, autonomy and trust and improving accessibility. The economic goals include implementing new business models, improving income generation and productivity improvement and improving regulatory and technical standards.

The core drivers for digital transformation is depicted in Figure 1.1.

The main driver for organizations is to implement their **business strategy**. We can assess the digital maturity of the organization through attributes such as clear overall strategy, transformation strategy, availability of skills, leaders having skills and management support for digital technology use [19]. The business strategy includes vision, management and leadership [12]. The digital leaders like to leverage the appropriate digital technologies to implement their long-term vision. Digital leaders need to commit to the digital transformation program and align the organization structure to implement the vision. Business models should be reinvented

01 Implement Business Strategy
- Enable long-term vision
- Align organization structure
- Business Process Transformation
- Improved decision making process

Drivers for Digital Transformation

02 Customer Centricity
- Customer behavioral analytics
- Self service tools enablement
- Relevant recommendations
- Prediction of customer needs
- Increased customer engagement

03 Technology & process Infrastructure Alignment
- Business Process Management
- Alignment of technical resources
- Digitization of products & services
- Data protection

04 Culture Alignment
- Reskilling
- Innovation focused
- Agile Delivery
- Collaboration focused

05 Improved Efficiency
- Optimal total cost of ownership
- Automation
- Faster access to relevant information

Figure 1.1   Drivers for Digital transformation.

and aligned to the changing market dynamics using digital technologies. Improved decision-making is required for implementing the digital strategy in the digital transformation journeys [19]. As part of their business strategy, few organizations want to expand their geographical footprint or explore newer markets that drive them to embark on digital transformation journey [40] and few organizations want to experiment with the emerging technologies for their use cases and avoid being disrupted [40].

Modern organizations strive on **customer centricity**. Most organizations take the digital transformation journey to improve the customer experience and customer engagement [19]. Customer-centric approach includes monitoring of customers' experiences, prediction of their needs [12] and improved customer engagement. Organizations like to leverage digital technologies to monitor customer behavior and thereby enable self-service tools and relevant product recommendations. Analytics and machine learning technologies come handy in predicting customer needs and anticipating customer behavior. Organizations like to increase the customer engagement through digitization.

The third main motivator for organizations to take up digital transformation is **Information and Communication Technology (ICT) and process infrastructure alignment**. ICT includes managing the business process changes [12] and optimizing the agility of the infrastructure. In the process, organizations aim to digitize their products and services and launch new offerings based on digitization. Organizations also aim to align the technical resources as part of the digital transformation program. Rapid advancements in technology and innovations, such as Artificial Intelligence (AI) and Industry 4.0, are also a key driver for embracing the digital transformation programs [43].

Culture alignment is a crucial aspect of the digital transformation process. Organizations need to align their culture to embrace change, take risks, fail faster and innovate faster. Talent, capability and capacity strengthening (reskilling), innovation culture and organizational commitment [12] are some of the key elements in this culture alignment. Agility and collaboration are the cornerstones of a truly digital mature organization. Digital leaders also need to be prepared to handle the resistance to change.

Increased efficiency is an ambitious goal that includes automation and quick access to relevant information [19]. Digital leaders aim to improve the overall productivity of the employees and end-users by providing faster access to relevant information. Quicker time to market, reduced cost, increased automation and improved processes are part of efficiency enhancement drivers.

Digital Transformation Roadblocks

The main roadblocks for achieving the digital maturity required for the digital transformation are lack of strategy, having too many priorities, insufficient technology skills and security concerns [19].

Dimensions of Digital Transformation

The dimensions of digital transformation cover the focus areas of the digital transformation. The paper [49] identifies six dimensions of digital transformation including business model (revenue streams), structure (organization structure), people (employees, partners), processes (business processes), offerings (products and services) and engagement model (how the organization engages employees, customers and partners). User experience, value proposition, digital evolution scanning, skills and improvisation are identified as key dimensions [50]. In another classification [51], the key dimensions of digital transformation are use of technology, changes in value creation, structural changes and financial dimension. The paper [52] identifies the key dimensions of digital transformation as marketing and sales (including offering and channels), engagement (engaging customers, partners and workforce), operations (processes and IT capability), organization (including customers, partners, workforce) and digital agility [52].

In summary, the key dimensions of digital transformation are technology, end-user engagement, business model and revenue streams, user experience, products and service offerings, business processes and governance.

Pillars of Digital Transformation

We have detailed the core motivations for digital transformation in Figure 1.1. The core drivers help us to define the pillars of digital transformation. To implement

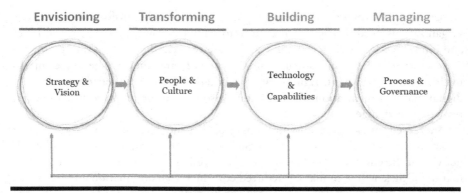

Figure 1.2   Pillars of Digital transformation.

business strategy, we need a *strong vision*; to ensure the customer centricity and culture alignment we need to transform the *people and culture* of the organization; for technology and process infrastructure alignment we need to enhance the *digital technology capabilities* and to improve efficiency we need robust *process and governance* practices.

We now define the main pillars of digital transformation as strategy and vision, people and culture, technology and capabilities and process and governance. We have depicted the main pillars of the digital transformation in Figure 1.2.

The starting stage of the digital transformation journey is to define the overall strategy and vision of the program. Digital leaders need to sponsor the investment needed for the program, commit to the digital transformation journey and motivate the employees. The "people and culture" pillar is all about enabling the employees and aligning the organization culture to make them ready for the transformation. Leaders need to lead the way by achieving the digital fluency and enabling the training and mentoring programs for the employees. Innovation and collaboration need to be integrated into the overall organization culture. As part of technology and capabilities, the organization needs to embrace and experiment the disruptive technologies and use agile delivery models. The digital technologies disrupt the status quo by providing early value delivery, providing applications in new domains or using unpredicted combination of technologies [16]. Leaders and employees need to master the digital services and understand the capabilities of digital technologies to build the digital platforms and refine the business models. Data, analytics and innovation are essential to digital transformation technology capabilities [17]. The process and governance pillar include change management process and efficient governance [14]. The study [44] identifies customer and ecosystem as additional dimensions of digital transformation, in our model, customer is part of the "strategy and vision" pillar and ecosystem is covered in the "process and governance" pillar.

In the subsequent sections we shall have a closer look at each of these pillars.

Strategy and Vision

Transformation of digital business strategy is required to adopt the digital technologies in formulation and execution [9]. Digital transformation strategy cuts across organization's operational strategy (such as products, markets) and functional strategy (such as sales, marketing) [15]. Finalizing the business strategy always precedes selecting the digital technologies [21]. The integration of strategy, culture and leadership are required to harness the full potential of digital transformation. Customer and partner focus, delegation, boldness and risk-taking attitude, bias for action and focus on collaboration are often included into the strategy [38]. The business model and revenue streams, user experience, products and service offerings dimensions and end-user engagement are covered in this pillar.

The key elements of digital transformation strategy and vision is depicted in Figure 1.3.

The digital transformation strategy and vision elements can be broadly classified into process- and culture-related and technology-related categories. Digital transformation is mainly happening across areas such as customer experience, processes, disruptive technologies and value chain impact [10] [15] [20] [21]. Finance also play a major role in accelerating the digital transformation process. Financial impact results in financial pressure for the organization to embark the digital transformation journey. Higher financial pressure expedites the digital transformation programs. Once we decide the business strategy, we need to decide the specific objectives, goals and action plan [30] based on the chosen strategy.

Process and Governance Changes

Process changes are essential part of the digital transformation strategy. As part of the process changes, we relook at the existing processes and reimagine the processes to augment the digital opportunities. We can transform the operational process through process digitization and automation. Another dimension of the operational process transformation is to enable employees through collaboration tools and productivity improvement tools. Performance management tools, such as analytics, reports and collaboration tools, play a vital role in improving the operational process. Transforming business models require globalizing the businesses and digitization of business processes and innovating new business models. Technology modernization, technical debt reduction, technology standardization and flexible integration solutions are included in process changes.

While defining the business strategy, we should relook at the existing **business models**. We can explore the digitization touchpoints for the existing business processes. Automation is one of the key levers for productivity improvement and cost optimization. Structured activities that are repetitive in nature are ideal candidates for automation. Digital leaders can explore tools such as Robotic Process Automation (RPA) for automation.

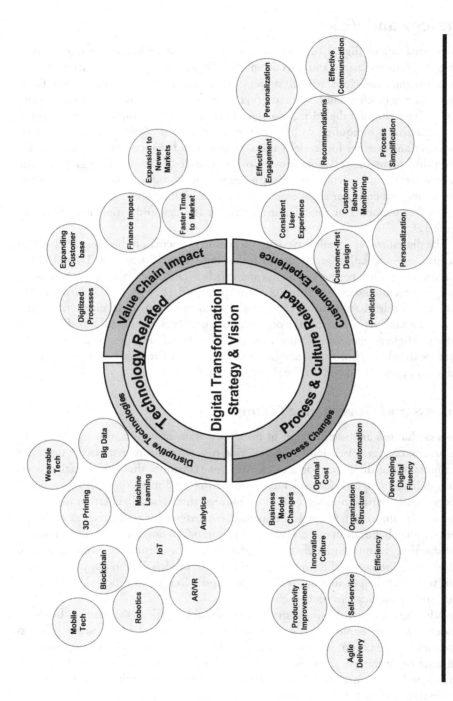

Figure 1.3 Digital transformation strategy and vision.

The **organization structure** should be realigned to reflect the changed business models. Organization restructuring includes creating separate functions or spinning up new subsidiaries to support the digital enhancements. Digital leaders should define the roles and responsibilities for the new organizations and provide the required financial support.

Productivity improvement is at the heart of the transformation journey. Simplified processes, self-service, automation, more efficient tools and agile philosophy are some of the key levers in achieving the productivity improvement. Digital leaders should map the process improvements and tools required for the productivity improvement.

Achieving **digital fluency** across the organization is a key enabler for the digital transformation. The organizations that have great amount of digital fluency among its digital leaders is able to achieve a high degree of success in the digital transformation programs [19]. The digital leaders should also incorporate the digital fluency enablement as part of the overall strategy. Enablement programs, such as trainings, mentoring sessions, hackathons, certifications and enablement workshops, come handy in creating the digital fluency among the employees.

Continuous cost optimization is one of the key drivers of digital transformation. Digital leaders should evaluate various cost optimization measures and incorporate those cost optimization measures in the digital transformation strategy. To optimize infrastructure cost, cloud migration is one of the preferred options. To reduce the license costs, organizations can consider using open-source platforms such as MySQL or PostegreSQL Database, Kubernetes and Docker and others. Serverless functions is an emerging paradigm that allows developers to focus mainly on business logic while the infrastructure is fully managed by the cloud platforms. Serverless functions are billed per usage leading to optimal cost.

The culture of **innovation** is required to achieve the success of digital transformation engagement. The development team has to experiment more often and should employ the best practices to improve the overall efficiency of the process. The leaders should foster a culture of innovation through initiatives such as hackathons, idea hub (to invite and reward the ideas) and encourage the thought leadership initiatives (such as patents, blogs, webinars, workshops etc.).

Agile delivery is the key part of digital transformation [7]. Agile delivery involves development of minimum viable product (MVP) with iterative releases and incorporating the user feedback in subsequent iterations. Agile releases happen through 2-week sprints. To develop a sound digital transformation strategy, we need to firstly develop the digital competence among the team and then increase the flexibility of IT infrastructure that results in new digital products and services and digitally enhanced products and services [31]. To develop new digital products and services we need to incubate the idea into a concept and build a MVP. To digitize existing products and services we need to reimagine the product from the customer viewpoint and test the MVP. We can then iteratively refine the product based on customer feedback [31]. The strategy for digital transformation mainly involves in tightly integrating data into business processes and decision-making.

Customer Experience

To improve the **customer experience**, organizations adopt customer centricity and productivity-based goals, vision for growth in customer experience and efficiency and focus on transformation [19]. The digital transformation of customer experience includes understanding customer behavior through analytics and effective customer engagement through personalized messaging and process simplification. Analytics plays key role in recommendation and personalization. By monitoring the customer's usage patterns and transactions, analytics tools can predict the customer behavior using which the platform can provide relevant recommendations, promotions and offers.

We often use design thinking to implement the **customer-first design**. As part of design thinking process, we seek to understand the current challenges faced by customer and design the interfaces that best satisfies the customer needs. The design should provide the contextual information to the customer and customer should be able to get the relevant information quickly. We value customer feedback and optimize the user interfaces for smoother customer journey. We ensure that a customer advocate is present in all key decisions to talk on behalf of customer.

Process simplification also enhances the overall customer experience. As part of process simplification, we can introduce self-service tools and applications, automation, reduced process steps, self-approvals, search-driven knowledge base and such.

Customer experience can be enhanced by optimizing the customer touchpoints through multi-channel engagement and through effective communication [21]. The digital leaders should understand the usage patterns of the company's digital platform and based on the usage they should enable easy access for customers. Introduction of mobile apps and wearable apps are some of the ways to enhance the reach of the digital platform and engage the customers more actively.

The digital transformation strategy should focus on enhancing the **customer engagement and effective communication**. Organizations can enhance customer engagement through touchpoint optimization, customer journey optimization and providing high quality of service (optimal performance, high availability).

Disruptive Technologies

The use of technologies indicates the organization's willingness to leverage new technologies to achieve its business goals. Some of the key transformation strategies that can be used for research opportunities are understanding data value and data analytics, adopting disruptive business models and integrating culture, technologies and processes [17].

Organizations should be committing to experimenting on disruptive technologies such as cloud computing, mobile technologies, analytics, IoT, robotics etc. We discuss the role of the disruptive technologies in a separate section.

Value Chain Impact

Usage of new technologies impact "value creation" and the value chain of the organization that results in higher value such as newer monetization opportunities, expansion of business, new streams of revenue and increased customer base.

Digital leaders need to assess the impact on end-to-end value chain of the organization. For instance, we can get real-time updates of product in transit using IoT and Blockchain technologies. In e-commerce industry we can leverage digital technologies to engage customers actively and thereby winning new customers with this unique value proposition. Similarly, in manufacturing we can efficiently track and route the products to improve the delivery times.

We have depicted the disruption to the value chain of various industries caused by digital transformation [32] in Table 1.1.

Digital technologies have also impacted various stages of the manufacturing supply chain including product design and innovation, supply chain management and marketing sales [33]. The fourth industrial evolution (often referred to as "Industry 4.0") is mainly enabled by digital technologies such as cloud computing, robotics, mobile devices, IoT, Augmented Reality/Virtual Reality (AR/VR), Big Data, Analytics, cybersecurity and such [33].

Digital technologies are redefining the matching of supply and demand [34]. Digital technologies are at the forefront in reducing the cost structure through automation, virtualization on the supply end and enriching the product and service value to the customers on the demand end. In the process, digital technologies have found new and cheaper ways to connect supply and demand creating newer markets [34]. Digital technologies create hyper-scale platforms that can quickly onboard new capabilities and customers.

People and Culture

People and organization culture are quintessential part of the success of digital transformation. To fully realize the benefits of digital transformation, transformation of organization structure, processes and culture are required [39]. Many of the organization's internal factors, such as complacency, inflexible culture and lack of agility [40], impact the success of digital transformation programs. Hence it is crucial for organization to define a culture that is compatible with the needs for digital transformation. The digital transformation dimension related to skill transformation is covered in this pillar.

We have depicted the key attributes of people and culture in Figure 1.4.

Table 1.1 Impact of Digital Transformation across Value Chain

Industry	Value Chain Processes that Get Impacted	Digital Technologies Causing the Impact
Marketing industry	Better product research, improving pricing strategy, improving advertising and marketing campaigns	Big Data and video platforms
Product development	Improvised product pricing and manufacturing the products, demand forecasting	IoT, Blockchain and Big Data technologies
Sales	Improving customer acquisition, improving the after-sales support	Cloud technologies, chatbot, mobile apps
Underwriting process	Automated risk assessment, application processing, document processing	IoT, Blockchain, Artificial intelligence (AI), cloud computing technologies
Claims management process	Fraud detection and claim settlement	AI and machine learning
Information technology	Hardware procurement, resource allocation, support, application development	AI, IoT, conversational assistants
Manufacturing	Supply chain automation, employee training, equipment monitoring, proactive maintenance	Robotics, AI, AR/VR, IoT

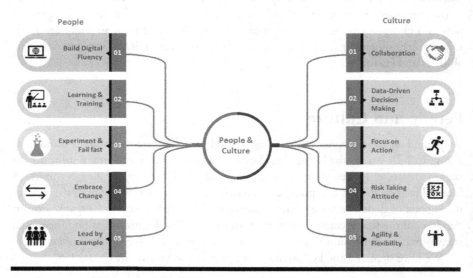

Figure 1.4 Key attributes of People and culture.

Digital Transformation Is More about People

Majority of the digital transformation is more about people and not technology [36] [40]. Organizations can adopt people-first policy to enable employees to embrace the digital transformation initiatives [36]. Organizations should invest in training, upskilling and coaching people to realize the full benefits of digital transformation. Organizations should also pick up the right talent who is curious to learn and match the skills to the organization's demand. The organization's leadership team should drive the change from the top; digital leaders should set the example by achieving the digital fluency. Employees are more likely to trust the digital strategy if the top leadership team has digital fluency [36].

The people involved in the digital transformation need to have continuous learning and growth mindset to succeed in the transformation journey. The people should be self-motivated and should have openness to change.

To achieve success in digital transformation initiatives, the people should be willing to share knowledge to achieve overall success. They must be willing to use collaboration tools and work as "one team" to achieve the goals.

Modern organizations need to be agile to respond quickly to market dynamics; they need to innovate faster to gain competitive edge. In order to innovate faster the organizations should adopt the agile culture and fail fast philosophy. The employees should be willing to take risks, experiment often, discard the plan that is not working and find the most appropriate business model.

Digital evangelists who pioneer the digital technology adoption in the organization should be in the forefront of the digital transformation implementation. Digital evangelists should lead the crucial parts of the program, setup center of excellence (CoE) practices, advocate, mentor and help the team achieve its goals.

The digital leaders who drive the digital transformation engagement should possess key skills such as transformative vision, forward-looking perspective, understanding of technology and championing the changes [40].

Culture

Culture defines the shared value system of the organization and motivates employees to achieve their excellence. Culture instills the behavioral patterns and drives the employees to reach the organization goals. A well-defined organization culture defines the code of conduct to achieve the long-term strategy. Culture enables organizations to continue their core values and motivate employees to participate with least resistance [35]. The organizations that focused on culture for digital transformation reported five times higher performance than those organizations that neglected culture [38].

The culture of the digital mature organizations (the organizations that effectively use technology for business transformation) includes digital fluency among the leaders and employees, collaborative spirit among the employees and management

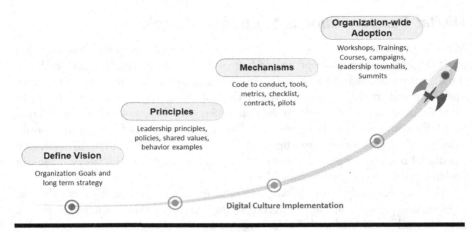

Figure 1.5 Digital culture implementation across the organization.

support for innovation [19]. Innovation is a creative destruction [37] and hence employees need to have high learnability to adopt and succeed in the culture of innovation.

The digital culture helps people to deliver the results faster [38] due to the flatter hierarchies and well-defined code of conduct. Employees can make quick decisions and be more agile to respond to dynamic scenarios. The digital culture also helps to attract and retain the talent [38].

We have depicted various steps for implementing the culture for the organization in Figure 1.5.

Digital leaders should articulate the long-term vision and strategic goals of the organization. Leaders should define the DNA and the key culture pillars of the organization. The employees should have clear understanding of the strategic and tactical goals of their organization. As a next step, the digital leaders need to define the principles that are aligned with the organization goals. Leaders should unambiguously define the principles and translate the organization goals to the key principles that help the employees navigate real-world scenarios. For instance, digital leaders can articulate the organization principles on agility, hiring and talent development, collaboration and innovation. Detailed policies that cover all the areas of the organization, such as information security, promotion, career development, performance management, job rotation and such, need to be detailed out with examples. This helps employees to align with the overall vision and practice the shared values of the organization. As a next step we should also define implementation mechanisms to implement the principles. This includes a structured code of conduct steps, collaboration tools, binding contracts for critical principles, job guides and such. Implementation mechanism provide tools to enforce and ensure that defined policies and principles are implemented. In order to scale and adopt the digital culture across the organization, the leadership team should carry out campaigns, workshops, leadership town halls (an event where senior organization leaders interact with employees), employee connects and trainings to create awareness and drive the adoption.

If the organizations are driving big change, it is recommended to test the change through pilot runs and understand the impact of the change. The learnings from the pilot can be used to scale the change across the entire organization.

Key Culture Elements for Digital Transformation

For organizations that embark on digital transformation adopting disruptive technologies few crucial cultural elements significantly impact the outcome of the digital transformation success. We have discussed some of the crucial cultural elements here.

Organizations should be open to change, embrace new ideas, innovate and experiment [39]. Organizations should be willing to test and adopt the changes. The second significant culture element is the customer centricity wherein the organizations should keep the customer at the forefront while designing and delivering their products and services. Focus on innovation is another key cultural element that helps organizations to deliver new products and services and grow. Agility is the essential culture element for all digital transformation engagements. Organizations should be agile and flexible in their structure and processes. Learnability focuses on continuously upskilling that helps in the long-term acquisition of skills. Trust, entrepreneurship, tolerance towards failure, risk affinity, collaboration and participation are other crucial cultural elements [39]. Passion for work, data-driven decision-making and distributed leadership structure are some of the other elements of the digital transformation [40].

Digital Transformation Technologies and Capabilities

Various technologies are disrupting the way enterprises deliver value to their customers. The key among them are cloud platform (that provides on-demand delivery of IT resources over the Internet with a pay-as-you-go model), wearable technologies (that include smart watches and fitbits to provide real-time health monitoring), Internet of Things (IoT) (that connect devices to Internet), Big Data (the set of technologies to manage huge volume of data), autonomous cars (cars with self-driving technology), robotics (managing robots), game technologies, AR/VR (technology to augment the real world with a digital world), Blockchain (managing transactions in a shared ledger) and 3D printing (creating a physical object from the model). Mobile technologies, cloud computing technologies, data and analytics, social media and collaborative technologies are widely used by digital mature organizations [19]. The technology transformation dimension is covered in this pillar.

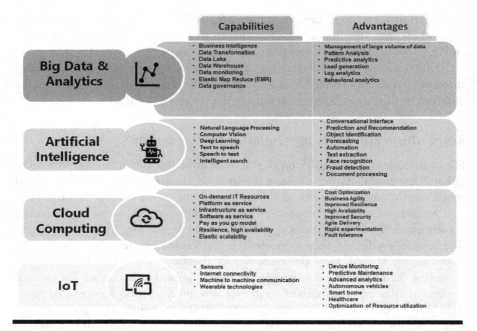

Figure 1.6   Core digital technologies.

Let us look at the core disruptive digital technologies of the digital transformation as depicted in Figure 1.6.

Cloud Computing

Cloud computing provides IT resources such as computing devices, storage devices, databases and other core services over the Internet. With a metered billing, organizations can focus on innovation while cloud platforms handle the infrastructure-related heavy lifting. Cloud computing provides freedom to innovate faster, experiment quickly and fail faster while optimizing the cost. Organizations can be more agile and productive using cloud computing [21].

Internet of Things

IoT is a network of connected devices that provides integration of the physical world into the digital space [21]. IoT technologies connect vehicles, buildings, factories through sensors and enable the devices to be monitored and controlled. IoT-enabled devices connect to the Internet and can exchange data and communicate with other devices. IoT is used for many use cases such as autonomous vehicles, equipment monitoring, real-time decision-making, process optimization and such.

Mobile Technologies

Mobile technologies, such as mobile apps, mobile devices and 5G networking, allow users to get and use information easily. Mobile devices, such as smart phone and tablets, are the most popular gateways for users to access information. Organizations can improve the productivity of users and enhance their reach through mobile technologies.

Big Data and Analytics

Big Data and Analytics technologies are designed to handle massive amount of data such as IoT sensor data, social media posts, real-time streaming data and such. Big Data technologies handle structured, semi-structured and unstructured data of massive volumes. Data lakes, cloud databases, data warehouse systems and business intelligence systems handle petabytes of data through parallel processing and flexible schemas. Analytics technologies provide real-time actionable insights based on the analysis of huge volumes of data that organizations can use to provide relevant recommendations. Big Data and analytics handle many business-critical use cases such as customer 360-degree view, fraud prediction, business intelligent reporting, churn prediction and such.

Artificial Intelligence

AI technologies can help train the machines based on the past data that can be used for variety of use cases such as trend analysis, product recommendation, forecasting, risk prediction, automation and such. Deep learning models power today's complex use cases such as real-time fraud detection, churn prediction, text to speech, speech to text, autonomous navigation and such. AI technologies are the key enablers of automation and efficiency improvement at an organization.

Augmented Reality/Mixed Reality (MR)

AR technologies overlays the physical world with virtual objects and provide enriching experience for the user. AR/MR users can get highly interactive experience of the real world. AR/MR technologies are used in virtual training, gaming, learning and entertainment industries.

Blockchain

Blockchain provides decentralized ledger of immutable records. Blockchain is serving many use cases such as cryptocurrencies, digital currencies, supply chain contracts etc.

Conversational Interfaces

Conversational interfaces, social media, video calling platform are other disruptive digital technologies that are impacting the social life of consumers [32].

Organizations can unlock values by weaving the key digital technologies such as cloud with AI and analytics [45].

We deep dive on digital transformation of technology in part 3.

Processes and Governance

Agile methods (that provide MVP on continuous and iterative basis) and design thinking (human-centric approach that uses technology, design and business factors in identifying and solving problems) support digital transformation [6]. In addition to the normal agile, we also adopt Scaled Agile Framework (SAFe) (Scaled Agile 2017) and Large-Scale Scrum (LeSS) in digital transformation projects [42]. The business processes and governance dimension is covered in this pillar.

Digital Transformation Process

Before we embark on the digital transformation journey, we need to define the overall program vision and strategy. Laying the groundwork for digital transformation process is a multidisciplinary approach involving participation of various teams with niche skill set.

The digital transformation process provides a broad framework covering all steps of the digital transformation program. The process acts as a blueprint to implement the overall strategy using digital transformation.

We have depicted the key steps of the digital transformation process in Figure 1.7.

Digital transformation process starts with the **planning** phase. We define the main roles and responsibilities of the key personnel and subject matter experts (SME) during this phase. We also plan various programs and initiatives that are required for the entire digital transformation and the main people responsible for it. We define the success metrics, key performance indicators (KPIs) and goals that needs to be tracked across the entire program. We lay out the digital transformation roadmap that defines the phases and sprints of the program. Digital leaders communicate the overall vision of the program to the organization and articulate the importance and support for the program. During this phase we also define the key business processes (such as change management process and incident management process) that align with the digital transformation. Ecosystems and marketplaces are essential components of modern digital platforms. We onboard and co-innovate with the partners, developers, academics, researchers, governments and other interested communities. We allow the communities to launch products and services in the marketplace.

The next phase is **building** where we build the products and services in iterations. We follow the agile philosophy wherein we are biased towards the action by building

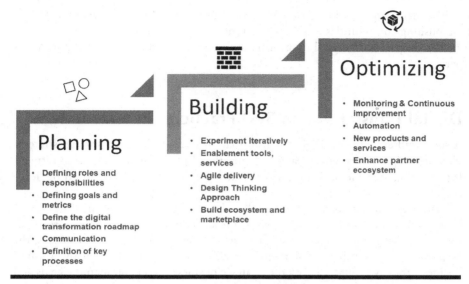

Figure 1.7   Digital transformation process steps.

the MVP. Modern digital programs adopt design thinking approach for designing the products and services. We iteratively improve the product based on the feedback and consumer expectations. The organizations should provide the teams with required tools and services.

Optimization is a continuous ongoing process wherein we continuously monitor the success metrics. We continuously improve the business process and automate the processes to improve efficiencies. We leverage the digital technologies to continuously digitize existing products and services and to deliver new digital products and services. We improve the ecosystem of interested communities.

Governance in Digital Transformation

Though agile methodologies are widely adopted in digital transformation programs, in the absence of proper governance large-scale digital transformation programs fail. The most common challenges we face in the large-scale agile implementations are misunderstanding of agile methods, poor customization of agile methods, inappropriate application area of agile methods, problematic coordination with other business units, inappropriate organizational structures, lack of top management engagement and such [42].

In order to address the common challenges, we need to use well-defined governance structure. Some of the best practices–based governance constructs to mitigate the risks are Integrated Agile Approach, focused in-depth trainings, establishing independent organization structure, establishing cross-function synchronization, establishing communities of practice and initiating agile pilots [42].

We deep dive on digital transformation of process and operations in part 4 and part 5.

Digital Transformation Best Practices

A successful execution of digital transformation needs technical planning, strategic planning, high performance teams, organizational planning and high commitment [8]. By using agile methodology, we can quickly iterate the releases and get the feedback from the audience [7].

The key success factors for the digital transformation programs are sound business strategy, leveraging the expert of the skilled individuals, involving the end-users in designing customer experience, addressing the fear of change among the employees and adopting the start-up like agile work culture [18]. Firstly, a sound business strategy should identify the strategic business vision and map the goals and metrics to achieve the strategic vision. Only after this we can evaluate the technologies that help us to reach the goals. Secondly, we should involve the subject matter experts and domain experts who have intimate knowledge of the business process or operations in the digital transformation program. The subject matter experts can validate the process changes that helps us to improve the process efficiency and productivity. Thirdly, while building the end-user experiences, the involvement of end-users is crucial. End-users can provide inputs on the challenges, goals, wish list of features and others. Additionally, end-users can also test the beta-version of the delivery and provide their feedback. The user-first approach helps us to iteratively build engaging user experiences. Fourthly, we can actively engage employees in the digital transformation process to address their fear of change. Training, coaching, mentoring and gamification are some of the means to overcome the resistance to change. Leaders should foster the culture of innovation and manage change by taking all employees onboard. Lastly, an agile culture where the team experiments often, innovates quickly and fail faster is required in a successful digital transformation program. Many of the technologies involved in the digital transformation initiatives are niche technologies that need to be evaluated through proof of concepts to understand their fitment.

The study [19] finds that the main success factors of large digital transformation programs are sound digital strategy driving the digital maturity, right scoping of digital transformation strategy, right skilling of the employees, risk-taking culture and digital initiatives that need to be led from the top with full executive support.

Efficient business process and operations also play a role in the success of digital transformation programs [29].

Due to the wide scope of the digital transformation program, a chief digital officer (CDO) is necessary to manage the digital transformation initiative at the organization [15]. The CDO is responsible for implementing the strategies to successfully carry out the digital transformation.

Summary

In this chapter we looked at various definitions of digital transformation. Essentially digital transformation uses digital technologies to impact the organization, business models and social spaces. We understand that the key drivers for digital transformation can be categorized into categories such as implementation of business strategy, customer centricity, technology and process infrastructure alignment, culture alignment and increasing efficiency. The four key pillars of digital transformation are strategy and vision, people and culture, technology and capabilities and process and governance. The key people-related aspects of digital transformation are building digital fluency, learning and training, experimentation, embracing change and leading by example. The culture aspects of the digital transformation are collaboration, data-driven decision-making, focus on action, risk-taking attitude and agility. The key elements of digital transformation strategy and vision are disruptive technologies, value chain impact, process changes and customer experience. Digital transformation process mainly involve three stages: planning where we define the roadmap and metrics; building where we iteratively build the products and services; and optimizing where we continuously monitor and improve the products and services. The key digital technologies that play a critical role in the digital transformation are Big Data and analytics, AI, cloud computing, IoT, Blockchain, mobile technologies, Augmented Reality and conversational interfaces.

References

1. The CSuite News Team. (April 18, 2017). "Why CIOs Have to Do More Than Just Keeping the Lights On." CSuite Retrieved from www.thecsuite.co.uk/cio/strategy-cio/cio-and-innovation-more-than-just-keeping-the-lights-on/
2. Forrestor consulting commissioned by Accenture Interactive. (October, 2015). "Digital Transformation in the Age of the Customer." Retrieved from www.the-digital-insurer.com/wp-content/uploads/2016/02/646-Accenture-Digital-Transformation-In-The-Age-Of-The-Customer.pdf
3. Vanson Bourne on behalf of Dell. (2020). "Digital Transformation Index 2020." Retrieved from www.delltechnologies.com/en-us/perspectives/digital-transformation-index.htm#scroll=off&pdf-overlay=/en-us/collaterals/unauth/briefs-handouts/solutions/dt-index-2020-executive-summary.pdf
4. Futurism Technologies. (November 6, 2019). "The Meaning and Importance of Digital Transformation." Retrieved from www.futurismtechnologies.com/blog/importance-of-digital-transformation/
5. RedHat team. (March 16, 2018). "What Is Digital Transformation?" Retrieved from www.redhat.com/en/topics/digital-transformation/what-is-digital-transformation
6. Gurusamy, K., Srinivasaraghavan, N., & Adikari, S. (2016). "An integrated framework for design thinking and agile methods for digital transformation." *International Conference of Design, User Experience, and Usability*. Springer, Cham, 34–42.

7. Sriram, N. (2015). *Agile IT Organization Design – For Digital Transformation and Continuous Delivery.* Addison Wesley, Reading.
8. Baker, M. (2014). *Digital Transformation – 4th Edition.* Buckingham Monographs. CreateSpace Independent, Scotts Valley, CA.
9. Goerzig, D., & Bauernhansl, T. (2018). "Enterprise architectures for the digital transformation in small and medium-sized enterprises." *Procedia Cirp* 67, 540–545.
10. Matt, C., Hess, T., & Benlian, A. (2015). "Digital transformation strategies." *Business & Information Systems Engineering* 57, 339–343.
11. Schallmo, D. (2016). *Jetzt Digital Transformieren.* Wiesbaden: Springer.
12. Pihir, I., Tomičić-Pupek, K., & Furjan, M. T. (2018). "Digital transformation insights and trends." *Central European Conference on Information and Intelligent Systems.* Faculty of Organization and Informatics Varazdin, 141–149.
13. Westerman, G., Bonnet, D., & McAfee, A. (2014). *Leading Digital—Turning Technology into Business Transformation.* USA: Harvard Business Review Press.
14. Evans, N. (2017). "Assessing Your Organization's Digital Transformation Maturity." Retrieved from www.cio.com/article/230462/assessing-your-organization-s-digital-transformation-maturity-2.html
15. Matt, C., Hess, T., & Benlian, A. (2015). Digital transformation strategies. *Business and Information Systems Engineering.* 57(5), 339–343.
16. Ebert, C., & Duarte, C. H. C. (2018). "Digital transformation." *IEEE Software* 35(4), 16–21.
17. Gudergan, G., & Mugge, P. (2017). "The gap between practice and theory of digital transformation." *Proceeding Hawaii International Conference of System Science, Hawaii,* 4–5
18. Tabrizi, B. et al. (2019). "Digital transformation is not about technology." *Harvard Business Review* 13, 1–6.
19. Kane, G. C., et al. (2015). "Strategy, not technology, drives digital transformation." *MIT Sloan Management Review and Deloitte University Press* 14, 1–25.
20. Westerman, G., Bonnet, D., & McAfee, A. (2014). "The nine elements of digital transformation." *MIT Sloan Management Review* 55(3), 1–6.
21. Schwertner, K. (2017). "Digital transformation of business." *Trakia Journal of Sciences* 15(1), 388–393.
22. Reis, J., et al. (2018). "Digital transformation: a literature review and guidelines for future research." *World Conference on Information Systems and Technologies.* Springer, Cham, 3–4
23. Fitzgerald, M., Kruschwitz, N., Bonnet, D., & Welch, M. (2013). Embracing Digital Technology: A New Strategic Imperative. MIT Sloan Management Review, Research Report.
24. McDonald, M., & Rowsell-Jones, A. (2012). *The Digital Edge: Exploiting Information & Technology for Business Advantage.* Gartner Inc., Stamford, CT.
25. Solis, B., Lieb, R., & Szymanski, J. (2014). *The 2014 State of Digital Transformation.* Altimeter Group.
26. Martin, A. (2008). "Digital literacy and the 'digital society'." *Digital Literacies Concepts Policies Practices* 30, 151–176.
27. Westerman, G., Calméjane, C., Bonnet, D., Ferraris, P., & McAfee, A. (2011). *Digital Transformation: A Roadmap for Billion-Dollar Organizations,* pp. 1–68. MIT

Sloan Management, MITCenter for Digital Business and Capgemini Consulting, Cambridge, MA.

28. Stolterman, E., & Fors, A. (2004). "Information Technology and the Good Life." *Information Systems Research*, pp. 5–6.

29. Dremel, C., Wulf, J., Herterich, M., Waizmann, J., & Brenner, W. (2017). How AUDI AG established big data analytics in its digital transformation. *MIS Quarterly Executive* 16(2), 81–100.

30. Zaoui, F., & Souissi, N. (2020). "Roadmap for digital transformation: a literature review." *Procedia Computer Science* 175, 621–628.

31. Chanias, S., Myers, M. D., & Hess, T. (2019). "Digital transformation strategy making in pre-digital organizations: the case of a financial services provider." *The Journal of Strategic Information Systems* 28(1), 17–33.

32. Eling, M., & Lehmann, M. (2018). "The impact of digitalization on the insurance value chain and the insurability of risks." *The Geneva Papers on Risk and Insurance-Issues and Practice* 43(3), 359–396.

33. Savastano, M., Amendola, C., & D'Ascenzo, F. (2018). "How digital transformation is reshaping the manufacturing industry value chain: the new digital manufacturing ecosystem applied to a case study from the food industry." *Network, Smart and Open*. Springer, Cham, 127–142.

34. Dawson, A., et al., (2016). "The economic essentials of digital strategy." *McKinsey Quarterly*, April.

35. Gürkan, G. Ç., & Gülsel Ç. (2020). "Developing a supportive culture in digital transformation." *Digital Business Strategies in Blockchain Ecosystems*. Springer, Cham, 83–102.

36. Frankiewicz, B., & Chamorro-Premuzic, T. (2020). "Digital transformation is about talent, not technology." *Harvard Business Review* 6(3), 3–4.

37. Reier, S. (2000). "Half a century later, economist's 'Creative Destruction' Theory is apt for the internet age: Schumpeter: the Prophet of Bust and Boom." *The New York Times*.

38. Hemerling, J., et al. (2018). "It's not a digital transformation without a digital culture." *Boston Consulting Group*, 1–11.

39. Hartl, E.va, & Hess, T. (2017). "The role of cultural values for digital transformation: Iinsights from a Delphi study." *Conference: Proceedings of the 23rd Americas Conference on Information Systems (AMCIS 2017)*, Boston, MA.

40. Kane, G. (2019). "The technology fallacy: people are the real key to digital transformation." *Research-Technology Management* 62(6), 44–49.

41. Del, R. S. (2017). "Digital transformation needs to happen: the clock is ticking for companies that have been unwilling to embrace change." *CRM Magazine*, 21 (10). Retrieved from www.destinationcrm.com/Articles/Editorial/Magazine-Features/Digital-Transformation-Needs-to-Happen-Now-120789.aspx

42. Fuchs, C., & Hess, T. (2018). "Becoming agile in the digital transformation: the process of a large-scale agile transformation."

43. Ulas, D. (2019). "Digital transformation process and SMEs." *Procedia Computer Science* 158, 662–671.

44. Ivančić, L., Vukšić, V. B., & Spremić, M. (2019). "Mastering the digital transformation process: business practices and lessons learned." *Technology Innovation Management Review* 9(2), 3–4.

45. Gens, F. (2013). *"The 3rd Platform: Enabling Digital Transformation."* USA: IDC 209.
46. Yoo, Y., Boland Jr, R. J., Lyytinen, K., & Majchrzak, A. (2012). "Organizing for innovation in the digitized world." *Organization Science* 23(5), 1398–1408.
47. Holotiuk, F., & Beimborn, D. (2017). Critical success factors of digital business strategy.
48. Unruh, G., & Kiron, D. (2017). Digital Transformation On Purpose. MIT Sloan Management Review, 6th November 2017. [online] Available: https://sloanreview.mit.edu/article/digital-transformation-on-purpose/
49. Wade, M. (2015). *Digital Business Transformation: A Conceptual Framework.* International Institute for Management Development.
50. Nylen, D., & Holmstrom, J. (2015). "Digital innovation strategy: a framework for diagnosing and improving digital product and service innovation." *Business Horizons* 58(1), 57–67.
51. Hess, T., Matt, C., Benlian, A., & Wiesböck, F. (2016). "Options for formulating a digital transformation strategy." *MIS Quarterly Executive* 15(2), 123–139.
52. Udovita, P. V. M. V. D. (2020). "Conceptual review on dimensions of digital transformation in modern era." *International Journal of Scientific and Research Publications* 10(2), 520–529.

Chapter 2

Digital Transformation Framework

Introduction

Digital transformation at an enterprise spans various areas such as business process transformation, operations transformation, technology transformation, culture transformation and such. To define an effective digital transformation strategy, we need to identify the methods and best practices for digital transformation in each of those areas.

Digital transformation framework defines the core building blocks for digital transformation. We identify main categories that will be transformed as part of the overall digital transformation along with the examples. In each of the building blocks we discuss the common trends, best practices and methods adopted during the digital transformation.

In this chapter we define the core building blocks of digital transformation including the business process transformation, operations transformation, technology transformation and infrastructure transformation. We have dedicated chapters to discuss each of the building blocks in greater details.

DOI: 10.1201/9781003390893-3

Building Blocks of Digital Transformation Framework

Building blocks are essential elements that get transformed as part of overall digital transformation. We have depicted the four main building blocks of digital transformation in Figure 2.1.

Business process transformation (transforming existing business processes to make them more agile and customer engaging), infrastructure transformation (transforming the infrastructure to make them highly available, scalable, resilient and cost-effective), operations transformation (transforming the governance and operations processes to make them agile and nimble) and technology transformation (transforming the existing technologies to reduce technical debt, accelerate innovation and scale) are the main building blocks of digital transformation.

Let us look at some of the use cases of digital transformation and the core building blocks that are transformed as part of the transformation. Table 2.1 provides examples of various kinds of digital transformation.

Digital Transformation of the Business Processes

The existing business processes have to be redefined to become agile, responsive and nimble. Business process transformation is mainly about making the existing business

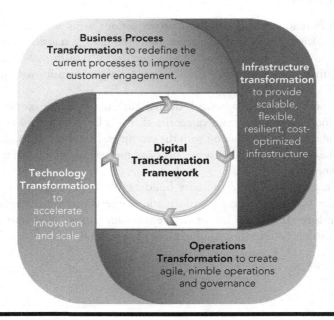

Figure 2.1   Building blocks of digital transformation.

Table 2.1   Examples of Digital Transformation

Use Case	Building Block	Digital Transformation Example
Learning and training	Technology transformation, business process transformation	Transform the learning and training process from in-person setup to digital learning with gamification.
Customer service	Technology transformation, business process transformation, operations transformation	Transform the human-based customer service into chatbots/virtual assistant-based servicing. Provide contextual search and automate the ticket handling using ticket handling bots. Leverage machine learning-enabled customer churn prediction to improve customer retention.
Shopping/Digital commerce	Technology transformation, business process transformation, operations transformation	Transform physical shopping into digital shopping experience through digital commerce portals enabled with intelligent search and recommendations.
Insurance processing	Technology transformation, business process transformation, operations transformation	Transform the in-person visit to online customer onboarding, online quotes, digital claims processing and digital claim settlement.
Banking transactions	Technology transformation, business process transformation, operations transformation	Transform the physical branches to digital branches providing services such as online account opening, online KYC, online lending and such.
Employee experience	Technology transformation, business process transformation	Transform the physical workplace into flexible work from anywhere workplace by enabling remote support, virtual desktops, digital learning experience.
Server maintenance	Operations transformation	Transform manual maintenance into automated and managed maintenance through cloud migrations.

(Continued)

Table 2.1 (Continued)

Use Case	Building Block	Digital Transformation Example
Customer onboarding	Technology transformation, business process transformation	Transform the physical visit process to online smart onboarding forms with intelligent document verification.
Healthcare use cases	Technology transformation, business process transformation	Transform the physical visit to hospitals into virtual consultation.

processes more efficient that ultimately improves customer engagement. Given below are the key digital transformation tenets for business process transformation:

Process digitization—The first step in business process transformation is to digitize the business process. Process digitization involves providing digital-first platforms that replace or complement existing non-digital processes. For instance, a banking organization whose current "account opening" process requires customers to visit the nearest branch can digitize the entire account process that enables customers to open account completely online. A paper form for opening account can be entirely digitized wherein customers can fill up the digital form completely online.

Process digitization also improves the customer engagement as we can improve the performance of the overall process. We can also gather insights from digital channels to further improve the customer experience. For instance, a digital account opening platform can track the customer preferences (such as phone or email or SMS) and accordingly send the notifications to the customer.

Process digitization also opens up opportunities for getting customer insights through analytics platform. The insights can be used for recommendations, cross-sell, up-sell and other customer engagement initiatives.

Process automation—We need to relook at the existing steps of the business process and the well-defined, rules-based steps should be automated. Business process automation (BPA) uses technology to automate the repetitive sequence of steps. For instance, the rules-based loan/credit decisioning process can be automated. Claims processing and settlement can be automated using the pre-defined rules.

Self-service—Few processes need users to wait for approvals or are dependent on other actions to be completed impacting the overall process time. We should enable end users through self-service mechanisms such as search, auto-approvals and such. For instance self-service portals, virtual assistants, chatbots, guided navigations, smart search and recommendations are various mechanisms that enable self-service leading to faster information discovery and improve customer satisfaction.

Faster data-driven decision making—Enterprises can use existing data to drive the decisions faster. Predicting loan default rate, calculating the loan eligibility, forecasting the inventory for the next week, predicting the customer churn are the main use cases for data-driven decision-making.

Machine learning–enabled processes—Machine learning (ML) uses statistical methods and data to "learn" tasks, such as inference, prediction and forecasting, based on defined set of goals. Some of the popular ML use cases are forecasting of sales and inventory, computer vision-based auto checkout, customer churn prediction, fraud detection, document digitization using OCR (optical character recognition), risk scoring, personalized recommendations, call center analytics, chatbots, intelligent document processing, smart search and such.

Process optimization—Existing business processes can be optimized through various mechanisms such as minimizing the process steps, process simplification, process digitization, self-approval and others. One-click checkout, simplified user registration and Service Level Agreement (SLA)-based auto-approval are few examples of process optimization.

Steps in Business Process Transformation

We begin the business process transformation by defining the success criteria for the business transformation. We define the key performance indicators (KPIs) and metrics to measure the success of business transformation. For instance, we can define the metrics such as process completion time, total cost saved per year, improved productivity in man hours and such.

We then identify the business processes that can be transformed. We prioritize the processes that impact the end-user experience and engagement (such as customer search, customer onboarding, customer checkout, product comparison etc.). We also prioritize the processes that impact the business revenue (such as ordering process or conversion process). The business transformation roadmap defines various business processes that will be implemented in different phases.

As a next step, we leverage the automation and other tools such as ML to augment, compliment or replace the existing business processes. We constantly look for new ways to reinvent the business process.

Digital Transformation of the Infrastructure

Digital transformation of infrastructure aims to reduce the overall infrastructure cost and make the infrastructure highly scalable, available and resilient. Virtualizing the physical servers and containerizing the applications forms the first level of infrastructure transformation.

The next level of digital transformation is to use cloud infrastructure to efficiently manage the operations. We adopt 5-R migration and modernization strategy for migrating the applications to the cloud. The 5-R migration strategy include *retire* (where we retire the old and unused applications), *retain* (where we retain the applications that have minimal business value and the ones that cannot be modernized), *rehost* (where we host the on-premise applications in cloud servers), *replatform* (where we modernize the platform) and *refactor* (where we redesign the applications using cloud native services). The cloud migration includes three main stages—assess (where we perform the TCO analysis and as-is infrastructure assessment), design (where we finalize the migration strategy and conduct migration proof of concepts (PoCs)) and migrate and modernize (where we execute the migration in iterations). We have discussed cloud migration in Chapter 4.

Digital Transformation of the Operations

Digital operations mainly involves managing the infrastructure hosting the digital platforms. Server maintenance, server patching, upgrades, availability testing, incident management, configuration management and change management are some of the key activities of digital operations. Organizations aim to be become agile and nimble post digital transformation. Hence the digital operations should naturally align with this strategic goal. Given below are key attributes of digital operations that we need to transform as part of digital transformation.

Automated operations—The structured and well-defined operations that are required for conducting business as usual (BAU) should be automated. For instance, the data backups, data synchronization, scheduled patching and such well-defined activities should be automated by using scripts, scheduled jobs or cloud-native and cloud-managed services.

Managed services—Cloud platforms provide managed platforms as services. For instance a database as service takes care of database maintenance activities such as daily snapshots, regular database backup, database failover, high availability, database security and such. Leveraging the cloud-managed service enables the development team to focus more on high value activities, such as business logic, schema definition, query fine-tuning, and be more agile.

Observability, continuous monitoring and notifications—Monitoring of end-to-end services enable the operations team to carry out proactive maintenance and to respond to incidents quickly. Continuous monitoring in real time provides granular view of performance across end-to-end request flow. The insights gathered from the monitoring helps us to identify the performance bottlenecks and to troubleshoot the issues.

Metrics-based tracking—We need to define the quantifiable metrics and KPIs to track the business goals. Once we define the KPIs and metrics across various categories, such as agility, performance, availability, resilience and cost optimization, we need to track it in real time and notify/alert the system administrators in case of any anomalies.

High availability—The infrastructure components and services should be designed for high availability. The high availability design includes redundant components, multi-instance clusters, automatic failover and health-check monitoring to automatically handle the component failures. The high availability should be tested across each of the application layers (such as high availability of the database, high availability of the services).

High resilience—Modern applications should be designed to be resilient for the failures through robust failure handling design. The digital services and applications should be tested for recovering from failures, handling failures and performance during failures. Modern applications should be tested for handling sophisticated scenarios such as simulated denial of service attacks, outage of dependent services and such.

Elastic scalability—The traffic for the modern applications is unpredictable and hence modern applications should be tested for on-demand scalability.

Continuous improvement—The operational procedures should be continuously improved using automation, operation run books, best practices and such.

Efficient incident management—Incident management for modern platforms can be optimized through various means such as automated triaging, self-service portals, incident avoidance architecture, shift left design, incident management bots and such.

We have discussed the digital transformation of the operations in Chapter 13.

Digital transformation of the Technology

Modern digital technologies are at the forefront of enabling enterprises to become more agile, innovate faster, become more resilient and scalable One of the main components of technology-related digital transformations is services transformation. In the traditional legacy platforms the business logic is tightly coupled with presentation layer components and data access layer components. As a result we face challenges during scalability and reusability of the business logic. Services transformation involves decoupling the business services from the application into granular, independently scalable microservices. As part of digital transformation, we transform the monolith to microservice using patterns such as strangler pattern, event-driven design pattern, CQRS (Command Query Responsibility Segregation) pattern and others. Enterprises also build open API platform to expose the services and build an ecosystem for other consumers to consume and build on the enterprise capabilities. We have discussed the services transformation in Chapter 5.

Reimagining user experience is another key aspect of digital transformation. Experience transformation creates user-centric design, enables multichannel delivery, provides personalized experience and enables quicker and relevant information discovery. As part of user experience transformation journey we perform user research to understand the needs, goal and challenges from end-user perspective. We model the user personas, journey map and do competitive analysis. Based on the user research, we iteratively build the low-fidelity and high-fidelity design, mockups and prototypes for faster experimentation. We have discussed the user experience transformation in Chapter 8.

As part of optimizing the development and delivery process, we should define architecture , design guidelines and use proven best practices that ensure high quality deliverable first time. We have discussed first time right framework in Chapter 7 to cover the guidelines and best practices under technology, operations and cost, security and customer experience pillars. We have discussed the first time right framework along with the tools in Chapter 7.

Legacy modernization is often a key exercise taken up as part of digital trans-formation journey. Legacy modernization exercise involves modernizing the legacy monolith platforms, legacy databases, modernizing mainframe systems and others. We have discussed the legacy modernization methods in Chapter 3.

We setup a digital factory to build a best practices–based automated way of man-aging digital resources and digital processes. Digital factory provides an automated platform for managing the digital resources and processes. We have discussed the digital factory in Chapter 6.

Summary

In this chapter, we discussed core building blocks of digital transformation including the business process transformation, operations transformation, technology trans-formation and infrastructure transformation. The main building blocks of digital transformation are business process transformation, infrastructure transformation, operations transformation and technology transformation. The key attributes of business process transformation includes process digitization, process automa-tion, self-service, faster data-driven decision-making, ML-enabled processes and process optimization. Digital transformation of infrastructure aims to reduce the overall infrastructure cost and make the infrastructure highly scalable, available and resilient. Digital operations mainly involves managing the infrastructure hosting the digital platforms. The key attributes of digital transformation of operations include automated operations, managed services, observability, continuous monitoring and notifications, metrics-based tracking, high availability, high resilience, elastic scalability, continuous improvement and efficient incident management. Services transformation, user experience transformation, first time right framework, legacy modernization and digital factory are the main attributes of technology transformation.

MIGRATION AND MODERNIZATION

Chapter 3

Legacy Modernization

Introduction

Big enterprises such as financial institutions who are using mainframes, legacy Enterprise Resource Planning (ERP) systems and legacy monolith applications often grapple with challenges such as longer release cycles, higher maintenance cost, shortage of skills, platform performance and scalability issues. To meet the expectations of today's customers enterprises need to innovate faster and release the products quicker to market. As a result those organizations embark on legacy modernization journey.

Modernization is a process wherein we iteratively transform legacy applications and data into modern platforms to reduce cost, accelerate innovation and realize the strategic business goals. The main goals for modernization are to improve maintainability, reduce time to market, reduce technical debt, improve scalability, improve quality, introduce new technology and prepare DevOps [1].

Enterprises modernize their core legacy platforms to increase their agility, reduce cost, improve overall security posture and achieve the strategic business goals. Meeting customer expectations, responding to market dynamics, improving profitability, improving resiliency and performance are other drivers for legacy modernization. During the legacy modernization process enterprises also reduce their technical debt.

Modernizing the legacy helps organizations to innovate faster and respond to market dynamics quickly. The modernization exercise enable organizations to

DOI: 10.1201/9781003390893-5

become more agile, scale dynamically and improve overall customer engagement and open up new revenue models and new digital engagement channels.

Adopting modern technologies such as cloud-native applications, analytics and machine learning (ML)-based platforms, DevSecOps-based release management and containers and serverless technologies enable organizations to accelerate innovation.

Modernization Strategies

Software modernization converts legacy systems into component-based modular systems. The process involves program understanding, business rules extraction, understanding interfaces and others [2]. Based on the use case, we need to use the appropriate modernization patterns, best practices and tools to modernize. There are primarily five modernization strategies (called 5-R strategy)—retire, retain, rehost, replatform and refactor. We have depicted the 5-R modernization strategies in Figure 3.1.

The first stage of modenization is to retire the unnecessary applications. Inventory analysis is carried out during the start of modernization journey. We get insights into the servers, infrastructure components and their utilization metrics from the inventory analysis. We retire the applications and solution components that are not used or has little business value. We analyze the dependencies of the applications to be retired and communicate the decision to all the stakeholders. We also retire applications that are not used or decommissioned, Legacy application that is nearing end of life, Duplicate functionality addressed by new application and applications with minimal business value.

As part of retain stage, few applications are retained in the current state and as such will not be modernized. Legacy-packaged applications and similar applications that have little or no modernization scope are retained. We retain the applications that have unsupported technology in target environment (such as cloud) or if there is no advantage or business justification for migration or if there is no skill set availability for the migration. Other scenarios for retaining the applications are applications that have stricter security and compliance requirements, applications that have many dependencies on the on-premise systems, or highly latency sensitive applications.

As part of rehosting stage, we lift and shift the existing applications to a newer host to optimize cost, improve scalability, availability and performance. For instance, we adopt the rehost strategy during the initial iteration of the cloud migration journey where we move the on-premise servers to the cloud-based servers to leverage the economies of scale and to optimize cost. We also move the physical servers to virtual servers to increase the scalability and optimize the cost. We leverage the Infrastructure as a Service (IaaS) of the cloud platform and automated migration tools for rehosting the servers.

During the replatform stage, we migrate the application to a different platform to improve the scalability, performance, availability and to reduce the cost. We change the underlying infrastructure during replatform exercise. Replatforming is also done to move to the open-source platforms and to migrate from proprietary standards to

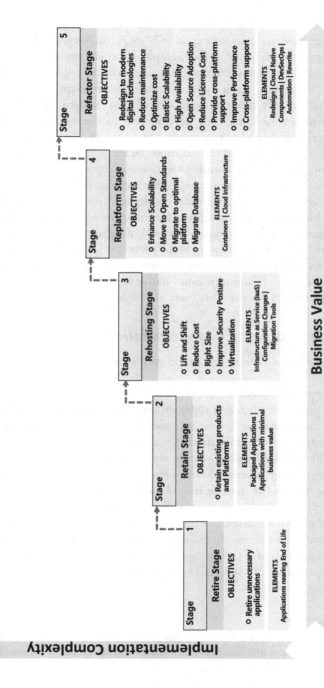

Figure 3.1 Modernization strategies.

open standards. For instance, we migrate the data from proprietary database engines to open-source database platforms such as MySQL or PostgreSQL. Containerizing the existing applications is one of the examples of replatform exercise.

Refactoring stage involves redesigning the existing application to a modern architecture. Refactoring is a type of white-box modernization that involves understanding the code that can be refactored into modern technology platforms [3]. Refactoring involves new code development in the modern technology platform. Refactoring is carried out to reduce the technical debt, make the application scalable, and to make the application more secure and improve the performance while reducing the cost. Transforming the monolith application to microservices to enhance the scalability is a common example of refactoring exercise. Other common examples of refactoring are migrating the legacy applications into cloud-native components like serverless functions; redesigning the legacy session–based security to stateless session model; migrating the SQL databases to more scalable NoSQL databases and migrating the existing build process to cloud-native DevSecOps and others. Other scenarios for refactoring are adding new functionality to the existing software, rewriting applications in cloud-native serverless platforms.

Table 3.1 provides the main use cases for the 5-R strategy.

Best Practices of Legacy Modernization

We have detailed the common best practices of legacy modernization in this section.

Migration Approach Validation through Proof of Concept

We need to validate the migration approach through proof of concept (PoC). We need to identify a complex use case for the PoC and use the selected migration tool or migration approach to execute the migration. The migration approach usually falls into these categories—lift and shift/rehost (wherein we migrate the existing applications to the new platform as is), replatform (wherein we migrate the legacy applications to the new platform) and refactor (wherein we rewrite the legacy application in the modern technology); the applications that are planned for retire or retain will not be migrated.

During the PoC, we assess the time taken for migrating a single functionality, business impact and the non-functional attributes such as security, performance, availability and scalability. The assessment helps us to finalize the most appropriate migration approach. Once the PoC is completed, we can explore options for automating the migration steps.

Iterative Migration

The initial iteration should focus on quick wins whereby we migrate non-critical applications and modules that have minimal dependencies. We should adopt the migration approach that is validated in the PoC. In subsequent migrations we migrate the applications with increasing complexity.

Table 3.1   Use Cases for 5-R Strategy

Migration Strategy	Main Use Cases	Example
Retire	Application not used, Legacy application that is nearing end of life, Duplicate functionality addressed by new application	Retire legacy reporting application not used by team, Duplicate application
Retain	Unsupported technology in target platform, no advantage or business justification for migration, no skill set availability for the migration	Legacy packaged application
Rehost	Supported applications in target platform, Cost advantage in target platform	Packaged software rehosted on new right-sized servers, migrate applications to virtual machines, dev and non-prod servers
Replatform	Achieve cost advantage, scalability and high availability in the target platform	Containerize the application, Move SQL database to NoSQL database, replace existing application with SaaS platform, change database or COTS platform, change OS
Refactor	Reduce technical debt, optimize cost, move to scalable modern technology stack, improve performance, improve security, add additional features	Migrate legacy application to serverless, migrade monolith to microservice, modernize existing application to cloud-native technologies, add new functionality to the existing software, applications nearing end of life, rewrite applications in cloud-native serverless platforms

Migration Planning

As part of migration planning, we compile the inventory of the legacy applications. The inventory should capture the hardware resource details (such as processor, network devices, hypervisor etc.), telemetry data (including the resource utilization of the servers), runtime libraries, OS, languages, middleware, packaged software and others. We also do the dependency mapping and create the "move-groups" (a set of applications that are closely dependent on each other and the ones that need a similar software stack). We then plan the iteration using the move-groups.

We identify the business priority of the applications and plan the iterations accordingly. We use the migration tools that are validated in the PoC and use the appropriate migration pattern.

Migration Automation
Tool-based automation is a common best practice we adopt to accelerate the migration and minimize the business impact. We develop the migration scripts to automate the data migration, application migration and other structured migration activities. We setup the DevSecOps pipeline to automate the testing and release management in the target platform.

Modernizing the Legacy Data Store
Migrate the data from the legacy data into modern data platforms, such as SQL and NoSQL databases, to improve the agility and scalability.

Database Modernization

Legacy applications use relational database for all the data-related use cases. Relational databases are good fit for management of structured data that requires strict schemas such as financial data. Modern applications handle large volumes of data and need to scale to millions of users. The velocity of data change and variety of data requires a different data management strategy.

Given below are the key database modernization strategies.

Migrate to Managed Open-Source Databases

As part of modernization journey we migrate from proprietary databases to managed open-source databases. This migration optimizes the license cost and helps organizations to adopt the open-source platforms and prevent vendor lock-in. Managed open-source platforms also provide enhanced performance. Modern cloud platforms provide managed open-source databases that can be leveraged for migrating the existing databases.

Best-fit Database Engine for the Use Case

Modern applications leverage structured, semi-structured and unstructured (such as documents, text files) data. Relational database engines are best fit mainly for structured data management use cases. For other data types, we need to use NoSQL or document databases to achieve the high scalability and performance.

Based on the use case, we select the most appropriate database engine. This strategy helps in high scalability and optimal performance for the use case. Table 3.2 provides the list of database engines that are appropriate for the use case.

Table 3.2 Database Fitment

Use Case	Suitable Database Platform	Example Database Engines
Manage structured, relational data. Schema on write, strong consistency and support for ACID transactions. For instance financial data	Relational Database Engines	MySQL, Oracle, SQL Server, PostgreSQL, IBM DB2, MariaDB
Manage documents and its metadata; search documents based on its metadata. For instance content management and document management systems	Document store	MongoDB, NoSQL Database, Amazon DocumentDB
Establish the relationship between data; use the relationship for recommendation	Graph Database	Neptune, GraphQL, Neo4j
Persist key value pair; need to provide eventual consistency and need fast reads and high throughput and high scalability. For instance session data	NoSQL database, Cache Platform	Amazon DynamoDB Redis, Memcached
Develop ultra-low-latency, highly scalable access store for data. For instance application cache and real time analytics	In-memory Database	Redis, Memcached
Manage time series data such as IoT event data	Time Stream Database	Amazon TimeStream
Legacy data stores (such as network database, indexed database, flat file, indexed database)	Relational Database Engines or NoSQL database engines	MySQL, Oracle, SQL Server, PostgreSQL, Amazon DynamoDB Redis

Table 3.3 Data Synchronization Approaches

Data Synchronization	Brief Details	Applicable Scenarios
Synchronous data replication	Synchronously replicate the data across the data stores in real time.	Strongly consistent transaction scenarios, Active-active database replication, Near Disaster recovery (DR) scenario, Low latency transactions
Asynchronous data replication	Data is replicated asynchronously.	Eventual consistent scenarios, Support automatic retry and automatic failure handling scenario, Far Disaster recovery (DR) scenario, High latency transactions, Event based architectures
Change data capture (CDC)	The changes to the data are captured as events and sent to the target database.	Near real time data replication, Analytical and reporting scenarios

Migrate to Cloud-Native Database

Public cloud platforms offer cloud-native databases that can be easily integrated with the cloud-based applications. Migration to cloud-native databases provide freedom and flexibility to the database developers to focus on the high-value activities such as core business logic, schema design, query tuning and the database manageability (such as backup, patching) are taken care by cloud. The cloud database engines are priced based on their usage and can be used in serverless mode as well.

Data Coexistence and Data Synchronization

During the modernization journey, the current database co-exists with new database till all the applications and data are fully migrated to the new platform. In such scenarios we need to do a bi-directional synchronization of the data across both the databases. Table 3.3 provides various approaches for data synchronization between databases.

Services Modernization

Services modernization essentially involves transforming the legacy monolith application into microservices. The main drivers for microservice adoption are high scalability and elasticity, high maintainability, shorter time to market, enabler for

DevOps, cloud suitability, polygot programming and polygot persistence [1]. We have discussed services modernization in Chapter 5.

Modernization Paths

Enterprises adopt various paths for modernization. In this section we have detailed the popular modernization paths.

Move to Open Source

Organizations migrate from licensed software or proprietary software to open source to eliminate vendor lock-in and to reduce the cost. Migration to open source helps organizations to standardize the technology stack and enables flexible integrations.

Serverless Functions

The serverless functions are accessible through a secure endpoint. Users can focus on developing the business logic while all other concerns, such as server provisioning, server maintenance, security, availability and scalability, is taken care by the serverless platform. Many of the public cloud platforms provide serverless functions. Users can innovate faster with serverless functions.

Cloud-Native Managed Services

Public cloud platforms provide managed services or platform as a service (PaaS) for core platforms like databases, middleware systems, document management systems and others. The cloud-native managed platforms ensure high availability, security and reduces the burden of system maintenance, such as patching, upgradation and others, from the user. Users can now focus on their core products and services by improving their time to market and optimizing their business logic.

Containerization

Containers are units that package the main application along with its dependencies. We can use containers to build auto-scaling and auto-healing applications across various environments. Legacy monolith applications are transformed into microservices and deployed as containers.

Low-Code No-Code Platforms

Low-code and no-code platforms provide users with visual interface for developing applications using intuitive user interfaces (UIs) such as drag and drop, point and

Table 3.4 Use Cases for Various Migration Paths

Migration Path	Use cases	Examples
Open-source Adoption	Standardize technology stack, reduce license cost, avoid vendor lock-in	Proprietary database to MySQL, Proprietary OS to Linux
Serverless Function	Avoid infrastructure management overhead and maintenance, focus on business logic	Batch jobs, data processing jobs
Cloud-native managed service	Avoid undifferentiated platform maintenance activities, faster time to market	Managed databases, managed middleware
Containerization	High scalability, resilience, high performance, high availability, batch processing	Legacy monolith migration to microservices running on containers
Low code no code	High user adoption, intuitive interface, business-friendly platform, no coding	Reporting systems, citizen applications

click features. Report builders, citizen application platforms and workflow modelers are few examples of low-code no-code platforms. Legacy applications can be migrated to the low-code no-code platforms to improve user adoption and user experience.

Table 3.4 provides details of use cases for various migration paths.

Modernization Scenarios

In this section we discuss various modernization scenarios such as legacy Java modernization, mainframe modernization, chip architecture change, batch job modernization, OS modernization and packaged software modernization.

Legacy Java Modernization

Enterprises have built legacy Java-based monoliths for various use cases such as web applications, server applications, batch jobs etc. The main modernization path for legacy Java-based monolith is to containerize the application. Containerization of the Java application helps organizations to improve the resilience (through the container based auto-scaling and self-healing features), scalability, availability and agility (container portability and DevOps automation reduces time to market). As it is possible to containerize a wide variety of applications organizations can use open-source technologies to reduce the cost.

The legacy Java-based monoliths can be transformed into microservices using framework such as Spring Boot framework. We have discussed the modernization

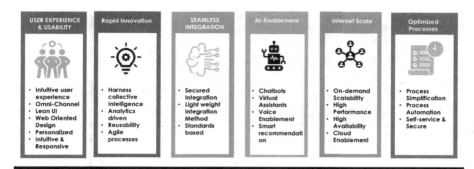

Figure 3.2   Core tenets of a modern platform.

of monolith to microservices in Chapter 5. The microservices are self-contained packages consisting of all the required dependencies and libraries. We bundle all the application dependencies into a container. Once an application or service is containerized we can adopt factory model to containerize more applications and services and deploy the containers. Post container deployment we monitor the container using various metrics such as performance, response times, availability, resource utilization and such.

Legacy Java Modernization Example

A typical legacy Java platform has tightly coupled presentation layer, business logic layer and the database layer as part of the monolith application. We modernize such legacy platforms using the core tenets such as user experience and usability, rapid innovation, seamless integration, AI integration and optimized processes as depicted in Figure 3.2. We modernize the legacy Java Server Pages (JSP)-based presentation layer using modern user experience and usability principles. We use modern lean and lightweight presentation components to provide intuitive and omni-channel user experience. We personalize the user experience based on the user preferences and transaction history.

We enable rapid innovation by using agile principles such as fail fast and learn fast. We use analytics to gather insights from the user data. We use open standards and light weight integration formats for enabling seamless integration. We AI-enable the modern applications using chatbots, virtual assistants, smart search and recommendations. We enable web scale for modern applications by providing on-demand scalability and high performance using the cloud. The processes are optimized through process simplification, process automation and self-service.

We have depicted a sample modernization roadmap for the legacy Java application-based on five transformation themes in Figure 3.3.

For modernizing a legacy web platform using legacy Java technologies, we start by identifying the transformation themes. We have depicted five main transformation

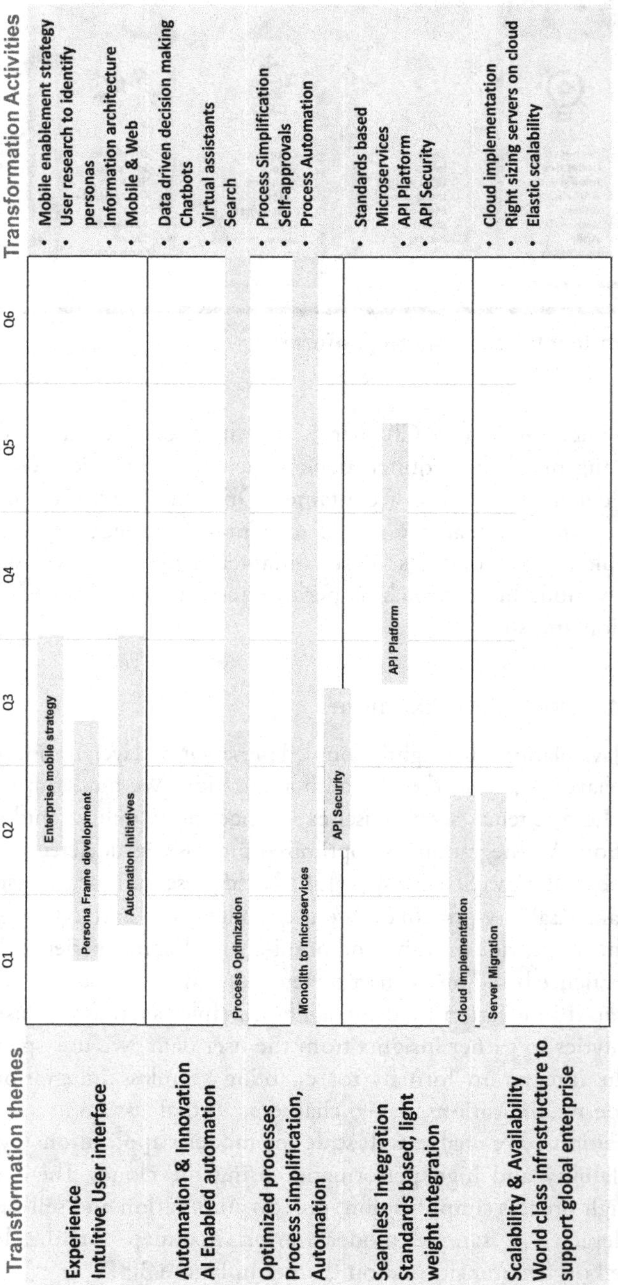

Figure 3.3 Transformation roadmap.

themes—experience, automating and innovation, optimized processes, seamless integration and scalability and availability. We identify the main activities for each of the transformation themes and the implementation is done through several stages, such as evaluation, planning, development, pilot, rollout and BAU (business as usual), as depicted in Figure 3.3.

As part of experience transformation theme, we perform the user research to define the user personas and design a personalized and mobile friendly user experience. This involves refactoring the JSP into modern JavaScript frameworks using responsive design. Other activities involved are creation of intuitive information architecture and designing visual themes and styles. As part of innovation and automation theme, we leverage various AI-enabled tools, such as chatbots, virtual assistants and analytics tools, for enhanced automation. As part of optimized processes transformation theme, we optimize, simplify and automate the processes. As part of seamless integration transformation theme, we migrate monolith to microservices and use open API standards and build an API platform. As part of scalability and availability transformation theme we do the cloud migration, install the right-sized servers on cloud and provide on-demand scalability.

Banking System Modernization

Banks are modernizing the digital platforms to provide personalized and engaging experience to their customers. We have discussed few modernization scenarios of modern banks.

Modernizing the core banking systems is a key digital transformational initiative for the banks. We can build digital interfaces on top of legacy core banking system. Modern digital banks also use dual core banking platforms—the cloud-native core to handle high volume transactions from the digital channels and the second main core for handling core banking transactions. Two cores synchronize in batch mode on frequent basis. We can also modernize core systems, such as the digital banking (including mobile banking, Internet banking), loan origination system (LOS), loan management system (LMS), customer relationship management (CRM), collections system and treasury system, KYC (Know your customer), video banking, by building them as cloud-native digital platforms.

Banks can leverage analytics and ML platforms to predict, forecast and automate the activities. Many banks build cross-sell, up-sell ML models and other predictive models to improve their profitability. Credit decisioning, loan underwriting, default prediction, document processing and personalized recommendations are few other use cases for ML. Customer services are powered by Artificial Intelligence and ML tools such as chatbots, voice bots, call center analytics, buy now pay later and others.

Digital experiences through WhatsApp banking, digital branches, online savings account and marketing automation are other modernization initiatives that banks plan for in their modernization journey.

Open banking platform is an emerging area through which banks expose and consume banking services through APIs. Banks create API marketplace platform to collaborate with fintech organizations. Open banking platforms enable integration with payment platforms and provide insurance and finance APIs as service to partners to build a banking eco-system. Modern banks also share and consume data securely through platforms such as Account aggregator to provide rich customer experience.

Mainframe Modernization

Legacy banking applications are built on mainframes (consisting mainly of COBOL code and CICS screens). Modernizing the mainframe applications has challenges, such as code complexity, skill set shortage, stringent security and storage requirements, and hence need careful planning for modernization.

During mainframe modernization, we transform the mainframe applications to scalable and secure modern applications. We start the mainframe modernization by analyzing the mainframe applications and its dependencies. We then identify the target technology platform (such as microservices) and execute a PoC to assess the feasibility, migration effort, security, performance and other parameters. Based on the successful completion of the PoC, we iteratively migrate other functionality.

UI modernization is used for mainframe systems wherein we build newer UIs that use services running on mainframe [3].

The key steps of mainframe modernization is depicted in Figure 3.4.

In the "*analyze*" stage, we perform the inventory assessment by compiling the application and server inventory. We gather the server details, utilization metrics, dependencies and others using application inventory template. We have provided a sample application inventory template in Appendix 3.1. We assess the applications

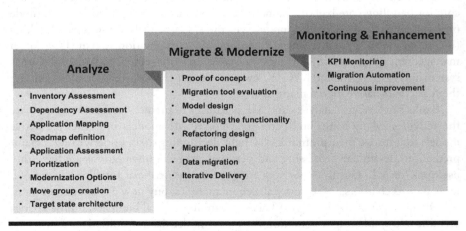

Figure 3.4   Mainframe modernization steps.

to understand their business criticality and the requirements from lens of security, infrastructure, DevOps and others. We have given a sample application assessment questionnaire in Appendix 3.2. Based on the application assessment, we prioritize the applications and create "move-groups" that migrates a set of closely related applications as part of a single iteration. We evaluate various migration and modernization options (such as lift and shift, refactor, replatform and others). We define the target state architecture and the migration roadmap identifying various migration batches and the applications that will be moved as part of each batch.

In the "*migrate and modernize*" stage, we execute the proof of concept (PoC) to validate the migration approach. We evaluate the migration tools that can be leveraged to automate the migration. We define the target state architecture including the target state domain model and target state application and database architecture. For the refactoring exercise, we decouple the modules and eliminate the dependency. We initiate the data migration and the iterative application migration.

In the "*monitoring and enhancement*" stage, we monitor the key performance indicators and metrics of the migrated application based on the non-functional requirements (NFR) we gathered during the assessment phase. We use the tools to automate the migration and explore continuous improvement options.

Table 3.5 provides common approaches for handling the mainframe modernization.

Chip Architecture Changes

One of the modernization initiatives is to migrate from legacy chip architectures to modern chips such as ARM-based chips or x86 architectures. The main drivers for such transformation are cost reduction, technical debt reduction, eliminating the aging hardware, avoiding risk of skill availability and to leverage the modern pay-as-you-go pricing models.

We start the migration using hardware emulation that emulate the legacy source systems (including the hardware, middleware and others). In the later stages we refactor the application code to the target chip platform. Modern application constructs such as containers are agnostic to the underlying hardware and hence become a popular choice for refactoring exercise.

Hybrid model of co-existence is another method of transformation wherein we iteratively migrate application and data from the legacy hardware platforms to the modern platforms. We start with non-critical applications that require less amount of refactoring effort to understand the feasibility of the migration. In the subsequent iterations we slowly migrate the remaining applications. Till all the applications are migrated, the application data is synchronized between both the platforms.

Refactoring approach is used for applications that are not compatible with the target platform. In such cases we rewrite the application manually or automate the refactoring using tools.

All the net new applications will be developed on the new architecture.

Table 3.5 Mainframe Modernization Challenges and Approach

Challenge	Brief Details	Modernization approach
Legacy hardware platforms	Modern software cannot run on legacy platforms, Scalability and availability issues	Hardware emulation(such as CICS or batch emulators) for the legacy applications, Service enable legacy application, replatform the applications wherever possible, refactor/rewrite the legacy applications
Complex Software	Monolith application with millions of lines of code, coupling between various modules	Leverage dependency mapping tools and iteratively migrate the applications starting with applications having low dependency
Mainframe language	Availability of people with COBOL, Assembler language skills	Leverage refactoring and conversion tools
Quality attributes	Performance and availability	Refactor into modern platform, such as containers and cloud-native applications, that provide elastic scalability and high performance
Impact to business	Impact to existing core business applications and users	Assess the migration feasibility through PoC, conduct iterative migration, co-existence of both the systems till final cutover
Legacy monolith application	Legacy COBOL monolith application	Refactor the monolith to microservices and use strangler pattern to iteratively migrate the microservices. Leverage automated COBOL to Java refactoring tools

Batch Job Modernization

Legacy batch scheduler applications that are developed using Job control language (JCL) or Control language (CL) normally invoke legacy programs and share the data. The legacy batch jobs are migrated along with the associated modules and are part of the same move-group.

We can execute a PoC to modern the legacy batch programs into modern batch frameworks, such as Spring Batch or Java-based platforms, and validate the performance.

Operating System Changes

Organizations migrate from proprietary operating system to open platforms such as Linux to drive the cost benefits. Interpreted language such as Java-based applications can be easily migrated to different OS (with exception for Java Native Interface (JNI), shared object dependency) whereas compiled languages such as C/C++-based applications need to be recompiled in the target platform.

Packaged Software Modernization

For modernizing the packaged software (such as Enterprise Resource Planning (ERP) platforms, reporting platforms) we need to work with the packaged software vendor to explore the opportunities to replatform them to the modern target platforms. The common packaged software modernization opportunities are replatforming it to Linux OS for cost optimization and containerizing the packaged application to improve the scalability and resilience.

We have discussed a legacy modernization case study of transforming a utilities portal in chapter 15.

Summary

In this chapter we discussed the legacy modernization scenarios and best practices. Modernization is a process wherein we iteratively transform legacy applications and data into modern platforms to reduce cost, accelerate innovation and realize the strategic business goals. Enterprises modernize their core legacy platforms to increase their agility, reduce cost, improve overall security posture and achieve the strategic business goals. The five modernization strategies are retire (decommission the applications and solution components that are not used or has little business value), retain (retain the applications that cannot be migrated), rehost (lift and shift the existing applications to a newer host), replatform (migrate the applications into newer platform) and refactor (redesigning the existing application to a modern architecture). The best practices for modernization are migration approach validation through PoC, iterative migration, migration planning and automation and modernizing the legacy data store. The key paths to modernization are the move to open source, serverless functions, cloud-native managed services, containerization, low-code no-code platforms.

Appendix 3.1
Application Inventory Template

General Metrics	Sr. No.	Example#1	Example#2
	Device Name	A	B
	PIP		
	Application Name	Example 1: Onboarding Portal	Example 2: Portal Database
	Technology Stack	Java Spring Boot	MySQL 8.0
	Device Type (Physical/ Virtual)	Virtual server	Physical
	vCPU	2	4
	Memory (GB)	16	16
	Storage (GB)	100	150
	OS Type	Windows	Linux
	Version	2019 Standard	RHEL 7.4
	License	Licensed OS	Licensed OS
	Number of operating hours/days	10	24
	Approaching refresh (Y/N)	N	N
	Criticality (High/ Medium/Low)	Critical	Critical
	Purpose	Application portal for onboarding users	Database for application portal
Utilization Metrics	**CPU (Peak)**	80	60
	CPU (Avg)	15	30
	Mem (Peak)	90	70
	Mem (Avg)	20	30
	Multi-Node (Yes/No)	Yes	Yes
Current Scaling Needs	**Number of nodes/ Instances**	2	2
	Maximum concurrent users/s	20	20
	Average concurrent users/s	1	2

	Can the application be deployed behind a load balancer? (Yes/No)	Yes	Yes
Security	Authentication	MS AD	DB Native
	Authorization	Roles	DB Roles
	Encryption	Data at rest encryption	Data at rest encryption
Backup	Back-up requirement (Yes/No)	Daily backup	Daily incremental backup, weekly full backup
Quality Metrics	Availability SLA	99.9	99.9
	Expected response time	<2 sec	<0.5 sec
Modernization	If the application is based on legacy technology, can we modernize it on cloud? (Yes/No)	Yes	Yes
	If yes, is it possible to provide details of the explored options	Use cloud-native serverless backend with React Frontend	Use managed cloud database
Dependencies	Integrations	Connects to MS AD hosted on premise	No dependency
	Support required	Yes	Yes
	File system	No	Yes
	Database	Yes	NA
	Is it possible to share the high-level application architecture	Yes	Yes
	Current challenges	Application has performance issues during peak load	Database faces deadlock often
	Data encryption needs	Encryption at rest	Encryption at rest
	Regulatory Requirements (reporting, monitoring, disaster recovery, backup)	Weekly reporting, DR with RPO/RTO of 5 mins	Weekly reporting, DR with RPO/RTO of 1 min

Appendix 3.2
Application Assessment Questionnaire

In this appendix we detail the questions we normally ask during application discovery process

Business-related

- What is the business criticality of the application?
- What is the expected application roadmap?
- What is the business impact if the application is down?

Stakeholder-related

- Who are the business stakeholders of the application?
- Who are the technology stakeholders of the application?

Application-related

- What is the core functionality of the application?
- What are the third-party libraries and dependencies of the application?

Product-related

- Is the product backlog maintained by the team?

Development methodology

- What is the development model adopted for the application (such as Agile, waterfall etc.)?
- Does the team maintain quality metrics (such as code coverage percentage, defect fix rate etc.)?

Security-related

- Is there a security design document?
- How is the authentication and authorization of the application managed?
- What are the encryption requirements of the application?
- What kind of security tests are performed (penetration testing, black box testing etc.)?

DevOps-related

- Is release management pipeline developed?
- What are the automated testing and code quality measures?
- What is the application deployment frequency?

Platform-related

- What is the OS used for the application?
- What is the development platform (Java, .Net, NodeJS etc.)?

Database-related

- What is the database engine and the version?
- How is the high availability achieved in the database?
- How is the disaster recovery managed in the database?
- What is the database backup strategy?
- What is the storage requirement of the database?

Infrastructure-related

- Is monitoring and notification setup configured?
- Is data backup configured?

NFR-related

- What are the requirements and Service Level Agreements (SLAs) related to availability, scalability?
- What is the performance SLA (latency, response time) of the application?
- What is the expected throughput of the application?

Disaster Recovery (DR)-related

- What is the Recovery Point Objective/Recovery Time Objective (RPO/RTO) requirements?
- What is the current DR strategy?

Architecture-related

- Can the architecture and design documents of the application be shared?

Integrations-related

- What are the systems, databases and APIs that the application depend on?
- Which application and services depend on the current application?

Miscellaneous questions

- What are the accessibility related requirements?
- What are the regulatory and compliance-related requirements?
- What are the various caching frameworks used at different layers?
- Is change management process document?

References

1. Knoche, H., & Hasselbring, W. (2018). "Using microservices for legacy software modernization." *IEEE Software* 35(3), 44–49.
2. Chiang, C. C., & Bayrak, C. (October, 2006). "Legacy software modernization." In 2006 IEEE International Conference on Systems, Man and Cybernetics 2, 1304–1309. IEEE.
3. Comella-Dorda, S., Wallnau, K., Seacord, R. C., & Robert, J. (2000). A Survey of Legacy System Modernization Approaches. Carnegie-Mellon University Pittsburgh P Software Engineering Institute.

Chapter 4

Cloud Migration

Introduction

Agility and cost optimizations are the key drivers for digital transformation for majority of the enterprises. Enterprises embark on migration of their main workloads to public cloud platforms to accelerate innovation, become agile, reduce cost and to improve availability and scalability. Modern applications receive unpredictable user loads and a sudden spike in demand requires on-demand scalability. Hyper scalar cloud platforms enable enterprises to handle the unpredictable user load.

The main advantages of cloud are cost efficiency, unlimited storage, automation, maintainability, quick deployment, elastic scalability, interoperability and faster delivery of new services [1] [2]. Optimum resource utilization and less maintainability are some of the other key drivers for cloud migration [3]. Additionally enterprises can innovate faster on cloud by experimenting more quickly and frequently. Public cloud also provides the flexibility of pay-as-you-go model that enterprises can use to optimize the cost. Organizations also aim to achieve the resiliency by moving to public cloud platforms. Organizations can also save cost by avoiding the over provisioning of the resources [2]. The main business values of cloud are improvement in staff productivity, reduced total cost of ownership (TCO), reduced risk, efficient operations and reduced downtime [4] [5].

We have depicted the cloud transformation themes and the cloud benefits across business, technology, operations and governance and security in Figure 4.1. The main

DOI: 10.1201/9781003390893-6

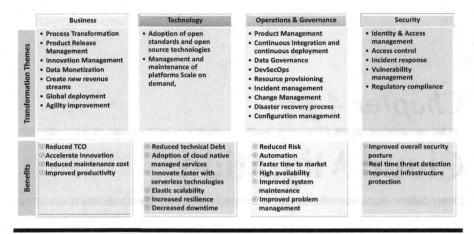

Figure 4.1   Cloud transformation themes.

transformation themes in business category are process transformation (through automation and improving the process efficiency using cloud services), product release management (by accelerating the product releases through automation and DevSecOps processes on cloud), innovation management (by experimenting faster on cloud), data monetization (by building data-based services) and creating new revenue streams (by building new services and enabling new channels). During the cloud migration process, the main business benefits that we can realize are reduced TCO, accelerated innovation, reduced maintenance cost and improved productivity.

The main transformation themes on the technology front are standardization (wherein we adopt open standards and open-source technologies), reduction of technical debt and improved maintenance of the application platform, faster innovation using cloud-native and cloud-managed service, elastic scalability (through scaling of resources on demand), improved resilience (through the redundancy offered by cloud resources) and decreased downtime.

On the operations and governance front, the main transformation themes are efficient product management, continuous integration and continuous deployment through DevSecOps, data governance, on-demand resource provisioning, incident management, change management, disaster recovery process and configuration management. We can achieve benefits such as reduced risk (through agile processes), automation (through machine learning (ML) methods), faster time to market, improved system maintenance and improved problem management.

On the security front, we can transform the identity and access management through cloud-native security services. We can also reimagine the security processes related to vulnerability management and regulatory compliance. The main security-related benefits are improved security posture, real-time threat detection through real-time threat intelligence and improved infrastructure protection.

In this chapter we discuss the cloud migration methodology, best practices and roadmap along with a cloud migration case study.

Cloud Migration Options

The papers [2] and [3] identify mainly four broad types of cloud migration options adopted by organizations:

- *Replace* where the the data or business layer components are replaced by cloud services. For instance replacing local Database with Amazon RDS.
- *Partial migration* where we migrate the solution components across multiple layers to cloud. For instance, use Amazon EC2 for application layer and Amazon RDS for database layer.
- *Full migration* wherein the entire solution stack is migrated to cloud using lift and shift methodology. For instance migrating the solution as-is to AWS by hosting them on virtual machines.
- *Cloudify* where the application is refactored into cloud using cloud-native components. For instance modernizing the solution to use serverless on AWS.

We can use the 5-R migration and modernization strategies we discussed in Chapter 3 for the cloud migration. We discuss the 5-R strategy in the context of cloud migration in Table 4.1.

Cloud Migration Use Cases

The end customer–facing on-premise applications receive unpredictable and spiky traffic and hence these applications are ideal for cloud migration as cloud platforms provide on-demand scalability and high availability. Other candidate applications for cloud migration are business critical applications that need high availability, applications that need to be released frequently to the market, applications that receive many change requests and applications that face frequent outages.

Cloud Migration Framework

We discuss various stages of the cloud migration exercise and we discuss the goals, activities and mechanisms for each of the stages.

We have depicted the stages and details of each of the stages in Figure 4.2. In the *assess* phase, we create a business case for cloud migration by mapping the strategic goals to the cloud benefits. In the *design* stage, we evaluate various migration strategies and design the operations and governance model. The *migrate and modernize* phase migrates the applications and data to cloud and performs continuous modernization on cloud.

We discus each of the phases in detail in subsequent sections.

Table 4.1 5-R Migration Strategy for Cloud Migration

Migration & Modernization Strategy	Cloud Migration Details	Applicable Use Cases
Retire	Do not migrate the on-premise applications that are nearing their end of life.	The legacy on-premise applications that are no longer used and applications that have functionality similar to the existing modern applications.
Retain	Do not migrate the on-premise applications that do not have modernization scope.	The packaged applications that have minimal business value and the applications that are difficult to extend and modernize.
Rehost	As-is migration of application to cloud servers using lift-and-shift strategy. Rehost the on-premise applications to right-sized cloud servers.	Custom applications, databases
Replatform	Modernize the OS, database platform, modernize the servers. Containerize the application.	Migrate from proprietary OS and database to managed platforms on cloud.
Refactor (cloudify, partially migrate)	Redesign and rewrite the applications using the modern cloud-native technologies.	New application development using cloud-native technologies and serverless technologies.

Assess Phase

The organizational stakeholders should be able to realize their strategic business goals with the cloud migration. We map the strategic organizational goals (such as cost optimization, agility, increased release velocity, reduced maintenance etc.) to the cloud solution elements.

The first step in the cloud migration journey is to secure the business stakeholder approval for which we should build a business case. The business case should quantify the cloud migration benefits by providing the application's TCO on cloud for five years and compare it with the on-premise cost.

For the cost benefit analysis, we perform application inventory assessment and as-is infrastructure assessment. We discussed the application inventory template and application assessment questionnaire in Chapter 3. We use the application inventory

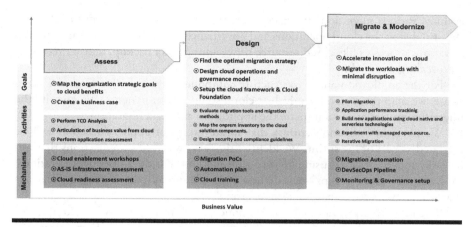

Figure 4.2 Cloud migration stages.

template to get the current utilization metrics and we collect the technology eco-system details using the application assessment questionnaire.

Once we get the application and server metrics, we use methods such as server right-sizing (finding the right capacity machine based on the average server util-ization) and auto-scaling methods (wherein we use fixed number of machines for steady-state workload and spin up new servers on-demand to handle the spikes) to calculate the cloud equivalent cost. As part of application assessment, we assess the license requirements and dependency requirements. We also add the cloud migra-tion cost to arrive at the Total Cost of Ownership (TCO) on cloud.

The organization leaders do the cost benefit analysis by comparing the cloud TCO with that of the on-premise cost. Once we get the business stakeholder buy-in for the cloud migration, we conduct cloud enablement workshops to enable the organization teams (such as application team, security team, infrastructure team, networking team etc.) about the cloud benefits. Each team can assess the cloud cap-abilities for their respective use cases.

We also assess the cloud readiness of the organization that includes the skill set assessment of the team, assessment of the process maturity, change management process, delivery process assessment and others. The cloud readiness assessment helps us in identifying the gaps and preparing the training plan.

Once we secure the business approval for cloud migration and post assessment completion, we move to the design phase.

Design Phase

In the design phase, we dive deep into the migration exercise. The primary goal is to identify whether we want to do partial migration or full migration and then evaluate various migration strategies (retire, retain, rehost, replatform or refactor). We also define the cloud operations and governance model to cover the automation of various processes like cloud resource provisioning, data backup, disaster recovery, auto-scaling and such.

For the application and infrastructure component list compiled from the assess phase, we map them to the equivalent cloud solution components. We identify the migration tools that can automate the application and data migration.

We plan the migration sprints that create group of applications that will be migrated as part of the sprint. We identify the "easy wins", the applications that can be easily moved to cloud using lift-and-shift method. For the subsequent iterations, we form the "move-groups" that defines a set of mutually dependent applications that will be migrated as part of a single group.

Based on the organizational security policies and the regulatory and compliance requirements, we define the appropriate security policies on the cloud infrastructure. Cloud-native security services enable the organizations to provide granular security controls such as role-based authorization, encryption, federated login and such. We also define the security guardrails for enabling new cloud resources (such as provisioning new virtual machine, starting database server, exposing the web service and such).

To assess the feasibility and the efficiency of the chosen migration method, we execute the migration proof of concept (PoC) to validate the migration approach and integrity of migrated data and other aspects.

Once the migration approach is finalized and validated, we perform the actual migration as part of migrate and modernize phase.

Migrate and Modernize Phase

The primary goal of migrate and modernize phase is to execute the migration with minimal disruption and to accelerate the innovation on cloud to unlock the business value.

We use the chosen migration method and execute the migration in phases. To minimize the business disruption, we use the dual-service approach whereby the service endpoint at both on-premise and at cloud are available simultaneously. Once we fully migrate the service to cloud, we shut down the on-premise service endpoint. We also do bi-directional synchronization of the data between on-premise and the cloud database till the migration is completed.

We build the new applications using the cloud-native technologies such as cloud-managed platforms and serverless technologies. We experiment with cloud-native technologies for new applications.

We setup the migration automation scripts (for automating the migration), DevSecOps pipeline (for seamless release management) and monitoring and governance setup (for real-time monitoring and notification).

Modernization, innovation and continuous improvement are ongoing processes and is done continuously to improve the agility, optimize cost and improve automation.

Cloud Migration Roadmap

The cloud migration happens in iterative phases to minimize the risk and business disruption. Enterprises pilot the migration of non-critical workloads for the initial sprint and based on the experience of migrating the initial workloads, the enterprises iteratively migrate other workloads.

We have depicted a three-year migration cloud migration roadmap in Figure 4.3 for a financial institution. We can broadly classify the migration dimensions into foundation, migration, modernization and innovation phases.

As part of the foundation phase, we do the cloud migration readiness assessment to understand the applications, servers and other network components that can be migrated to cloud. We gather the server metrics (including the resource utilization numbers) to get the right-sized solution component on the cloud. We create the initial foundation on cloud to define the secured, best practices–based cloud foundational building blocks (such as virtual network, authentication and authorization solution, core network connection). As part of cloud foundational building blocks, we create the cloud segments, network connectivity and security guardrails. We define the security controls and operations governance on the cloud infrastructure to implement the organizational security policies and to implement the regulatory compliance. We also create a cloud center of excellence (CCoE) that defines the cloud migration policies, migration approach, standards and implements the best practices across all migrations. In the subsequent years we integrate the cloud infrastructure with various fintech services.

As a part of migration phase, we execute the PoC to validate the migration method. We then pilot a small application migration. Post the successful pilot, we rehost the non-critical applications and workloads in the first year. We document the learnings, best practices and automation methods. During the subsequent years we migrate the critical applications using the best practices and the automation methods. While some applications and servers are migrated as-is using the "rehost" option, we refactor and modernize other applications as part of the cloud "Refactor and modernize" phase. We migrate commercial databases and operating systems to managed open-source platforms on the cloud to reduce the license cost and to innovate faster. We move from virtual machines to containers and serverless technologies on cloud to scale and optimize cost. The new innovations that are initiated on the cloud, we use cloud-native serverless and managed open-source platforms to exploit the cloud advantages such as elastic scalability, pay-as-you-go model and others.

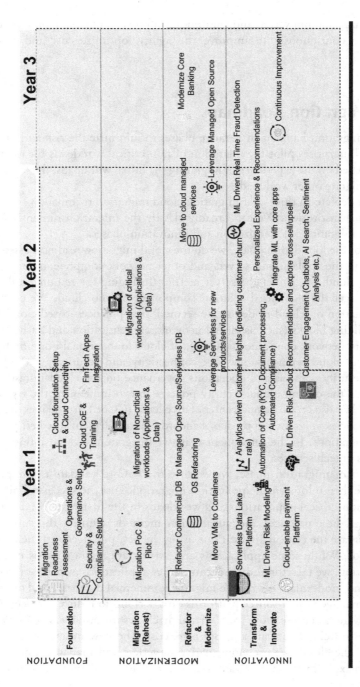

Figure 4.3 Cloud migration roadmap.

As part of "Transform and innovate" phase, we build new innovations on the cloud such as data lakes (for analytics and reporting use cases), ML models (for use cases such as cross-sell, up-sell, prediction, forecasting, product recommendations and others). We also enable the ML capabilities for the existing applications. We build deep customer engagement services such as chatbots, Artificial Intelligence (AI)-based search, AI-driven recommendation engines and such.

Innovation and optimization on cloud is a continuous journey. We iteratively enhance the existing applications using cloud-native components, open-source components and serverless components on cloud to improve performance and reduce the cost.

Cloud Migration Steps

We have detailed the sequence of steps adopted in a typical cloud migration journey in Table 4.2.

Key Success Factors for Cloud Migration

We have identified the key success factors for the cloud migration as follows:

- **Focus on customer engagement**—The success of cloud migration is measured in the impact it creates on the customer engagement. Improved customer experience, high availability, improved resilience and improved performance are the factors that play key role in customer engagement. The factors that influence customer engagement should be quantified and become the key performance indicators (KPIs) that we track during and post cloud migration.
- **Identify the business drivers for cloud migration and map it to migration solution components**—Before we initiate the migration, we should clearly identify the main business drivers for the migration. If an organization wants to move to cloud to reduce the maintenance cost; in such case we need to identify the current maintenance challenges (such as manual system maintenance) and map the business driver to the cloud solution components (such as automated patching, automated monitoring, managed server maintenance, serverless technologies).
- **Migrate in sprints**—Due to the variation of the migrated applications and due to the involved data migration complexity, it is recommended to assess the best suited migration options (retire, retain, rehost, replatform, refactor). Prioritize the applications that deliver most of the business value.

Table 4.2 Cloud Migration Steps

Sl No.	Category	Detailed Tasks
1.	Application identification and prioritization	■ Identify the potential applications for cloud migration ■ Run the telemetry tool to collect the resource utilization details and Identify the dependencies and the prioritized list of application groups
2.	Migration assessment	■ Identify the migration strategy ■ Identify the PII and sensitive data and the security controls for the same ■ Conduct cloud readiness workshops
3	Cloud Foundation Setup	■ Develop the cloud foundational building blocks such as cloud network, users and permissions, firewalls, single-sign-on (SSO) and Setup hybrid connectivity to the on-premise systems ■ Implement the security guardrails [6]
4	Pilot migration	■ Migration of the pilot application to cloud
5.	Security implementation	■ Implement the compliance and governance controls
6.	On-premise integration	■ Integrate cloud with on-premise applications such as SIEM, PAM, MS AD and others
7.	Application migration	■ Iterative migration of the applications
8.	Application modernization	■ Modernize the application on cloud – migrate monolith to microservices, move to managed open-source, move to serverless
9.	Continuous operational improvements	■ Use operations runbook to define and use the standard operation procedures (SOP)
10	Continuous cost optimization	■ Optimize the cost and right size the servers based on usage
11	Cloud center of excellence	■ Setup cloud center of excellence to drive the cloud migration

- **Migrate and modernize approach for full migration**—When we adopt full migration approach [2] to migrate all the applications to cloud, we can use the "migrate and modernize" approach wherein we initially do the as-is migration using lift-and-shift method and then modernize on cloud using managed services and cloud-native services.
- **PoC-based migration approach validation**—We need to validate the migration approach and the migration tool using a PoC. We should clearly define the success criteria for the PoC.

- **Robust migration plan**—The migration plan should identify the prioritized list of applications that deliver the business value. We create the application groups (or move-groups) based on the interdependency among the applications (for instance, the web portal and its database are part of the move-group). In the first iteration we include the quick wins that can be easily migrated to cloud without much changes. In subsequent iterations, we migrate applications based on business priority and complexity.

- **New development using cloud-native technologies**—All the net new development can be done cloud natively by leveraging the cloud-native services, cloud-managed platforms and serverless technologies.

- **Skills training and enablement**—As a part of migration planning we should do a learning and training assessment for the existing team. The learning assessment identifies the skill gap with the existing team members and based on that we can come up with training plan to enable the team members to accelerate the innovation on cloud.

- **Migration automation**—As part of migration design, we should identify the tools that can automate the migration activities such as data migration, data transformation, server migration, data backup and such.

- **Experiment fast, fail fast and win fast**—Use agile philosophy to experiment frequently using cloud to understand what works and what does not. Cloud minimizes the experimentation cost enabling organizations to innovate faster.

- **Design and monitor cloud security**—We start by replicating the on-premise security controls on cloud and then use cloud-native security to implement a comprehensive security posture. We use the security principles, such as defense in depth, layer-wise security, zero trust security model, to provide a robust security infrastructure on cloud.

- **Define and monitor KPIs**—We define the KPIs that measure the business goals and cloud migration drivers. The commonly used KPIs across various categories are cost-related KPIs (such as TCO for three years, cost savings for five years, maintenance cost savings per year), agility-related KPIs (release velocity, number of product releases per year), innovation-related KPIs (creation of new business models, creation of new revenue streams, revenue from data monetization) and non-functional requirements–related KPIs (availability metrics, performance metrics, scalability metrics and such).

Case Study Cloud Migration

In this section we discuss a case study of the cloud migration journey of a financial institution. We discuss the background, key business drivers, cloud migration process and the benefits.

Background of the Case Study

The financial institution provides various financial services, such as loan servicing, account opening, account management, customer onboarding and others, to its customers. The current technology ecosystem has a mix of home-grown custom applications, legacy portal and packaged reporting application running on-premises. As the financial institution aspires to scale and innovate, the organization has embarked on a cloud transformation journey.

Business Drivers

The organization has identified the below given business drivers for the cloud migration:

- Build a cloud-first agile solution platform to improve the customer engagement.
- Reduce the lead time for loan processing and decisioning—the current loan decisioning time is about 4 hours as it involves various manual processes and approvals.
- Accelerate the customer onboarding time and scale the solution to handle millions of customers. Currently the average customer onboarding time is 1 day.
- Create open API ecosystem for the financial institution and marketplace to expose the financial services as APIs to other fintech organizations to monetize the data and services.
- Remove the capital expenditure and reduce the TCO for infrastructure operations and maintenance.
- Increase the product release velocity from 2 months to 3 weeks.

Current Technology Stack

We have detailed the current technology stack in Table 4.3.

Cloud Migration Process

We have depicted the activities in various phases of cloud migration journey in this section.

Assess Phase

We have identified the strategic goals for cloud migration as given in earlier section. We assess the application and server inventory to identify the key metrics such as utilization metrics, performance metrics and others. The migration team is also trained on cloud skills such as cloud-managed platforms, serverless technologies, cloud security controls and others.

Table 4.3   Current Technology Stack of the Organization

Application	Technology Stack	Brief Details
Custom onboarding portal	Monolith built on enterprise Java technologies running on virtual machines.	Legacy application that currently has scalability challenges during high load.
Custom built services layer	Service components as part of monolith.	Heavyweight services that are tightly coupled with presentation layer components.
Enterprise database	Oracle database.	The database is used for managing onboarding portal data and the customer documents.
Reporting application	Custom packaged application running on virtual machine.	Third-party software vendor–provided application.
Middleware	Enterprise Service Bus (ESB).	Middleware for interacting with enterprise systems.
Credit decisioning engine	Rules-based system.	Currently the credit decisioning engine uses manual approvals.

Design Phase

We have depicted the migration strategy adopted for migrating various applications in Table 4.4.

Migrate and Modernize Phase

We use the chosen migration strategy in Table 4.4 to perform the migrate and modernization. We have categorized the migrate and modernize exercise into three categories as depicted in Figure 4.4.

During *foundation* stage, we setup the main building blocks needed for cloud migration. We setup the base cloud environment along with network and security baseline. We setup the CCoE at the organization to drive the cloud adoption and define the cloud governance processes and cloud policies. We execute the migration PoCs to validate the replatforming of the proprietary SQL database into cloud-managed open-source database and NoSQL database. We also plan the migration sprints in the migrate stage.

In the *migrate* stage, we start with easy wins by rehosting the packaged application on the right-sized cloud server. We migrate the data used by the packaged

Table 4.4 Migration Strategy

Application	Migration Strategy Adopted	Cloud Migration Details	Rationale for the Migration Strategy
Custom onboarding portal	Refactor	Redesign the front end using the modern UI frameworks such as ReactJS. Build the portal backend as serverless.	Modernize the legacy to scalable, cloud-native technology.
Custom-built services layer	Refactor	Redesign to microservices and deploy as containers.	Modernize into scalable microservices architecture.
Enterprise database	Replatform	Manage the relational data in cloud-managed open-source database; manage the documents in cloud-native NoSQL database.	Modernize into scalable and cost-effective database based on the use case.
Reporting application	Rehost	Lift and shift the application to the right-sized cloud servers.	Third-party application that cannot be modernized.
Middleware	Refactor	Use cloud-managed API gateway	Modernize the application to improve the scalability.
Credit decisioning engine	Refactor	Redesign the credit decisioning logic to use cloud-native machine learning technology.	Automate the credit decisioning process.

application as part of the same iteration. In subsequent iterations, we adopt the refactoring migration strategy. We refactor the user interface (UI) for custom onboarding application, proprietary database into cloud–managed open-source database for managing the structured data and NoSQL database for storing the documents. We replace the legacy middleware to a scalable cloud-native API gateway.

In the *modernize* stage, we use cloud-based ML features to automate the credit decisioning and other activities. We use cloud-native serverless technologies for net new development and continuously improve the performance of workloads on the cloud.

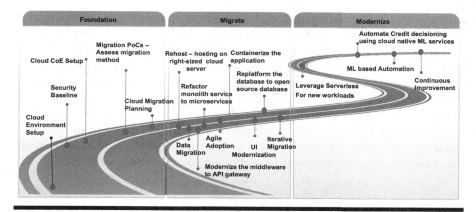

Figure 4.4   Migration and modernization phases.

Benefits

Cloud migration and modernization provided the below given benefits:

- The organization was able to release a product within three weeks due to automation measures and the agile processes on cloud.
- The scalability of individual solution components increased due to the containerization of microservices, usage of cloud-managed API gateway and NoSQL database.
- The organization was able to reduce the technical debt by migrating to the modern technologies.
- The customer onboarding time was reduced from 1 day to 5 minutes due to the self-service scalable onboarding platform.
- The organization was able to create an open API ecosystem.

Summary

The main cloud migration advantages are cost efficiency, faster innovation, unlimited storage, automation, maintainability, quick deployment, elastic scalability, interoperability and faster delivery of new services. On cloud the main transformation themes and benefits can be categorized into business, technology, operations and governance and security. The four broad types of cloud migration options are replace, partial migration, full migration and cloudify. The cloud migration stages are assess stage, design stage and migrate and modernize stage. In assess phase, we identify and map the organization's strategic business goals to cloud benefits. We perform the cloud TCO analysis, business value articulation and application assessment during this stage. During the assess phase, we evaluate various migration strategies, such as rehost, replatform and refactor, to determine the optimal migration strategy for various applications and platforms planned for migration. We map the on-premise inventory to the cloud solution components. During the migrate and modernize stage, we iteratively migrate the applications. We setup DevSecops and monitor the pipeline for continuous improvement. The key success factors for cloud migration are focus on customer engagement, identification of the business drivers for cloud migration and mapping it to migration solution components, sprint-based migration, PoC-based validation, robust migration plan, new development using cloud-native technologies, skills training and enablement, migration automation, robust cloud security, faster experimentation, definition and monitoring of KPIs.

References

1. Apostu, A., Puican, F., Ularu, G., Suciu, G., & Todoran, G. (2013). Study on Advantages and Disadvantages of Cloud Computing–The Advantages of Telemetry Applications in the Cloud. Recent advances in applied computer science and digital services.
2. Jamshidi, P., Ahmad, A., & Pahl, C. (2013). Cloud migration research: a systematic review. *IEEE Transactions on Cloud Computing* 1(2), 142–157.
3. Rai, R., Sahoo, G., & Mehfuz, S. (2015). Exploring the factors influencing the cloud computing adoption: a systematic study on cloud migration. *SpringerPlus* 4, 1–12.
4. Business value on AWS – Amazon Web Services, inc. (n.d.). Retrieved March 12, 2023, from https://pages.awscloud.com/rs/112-TZM-766/images/Business%20Va lue%20on%20AWS%20-%20Whitepaper%20%281%29.pdf
5. Carvalho, L., & Marden, M. (2015). Quantifying the business value of Amazon web services. *IDC White Paper*, 1–15.

DIGITAL TRANSFORMATION OF TECHNOLOGY

Chapter 5

Services Transformation

Introduction

Enterprises often use application modernization as part of their digital transformation journey. Application modernization is a process of progressively transforming their existing application and infrastructure to modern technologies to reduce technical debt, unlock new business capabilities, optimize cost and accelerate the innovation.

Application modernization commonly involves migrating to modern user interface (UI) technologies, transforming monolith to microservices, using cloud-native technologies, using serverless technologies and such.

Migrating existing monolith applications to microservices need careful planning. We should understand the key business drivers, and key performance indicators (KPIs) and success factors for the modernization. Based on this we define the migration plan, iterative microservice deployment and others.

In this chapter we discuss the core principles of microservices and the process steps for transforming monolith to microservices. We also discuss the patterns for microservices, microservices best practices, microservices testing and the case study for the monolith to microservice transformation.

Microservices

Microservice is an architecture pattern to build loosely coupled services [1]. Microservices provide modular service components that handle single functionality. Microservices are independently scalable, technology independent

DOI: 10.1201/9781003390893-8

and independently deployable and provides development agility and deployment flexibility. Microservices are modeled around a business domain and compartmentalizes complexity. As a result, we can increase the release velocity and scale easily.

Principles of Microservices

During the refactoring of the monolith to microservices we need to design the microservices that satisfy the core tenets of microservices. We discuss the core tenets of microservices in this section.

Core Principles

We have defined the core principles below:

Modeled around business functionality—The microservices are designed around the business functionality and hence have high cohesion. Hence all the service dependencies (such as database) should be part of the microservice deployment. The data is exposed to consumers through clearly defined interfaces.

Data ownership—Microservices own their data and hence the data stores used by the microservices are deployed along with microservice. Interested microservices can access through the APIs and cache the data.

Extensibility—We should be able to add new functionality to the microservices with minimal effort and minimal impact on existing functionality.

Single Responsibility Principle—The microservice should be able to handle single responsibility and own the data related for the use case. The separation of responsibilities should be clearly defined between microservices.

Evolutionary design—The functionality of the microservices is refined with each iteration. We can use blue/green deployment model and DevSecOps to roll out the features iteratively.

Design for failure—The microservices should be able to handle the errors gracefully and should prevent domino effect on the other microservices. Redundancy, auto-scaling based on demand, fault tolerance, health checks, auto-recovery, backup, decentralized data management, security testing, exponential back off and automated monitoring are factors that need to be considered while designing for failure.

Integration Principles

We have defined the integration-related principles for microservices below:

Asynchronous invocation—To enable loose coupling and event-driven architecture, the microservices should communicate asynchronously. The messages can be sent to queues (for point to point communication) and topics (for publish-subscribe use case) for providing high scalability of the system. Consumers should invoke the microservices through lightweight interaction protocols such as HTTP or REST.

Frequent, iterative changes—The changes to the microservices should be released frequently so that we get faster customer feedback and reduce the integration and deployment risk.

Loose coupling—The microservices have high cohesion and low coupling. The microservices should not have any dependencies on other services. At runtime, the microservices use asynchronous communication mode and publish or subscribe to events. Loose coupling also improves the availability and scalability of the microservices.

Encapsulation—The microservice should provide well-defined API contracts and should not expose the internal business logic. The changes to internal business logic should not change the API contract.

Statelessness—The microservice should not manage any state data to eliminate the resource overhead for state management. Stateless microservices are much easier to scale.

Security—The microservices should be accessible only from authorized users and should support token-based security.

Autonomous—The microservices are self-contained services that own a business capability that own its own data and evolve independently. Microservices are independently deployable and independently scalable.

Infrastructure Principles

We have defined the infrastructure-related principles for microservices below:

Independent scalability—The microservices are independently scalable. We can develop, deploy and change the individual microservice without impacting other services. Individual microservice can be selectively scaled based on the load requirements specific to the microservice.

Distributed—The microservices should be horizontally scalable and should be deployable across various instances/nodes.

Decentralization—The microservices should be decentralized without any single point of failure by distributing the requests. Decentralization can be achieved through database-per-service pattern (to avoid single point of failure for databases and for decentralized data management) and DevSecOps (for automated release management).

Independently deployable—The microservices should be independently deployable without any dependency on other services.

Automation through DevSecOps—The build, test, deployment and monitoring of the microservices should be automated through DevSecOps pipeline. The continuous delivery and continuous integration should be supported for microservices.

Drivers for Transforming to Microservices

Monolith to microservice transformation is one of the core modernization initiatives undertaken by organizations. We have compared the key characteristics of monolith and microservices in Table 5.1.

Monolith to Microservice Transformation

Legacy monolith applications are built with tightly coupled modules that performs all the required functionality. Monoliths have the presentation modules and business logic in a single tier. Due to the nature of tight coupling, even a small change in one of the modules require deployment of the entire monolith application thereby impacting the release velocity. Monoliths are also difficult to scale and a failure in one module impacts other modules.

Monolith to Microservice Transformation Patterns

We adopt multiple patterns to transform the monolith into microservices. In this section, we discuss the key patterns with examples.

For discussing the monolith to microservice transformations, we have considered a payment monolith application as depicted in Figure 5.1. The payment monolith is built on legacy UI platform using Java Server Pages (JSP) and the business services, such as payments, account and registration services, are developed as tightly coupled software modules. The data is centrally managed in a centralized master SQL database

In the subsequent sections we have described the migration patterns.

Strangler Pattern

In strangler pattern we iteratively transform the monolith modules into microservices [2]. We gradually replace the monolith with the microservices. We start with the monolith module that has least dependencies with other modules. We develop the new capabilities as microservices. Until all the existing monolith modules are fully transformed into microservices, both the newly created microservice and the existing monolith modules co-exist.

Strangler pattern is often used as a starting point of the monolith to microservice modernization journey as it provides a low-risk migration option.

We have depicted an example of strangler pattern-based refactoring in Figure 5.2

In the first iteration we isolate the payment module into payment microservice (that has least dependencies) with its own payment database. Since the registration module and account modules are part of monolith application that stores the data in the master database, we synchronize the master database with the payment database.

Table 5.1 Monolith vs. Microservices

Architecture Characteristic	Monolith	Microservice	Microservice Advantage
Deployment	Entire monolith is deployed as single code base impacting the release time.	Individual microservice deployment. Easier, faster and quicker deployment.	Faster release time
Agility	Low modularity and changes need redeployment of entire monolith.	Individually developed and deployed and changes are absorbed easily.	Faster time to market
Scalability	Stateful with limited scalability	Stateless and independently scalable.	Higher scalability
Cost	High due to maintenance and enhancement cost.	Low	Lower cost
Maintainability	High due to the cost of change.	Low	Easy maintainability
Testability	Higher testing efforts.	Lower testing efforts due to automation.	Easy testability
Resiliency	Fatal error in single module can bring down application due to tight coupling.	Failures are localized and does not impact other services.	High resiliency
Flexibility	The choice of programming language, framework and database is fixed for the entire application.	Developers can chose their program and platform of choice and use most appropriate database for the use case (Polygot persistence).	More flexibility

(Continued)

Table 5.1 (Continued)

Architecture Characteristic	Monolith	Microservice	Microservice Advantage
Data management	Centralized master database with rigid schema poses challenges during schema changes, scaling and acts as single point of failure.	Polygot persistence (use case-specific database) provides flexible schema changes, high scalability and high performance.	Flexible, scalable and manageable database.

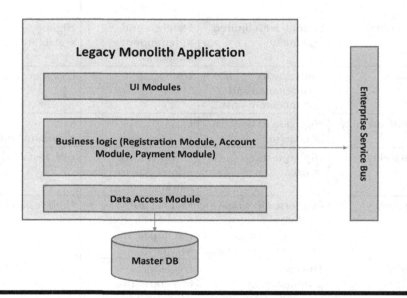

Figure 5.1 Typical monolith application.

In subsequent iterations we also create separate database for registration microservice and account microservice.

Decomposition by Business Capabilities Pattern

We identity the business context and logically group the modules and events based on the business context. The business context has a clearly defined boundaries that also specifies the ownership. The business capability-based decomposition achieves loose coupling.

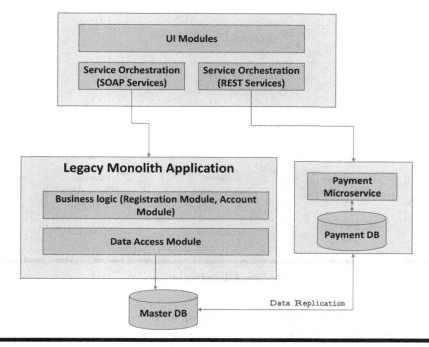

Figure 5.2   Strangler pattern.

In Figure 5.3 we have created registration, account and payment transactions as distinct microservices as registration, account and payment are distinct business functionality. As the microservice owns its business data, each of the microservices manages its data in a separate data store.

Event-Driven Architecture Pattern

Event-driven architecture is used for integration at scale for microservices. We identify the business events based on their business domain and the services can both post events and subscribe for the events.

Event sourcing is one of the popular patterns used in the event-driven architecture. In event sourcing pattern, a command generates an event which is stored in an immutable append-only event store. Current state is derived by replaying the sequence of events that are added over a period of time.

For the payment monolith depicted in Figure 5.1, we group the events into three business domains—payments, account and registration. All the account-related events (such as account created, account updated, account deleted) are grouped into account domain; similarly, payments events (such as payment completed, payment

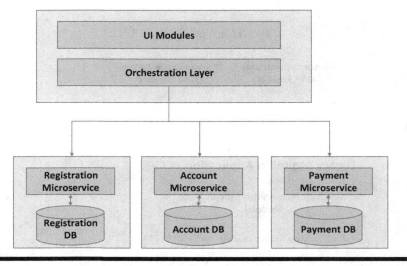

Figure 5.3   Business capability-based decomposition.

pending) into payment domain and registration events (such as approval required, registration completed) are grouped into registration domain.

Each of the microservices subscribe to a highly available and highly scalable event store as depicted in Figure 5.4. The event store has immutable append-only list of events. When the user registers to the platform, the registration service posts the event (that has newly registered user details) to the centralized event store. The account service that has subscribed to the event store gets the notification about the new user and uses the registration data to create the account. When the user makes the payment, the payment service handles the payment data.

Database Per Service Pattern

To address the scalability challenges with the monolith, we use the polygot persistence wherein we have database per service pattern. Each microservice chooses the most appropriate database relevant for its use case to make it independently scalable. For instance, a recommendation microservice uses graph database whereas a document management microservice uses document database, a shopping cart service uses NoSQL database and an account management service uses a relational database.

In the distributed database scenario, the transactions are handled through eventual consistency. Each transaction that spans multiple microservices are correlated through a unique correlation ID. Each microservice provides a rollback function. During the failure, transaction manager invokes the rollback function of all the involved microservices using the correlation ID.

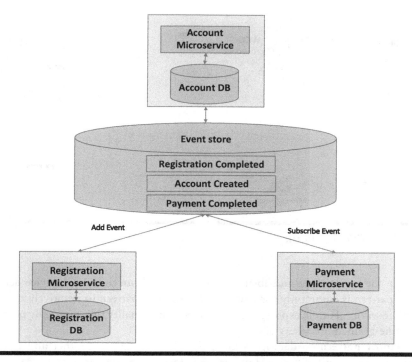

Figure 5.4   Event-driven architecture.

Command Query Responsibility Segregation (CQRS) Pattern

The data stores achieve high scalability by decoupling read and command (insert, update, modify, delete) operations so that read and write operations can scale independently. CQRS pattern helps in polygot persistence and enables eventual consistency. Figure 5.5 depicts the CQRS pattern with event sourcing where we use an event store to store the write events and a cache for read events. We have depicted the CQRS with event sourcing in Figure 5.5.

When the client invokes the write commands (such as data insert, update, delete) on the write microservice, it stores the write events in the event store. The data from the event store is synchronized with the cache. The read microservice uses the data from the cache for the read operations and queries.

Other Patterns

We have given some of the other patterns commonly used while transforming from monolith to microservice below:

Façade pattern—A façade acts as a single point of entry and gateway for all the client requests. The façade routes the request to the monolith or microservice

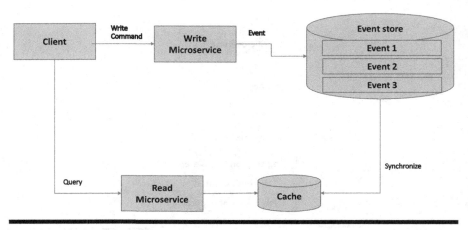

Figure 5.5 CQRS pattern.

based on the request type and abstracts the requestor from the actual service details. Façade pattern is commonly used along with strangler pattern to iteratively migrate the microservice. Façade exposes coarse-grained functionality that internally maps to many fine-grained microservices.

Adaptor pattern—Adaptors convert one data format to another and is used when two services use different data exchange formats for interaction.

Saga pattern—In orchestrator type of Saga pattern, a central orchestrator coordinates the sequence across all the microservices. In the choreographer type of Saga pattern, the microservices send and respond to the events. The microservices broadcast the events to a message broker and interested microservices consume them. The Saga pattern also supports compensation events to handle the rollback and failure.

Observability: Monitoring, logging and tracing—A transaction across microservices should be traced using correlation ID to get the visibility across various microservices. The log data should be aggregated across various microservices into a centralized location. The unified view of the end-to-end performance helps in identifying the performance bottlenecks and troubleshoot quicker.

Resiliency Patterns—To ensure resiliency of microservice, we should implement patterns such as circuit breaker (that avoids an operation that is likely to fail), timeout (stop the wait after a pre-configured time duration), asynchronous communication (in which the services are invoked asynchronously) and exponentially back off (where requests are retried with increasing wait times between each retry).

Monolith to Microservice Transformation Phases

The monolith to microservice transformation exercise involves extensive planning. We have detailed the prerequisites and key stages of the transformation plan based on the proven best practices.

We have discussed the plan for transforming the typical monolith application into microservices along with applicable patterns and various stages.

Context

A monolith application has tightly coupled components. The solution components addressing various concerns, such as security, presentation and business logic, are part of a single application.

Prerequisites

Before we kick-off the transformation engagement, we need to analyze the existing monolith application. Given below are some of the prerequisites we need to complete before the start of the transformation engagement.

As-Is Analysis

We should analyze the existing landscape to understand the underlying platform and frameworks. We should also understand the challenges (such as scalability-related challenges or performance-related challenges) with the current platform. We also assess the organization readiness to define the governance model and training plan.

Skill Set Analysis

The project manager should assess the skill set of the current project team. This helps us to create the learning and training plan to enable the existing project team on the microservices and modern technologies (such as containers, NoSQL databases) targeted for the migration.

Success Factors Metrics

The project manager should have clear visibility of the success factors for the migration. The project manager should identify the business drivers and the success metrics (such as time to market, delivery quality and others).

Monolith to Microservice Transformation Phases

We start with the deeper understanding of the existing monolith landscape and subsequently we design the modernization plan. The monolith to microservice transformation has several stages as depicted in Figure 5.6.

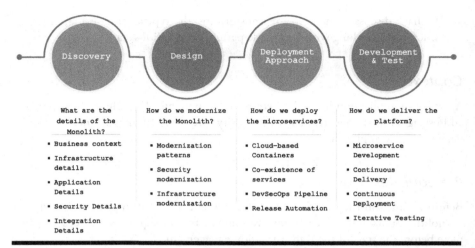

Figure 5.6 Monolith to microservice transformation phases.

Discovery Phase

In the discovery phase, we gather all the details of the monolith ecosystem including the infrastructure, application, security and integration. We gather and analyze the application architecture, infrastructure architecture and security architecture of the existing platform.

We mainly understand the business context, business domains and subdomains. This insight helps us in designing the microservices. We also understand other details such as multi-lingual requirements and channel preference (web app or mobile app).

On the infrastructure front we gather the below given details:

- Core infrastructure details: We gather the server details (such as size and capacity of web server, application server, database server, file servers and others). We also gather details of network components (such as switches, routers), security components (such as firewall, Web Application Firewall user directory) and all other components involved.
- Infrastructure telemetry: We gather the utilization metrics of the infrastructure components. The metrics are used to create right-sized infrastructure components in the target environment.
- Traffic metrics: We gather the key traffic metrics, such as maximum concurrent users per second, maximum transactions per second, average and peak load and required input/output operations per second (IOPS), for various servers.
- Other infrastructure components: In this category we gather details of existing backup jobs, synchronization jobs.

- Disaster recovery (DR) and business continuity process (BCP): We understand the Recovery Point Objective (RPO), Recovery Time Objective (RTO) and the disaster recovery processes. This helps us to setup the equivalent DR processes and synchronization jobs in the target platform.
- Non-functional requirements: In this category we gather the details of availability metrics, scalability metrics (such as maximum supported concurrent transactions), performance metrics (such as response times, download times).

We conduct the application portfolio analysis to understand the following details:

- Solution component details: The details of solution components and the business logic handled by the solution components.
- Security component details: The details of the security components handling the authentication, authorization and role-based access in the application.
- Utility component details: We gather details about the utility components like caching module, logging module, encryption module, exception handling module and such.
- Integration details: We analyze the APIs and API contracts, protocols, data transformation requirements and such.
- Core application details: We gather the details of state management (stateless/stateful), API design and storage,

On the database front, we understand the data model, schema details, stored procedure details, data backup details and other details.

We get the existing test cases for the application to understand the test scenarios.

Design Phase

For refactoring monolith to microservice, we mainly evaluate various modernization patterns such as strangler pattern, façade pattern, decomposition pattern and others. For data access and for distributed data use cases, we evaluate various patterns such as CQRS, event sourcing, Saga and others. For service integration we shall evaluate protocols such as REST and GraphQL in synchronous or asynchronous mode. For security modules, we evaluate various authentication and authorization methods such as the stateless security model, OAuth 2.0 flows, short-lived tokens and such. For service documentation we use OpenAPI, Swagger and others.

We also evaluate tools that can help with refactoring the existing monolith code to the microservices. Each of the programming languages has frameworks that support microservices (for instance Spring Boot in Java, Flask in Python) that can be leveraged for this effort. On the database front, there are tools that can migrate data and schema across heterogeneous databases.

As this phase need deep-dive analysis, we have discuss the methodologies and patterns in microservice design section.

Deployment Design Phase

In this phase, we evaluate the deployment options. Microservices are best deployed using cloud-based containers (such as Docker containers with Kubernetes orchestration engine). Containers provide faster startup, high scaling and isolated execution environment for self-contained microservices. During iterative migration of services from monolith to microservices, we have to design for co-existence of services across both monolith and microservices layers. To accommodate this, we evaluate patterns such as API gateway. Similarly, we also evaluate various service discovery patterns for microservices to communicate with each other.

The important aspect of the deployment is the DevSecOps pipeline that automates the build, test, deployment and release activities. We design various components of the pipeline.

Development and Test Phase

Once the design activities are completed, we refactor the existing monolith to microservices iteratively. We leverage the DevSecOps pipeline to continuously build, test and deploy the microservices.

Microservice Design

For microservices design, we have identified four key stages as depicted in Figure 5.7.

During the "analyze" phase, we identify the business domain and define the primary candidates for microservices. We identify the microservices across various layers (such as authentication, business logic, data, integration and such).

The next step is the "design" phase wherein we start with business functionality that has least dependency on other functionality (like authentication service, logging

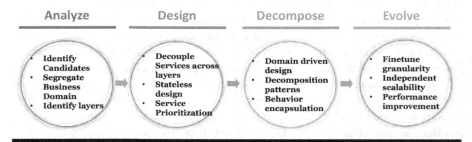

Figure 5.7   Microservices design.

service, caching service etc.). We use one of the patterns, such as strangler or business-capability-based decomposition, to define the initial list of microservices. We then define the main payload structure, and API contracts. We start decoupling the microservices from the monolith by breaking the dependency. As the microservices need to be independently scalable, we also extract the data requirements for each of the microservices and use the appropriate data persistence platform (such as SQL or NoSQL databases) bundled with the microservice. Creating a microservice specific data storage also requires the data migration from existing database. During the microservice design process we ensure that new services are stateless and prioritize the services based on their business criticality. We use 12-factor apps [3] guidance to design the microservices to provide high scalability and high resilience.

We start with macro services that are logically related to a business domain and follow the domain driven design concept. The defined microservices should encapsulate the business functionality and behavior. To start with, we start with a larger business domain and later create granular microservices iteratively. For instance, we start with Account domain to create a macro service and later create granular services, such as Savings Account, Current Account and such, iteratively based on the business requirements.

"Evolve" phase is an ongoing optimization and fine-tuning stage where we continuously monitor the microservice and improve its scalability and performance based on the requirements. We must ensure that the microservices should be independently deployable. We normally use API gateway to deliver the microservices and events for exchanging data between microservices.

We continue to evolve till all the functionality in the monolith is transformed into microservice.

Microservice Best Practices

Given below are the key best practices while designing microservices.

API contract—Create microservices and APIs with well-defined contracts and payload structure. The input and output parameters, parameter data types, size limitations should be clearly defined.

Abstraction—The microservices should abstract the business logic from the consumers.

Open standards—The microservices should adopt the open standards such as HTTP, REST-based protocols; JSON, XML-based data exchange formats and security processes based on OAuth/SAML/OpenID standards. Adherence to open standards helps in easier integration with external services and provides scalability.

Well-defined response code—The microservice should provide a well-defined response code.

Table 5.2   Implementation of 12-Factor App Principles

12 Factor App Principle	Microservice Implementation
Code base	Version control system (such as Git). DevSecOps pipeline-based automation. Branching strategy.
Dependencies	Declare dependencies in configuration file (e.g. Package.json of node.js). All the dependencies are packaged as part of the application container.
Config	Environment-specific configuration which is deployed on host.
Backing services	Use resolvable name for the service. Use the local services like the remote service.
Build, release, run	Use container build tools and release management tools.
Stateless processes	The microservice persists state in an event store or a cache platform (like Redis).
Port binding	Run containers on specific port.
Concurrency	Run concurrent microservices on containers based on the host capacity.
Disposability	The container orchestration should be able to shut down and start new container on demand.
Dev/Prod parity	Use the same image on containers for both development and production environments.
Logs	Securely store the logs in a centralized location.
Admin processes	Run the admin microservices like regular microservices.

Naming convention—For REST microservices use nouns (such as account, order, cart) as resources and the verbs (HTTP GET, POST, DELETE) on the resources to perform the appropriate CRUD (Create, Read, Update, Delete) operations.

12-factor app principles—Implementing the 12-factor app principles along with the microservice principles provides us a scalable and resilient microservices. Table 5.2 provides the microservice best practices to implement the 12-factor apps.

Microservice Testing

Each of the microservices are individually unit tested through automated unit test cases. For end-to-end testing we test all the microservices involved in the use case.

Table 5.3 Microservice Testing Tools

Testing Category	Tools/Frameworks
Unit testing	Junit, Mockito
Mocking services	Dbunit, mockaroo
Integration testing	TestNG, Spring Boot Test, REST-assured
Functional testing	Selenium, Cucumber
Load testing	Apache JMeter, LoadUI
Chaos engineering tools	Gremlin, Chaos monkey
Security testing	Synk, OWASP Zed Attack Proxy (ZAP), Burp suite

We can integrate the testing as part of CICD pipeline to automate the testing. We have depicted the main testing tools in Table 5.3.

Unit Testing

The unit testing of microservices test the individual methods or classes of the microservice. All the dependencies are mocked. It is recommended that unit tests are automated, isolated (validates specific method or class), idempotent (can be invoked without impacting the state) and invoked frequently.

Integration Testing

Integration testing validates the service contracts of the APIs. It validates the API and its dependencies.

Functional Testing

The functional testing validates the specified functionality of the component. The functional test cases validate the positive flows and error handling flows of the component. A black box testing is a type of functional testing wherein the tester treats the component as a black box without any knowledge of the inner working of the component and validates the behavior of the component.

Non-Functional Testing

As part of non-functional testing, we validate the quality parameters of the application such as performance, scalability and availability. The main non-functional tests are load testing, stress testing, resiliency testing and performance testing.

Load Testing

We test the microservices with the average and peak load and monitor the resources. We monitor the response times, resource utilization and auto-scaling of the compute resources to handle the peak load. We report the below given metrics in load testing:

- Concurrent transactions—the maximum number of concurrent transactions that the microservice can process simultaneously.
- Transactions per second (TPS)—The total number of transactions that are completed in one second.
- Latency or transaction completion time—The total time taken for the completion of the transaction.

Stress Testing

The stress testing aims to understand the breaking point of the application and tests the exception handling capability of the microservice. For stress testing, we test the microservice with load higher than the expected peak load to overwhelm the resources and test the graceful failure behavior of the microservice. For instance, if the expected peak load is 100 concurrent users per second, we use 200 concurrent users per second in stress testing and monitor the resource utilization.

Resiliency Testing

Resiliency testing aims to validate the ability of the microservice to recover from the failure. We use chaos engineering to inject the failures to simulate the real-world failure scenarios. For instance, a chaos engineering tool turns off the machines randomly, blocks the ports, shuts down the router, kills the process, terminates the load balancers and perform activities to simulate the failures. We then test the resiliency of the microservice on how well it handles the failover, auto-scaling and such.

Performance Testing

Check the response time of the APIs during average and peak loads. We compare the 95 percentile and 99 percentile response time numbers with the baseline performance SLAs.

Security Testing

The security testing is carried out to uncover the security vulnerabilities in the microservices. We test the OWASP top ten vulnerabilities [4] such as injection attacks, cross-site scripting (XSS) attacks, privilege escalation attack, weak security configurations, broken authentication, weak passwords and such.

Monolith to Microservice Transformation Case Study

In this section, we discuss a case study to transform the monolith to microservice hosted on cloud. We discuss the transformation steps and patterns for transforming the monolith to microservice in this case study.

Background of the Monolith Application

We have depicted the monolith application in Figure 5.8.

The loan handler application is developed in PHP technology and is widely used by the organization for managing the loans. The loan handler application has modules to register the borrowers, manage the end-to-end life cycle of the loan and collections. Both the UI and the business logic are tightly coupled and is developed in PHP. The mobile interface uses the PHP web page by field agents for handling loan transactions. The loan documents and media files (such as agreement copies, identity documents and others) are stored in the local storage of the application server. The application uses in-process state management, stores user's logged-in state inside web server's memory and leverages MySQL database for persistence.

Challenges with the Current Monolith Application

Given below are the main challenges with the current monolith application:

- The monolith application is not able to scale to handle high users.
- Performance issues with the loan handler applications especially when accessed from mobile device.

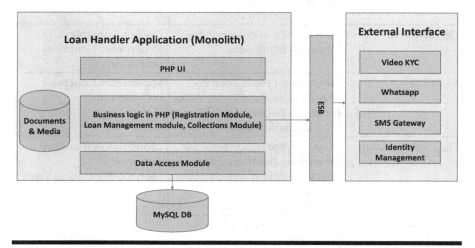

Figure 5.8   Loan handler monolith.

- Lack of traceability leading to higher lead times during debugging.
- Performance challenges during database transactions.
- Frequent availability issues with the application.

Modernization to Microservices

We have defined the modernization approach for the legacy application in Table 5.4.

Modernization Patterns

During modernization, we use the API gateway as the entry point for the microservices. We use strangler pattern to progressively extract the microservices

Table 5.4   Modernization Approach

Monolith Module	Modernization Approach	Modernization Tools and Platforms
PHP-based UI module	Refactor into React-based responsive UI to provide mobile friendly interface.	React Framework
PHP-based business logic	Refactor into Spring Boot-based microservice.	Spring Boot
State management	Refactor stateful state management into stateless microservices. Use a scalable caching platform for optimal management of state.	Redis Cache
Deployment	Deploy the microservice through containers.	Docker Containers Kubernetes Container orchestration
Scalability	Implement Horizontal Pod Auto scaler and Cluster Auto scaler in Kubernetes while deploying services.	Kubernetes Container orchestration
Data management	Use polygot persistence for managing the transaction data in cloud-native database and document data in NoSQL database.	Cloud native managed database MongoDB for documents
Integration	Use API gateway to expose the APIs	API Gateway Apache ActiveMQ

from the monolith. We implement microservices Observability by tracking metrics, traces and logs for end-to-end transactions.

DevSecOps

We also implement the DevSecOps processes to automate the build, test and deployment using the pipeline. The DevSecOps processes helps us to quickly deploy the enhancements.

Open API Platform

Open API platform enables enterprises to democratize access to their existing assets and capabilities by integrating the digital services through APIs while augmenting the external capabilities to offer best-in-class experience. Open API platform exposes the APIs to registered users to access the core functionality and data in secured way. Open API platform enables enterprises to monetize the data.

Enterprises provide marketplace and Developer Portal as part of open API platform. Marketplace allows enterprises to offer a curated set of products and integrated experiences reflecting the brand value proposition and their partnerships with customers and partners, while enabling in-app management and interaction. Developer Portal is a public platform that technology partners and providers visit to discover and explore APIs, resources and knowledge base to help them implement and integrate their product or service into the enterprise's open API ecosystem.

We have depicted the key elements, such as business outcomes, technology delivery, optimized operations and optimized governance, of open API platform in Figure 5.9.

The main business outcome of the open API platform is that it enables enterprises to build an API ecosystem and a new business model using API monetization. The open API platform helps enterprises to create new age marketplaces that help partners, customers and enterprises to consume and contribute the applications built on top of the enterprise APIs.

The technology delivery dimension involves building an API-first design platform and its roadmap. The integration are driven by API. We use open standards, such as HTTP(s) or REST, for integration that offer flexibility for future integrations.

As part of an optimized governance dimension, we define the standards for the platform and API governance (security guardrails and API management processes). We also define a self-service model wherein the developers can register themselves in the Developer Portal and use the APIs.

As part of an optimized operations dimension, we use DevOps to automate the build and management of APIs to drive operational efficiency and cost savings.

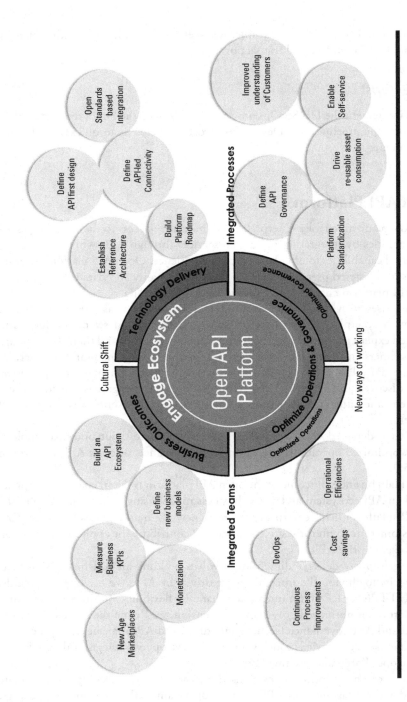

Figure 5.9 Open API platform ecosystem.

Based on the API analytics we drive continuous process improvements to improve the API performance, scalability and maintenance cost.

Open API Platform Goals

We have listed the key goals of open API platform as follows:

- "Power of choice" for customers, partners and enterprise by building on the APIs.
- Market growth and penetration through efficient collaboration with partners, customers and developers.
- Increased speed and scale of innovation through standards-based integration.
- Enablement of productive and disruptive innovation.
- Business model agility by being able to quickly incorporate the changes.
- Leverage "data" as a competitive differentiator.
- Partnering with "best-of-breed" solutions.
- Bidirectional exchange of data and capabilities.
- Increased interoperability across various platforms and services.

Open API Platform Capabilities

In order to build an open API platform, we use platforms such as API gateway, active directory, logging and others. We have listed the main capabilities that an open API platform supports below.

1. Developer, partner, and app onboarding by providing features such as client ID/app key generation, interactive API console, user registration, user approval and others.
2. Traffic mediation such as SOAP to REST mediation, data format transformation, legacy application integration and others.
3. API life cycle governance to support the below given features for API:
   a. Create
   b. Secure
   c. Document
   d. Test
   e. Versioning
   f. Publish
4. Analytics engine for providing insight for business owners, operational administrators, and developers into how much traffic APIs are getting.
5. API security through features such as SSL, PKI, threat protection, schema validation, encryption, signatures etc.

6. API identity by supporting AuthN & AuthZ, API key, OAuth, SAML, LDAP, proprietary IAM, multifactor, token translation and management.
7. API orchestration through adaptation of multiple services, workflow operations, branching policies etc.
8. Rate limiting by allowing defined number of concurrent APIs for specified time period.
9. Data protection through data encryption, data masking etc. for PCI/PII compliance.
10. Logging, monitoring and alerts by monitoring and logging various metrics such as API errors, user-specific API metrics, API performance and others.

Open API Platform Design

We have depicted various components of a digital enterprise in an e-commerce domain with an API platform in Figure 5.10. The e-commerce products, such as product management, search engine, recommendation engine and portals, are offered to the customers. These products internally use the B2B (business to business) and B2C (business to consumer) capabilities such as seller onboarding, marketing service, lead management and performance management for B2B and capabilities such as product management, shopping cart, search, order management and recommendation service for B2C domain.

The capabilities use the open API platform that provides API governance, API management capabilities and Developer Portal. The API management capability provides the core building block API functionality such as API gateway (the main entry point for all API invocation), API security (authentication and authorization of APIs), API creation and deployment (process of creating and deploying the APIs), API policies (that supports the features such as rate limiting/throttling, integration, data transformation, protocol translation and others), API monitoring (real-time monitoring of API metrics) and API analytics (such as user-specific API calls and others).

The Developer Portal enables the developers to register and build using the exposed APIs. Developers can register on the Developer Portal and start using the SDK on the sandbox environment. Developers can use the API documentation and discover or browse the available APIs. The Developer Portal also provides opportunity for developers to collaborate with the community.

The API hierarchy is divided into three main categories—experience APIs, process APIs and system APIs. The experience APIs are designed to cater to experience channels such as web platform and mobile platform. The granularity of the experience APIs are designed to serve the functionality of a specific web fragment or a mobile screen. The experience APIs provide the user context (such as user role, category) to the underlying APIs and will use the process APIs to get the required data.

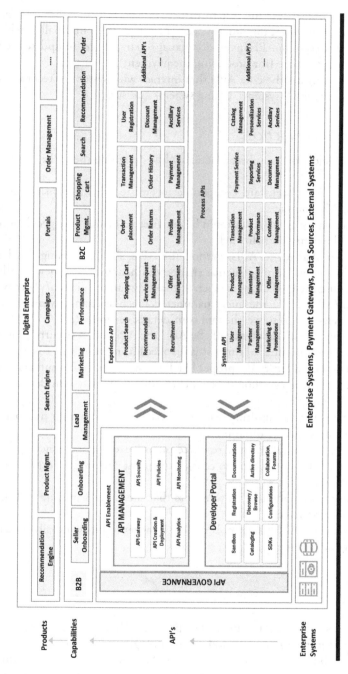

Figure 5.10 Digital enterprise ecosystem.

Process APIs orchestrate the system APIs to aggregate data and fulfil a business functionality. For instance, the order placement process API internally orchestrates the order details to system APIs inventory management service (to update the inventory) and payment service (for processing the payment).

The system APIs are the core APIs that interact with system of records (such as enterprise database, ERP systems, billing systems and such).

API Design Best Practices

We have listed below the core best practices while designing the APIs:

- Make the APIs backward compatible to ensure existing consumers use the defined API contracts.
- The granularity of the API should be designed to handle the specific functionality of the requesting channel.
- For major changes to APIs, version the APIs. API versioning can be done using domain versioning (such as change weather.api.com to new-weather.api.com) or use the URI changes (such as change weather.api.com/v1/ to weather.api.com/ v2/) or use the query parameters (such as change weather.api.com/details?version=1.0 to weather.api.com/details?version= 2.0)
- Implement the idempotency of the API (the API action occurring only once irrespective of number of times it is invoked) using the client tokens.
- The APIs should return the proper HTTP error codes for consumers to handle it. The error message should not include the internal system details (such as server details).
- Implement the rate limiting feature to restrict the maximum number of API calls during a specific duration.
- For APIs that implement a resource-intensive operation (such as complex table joins or a costly remote calls) implement caching to improve the API performance.
- Handle the timeout at APIs to ensure that the issues with one API does not cause domino effect.
- Document the APIs using tools such as Swagger to make it easily understandable by the developers.

Summary

Application modernization is a process of progressively transforming their existing application and infrastructure to modern technologies. Microservice is an architecture pattern to build loosely coupled services. Microservices provide modular service components that handle single functionality. The main microservice principles are modeled around business functionality, data ownership, Extensibility, Single Responsibility Principle, Evolutionary design, Design for failure, Asynchronous invocation, Frequent, iterative changes, Loose coupling, Encapsulation, Statelessness, Security, Autonomous, independently scalability, Distributed, Decentralization, Independently deployable and Automation through DevSecOps. The key patterns we use for transforming the monolith to microservices are strangler pattern (where we iteratively transform the monolith modules into microservices and gradually replace the monolith with the microservices), decomposition by business capabilities pattern (where we define microservices based on the business functionality handled by the microservice), event sourcing pattern (where a command generates an event that is stored in an immutable append-only event store), database per service pattern (where each microservice gets its own database), Command Query Responsibility Segregation (CQRS) Pattern (where read and write operations are decoupled), façade pattern, adaptor pattern, Saga pattern and Observability pattern. The main stages while transforming the monolith to microservice are discovery phase, design phase, deployment approach phase and development and test phase. The phases during microservices design are analysis, design, decompose and evolve.

References

1. What are microservices? (n.d.). microservices.io. http://microservices.io/index.html
2. Fowler, M. (June 29, 2004). StranglerFigApplicationhttps://martinfowler.com/bliki/StranglerFigApplication.html
3. Wiggins, A. (n.d.). The Twelve-Factor App. https://12factor.net/
4. OWASP Top Ten | OWASP Foundation. (n.d.). In *OWASP Top Ten | OWASP Foundation*. https://owasp.org/www-project-top-ten/

Chapter 6

Digital Factory for Digital Transformation

Introduction

The rapid innovation in the technology brings in its own set of challenges. Various business units within a large organization use different technologies that are best suited for their solutions. As a result, at the organization level, we lack a consistent set of standards, uniform set of integration methods, consistent delivery processes. As a result, delivering the business value consistently and predictably becomes one of the key challenges that organizations need to tackle. When the organization wants to innovate faster or to integrate quickly or to roll out the products quickly, the heterogeneous technologies, standards and processes come in the way of achieving the business goal. The non-standard processes also becomes an impediment for the organization's automation efforts.

In order to tackle the challenges posed by integration and roll out of heterogeneous technologies, we need a consistent, standards-based and uniform processes, tools, standards and technologies.

Digital factory leverages the methods of the manufacturing domain's assembly line delivery where the manufacturing of the products is automated using the assembly line. Digital factory model is heavily used in automotive industries [1] and manufacturing industries [2].

In this chapter we discuss a digital factory model that automates the delivery of software products in predictable and consistent way.

DOI: 10.1201/9781003390893-9

Digital Factory

A digital factory is defined set of processes, methods and tools that can be used to deliver high quality software product repeatedly and reliably. An organization can define the digital factory to consistently release high quality software using a standard set of standards, governance processes, best practices and tools.

Drivers for Digital Factory

Large organizations with multiple business functions often face challenges with integration and delivery timelines due to the heterogeneous technology stack. The main drivers for digital factory are given below:

- The organization hosts various applications to cater to the different business units that are built on multiple technology stacks. Each of the business units follow a different technology stack and development processes leading to integration challenges and impacting the delivery timelines.
- The development cycles are longer as multiple functionalities or use cases are part of an application development. This also results in repeated activities, similar in nature, but cannot be automated/standardized due to the varying complexities of the applications
- The organization is looking for an approach to simplify and standardize the development process—make it leaner and agile, so that the focus is on a single use case development. This allows greater efficiency through standardization and automation
- The organization is looking for a software playbook that can standardize the development process, tools and technologies
- The organization wants to implement a digital factory model to provide a consistent, standardized tools and processes

Digital Factory Phases

Digital factory aims to standardize and automate the software processes to build the software more reliably and quickly. At each of the phases, we define the templates and best practices that can be replicated across the organization. We have depicted the different phases of digital factory in Figure 6.1.

Firstly during the software product planning phase, we standardize the project management tools (such as Jira) at the organization level. We then define the methodology to prioritize the product features (for instance we prioritize based on business value, usability value and such). The finalized prioritization methodology is followed across all functional units within the organization. We then build the product roadmap defining the timelines, sprint wise features and so on. We can leverage the existing product roadmap template and the project management

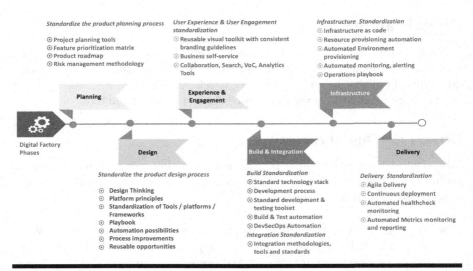

Figure 6.1   Digital factory phases.

tools for the same. We define the methodology to handle the risks of the project (including risk prioritization, contingency plan for the risks, risk communication and such). The risk methodology template can be reused by different business units.

During the design phase, we aim to standardize and automate the software product design process. We use design thinking methodology to identify the right set of questions to understand the user requirements and use iterative prototyping to incrementally build the product. We define the core platform principles (such as principles for front end design, principles for services design and such). We define the main tools, frameworks and platforms that will be used for product development. The platform principles, tools and frameworks are reusable across all the projects enabling faster and standardized way of integration and product rollout. We also define the reusable playbooks (such as tool assessment playbook, tool comparison playbook and such). We explore process optimization opportunities (such as automating the design to prototype conversion process).

The experience and user engagement phase mainly standardizes the user interface components. We develop the visual toolkit (consisting of style guides, images, fonts, branding elements and others) to provide a uniform and consistent branding across all the organizational channels. We also design for business self-service (such as search, product comparators, chatbots and such). We identify the appropriate tools for collaboration, analytics, search and voice of customer (VoC) that can be reused across the organization.

During the build and integration phase, we mainly standardize and automate the build and integration-related processes. As part of build standardization, we identity the primary development tools, frameworks and the development process. We then identify and use automation tools (such as code generators, code co-pilots) to automate the build process. Similarly, testing tools (unit testing tools such as Apache JUnit, functional testing tools such as Selenium, performance testing tools such as Apache JMeter) are used to automate the testing. DevSecOps is a set of tools and processes that automates the build, test, deploy and release activities. We define the DevSecOps tools and processes that can be replicated and reused across the organization. We define the integration methodologies (such as using REST APIs), integration tools and standards (such as JSON-based payload). The standardization of the integration methodologies enables faster integration with internal and external systems.

During the infrastructure standardization phase, we use Infrastructure as Code (IaC) as a mechanism to provision and deploy the complete infrastructure in automated way. We identify the approved infrastructure resources (such as a specified version of machine images, secure version of router and such) and automated provisioning of the infrastructure resources from the organizational infrastructure library. We also setup end-to-end monitoring for monitoring the key metrics and alerting.

During the product delivery phase, we setup the continuous deployment that automates the deployment based on the defined standards. We also setup the health check monitoring (to continuously monitor the performance, availability of the product). We also define the monitoring metrics (such as response time, error rate and such) and configure the monitoring setup to use the metrics for continuous and real-time monitoring and alerting.

Governance (set of processes, procedures and policies) and security are horizontal concerns that is applied across all the phases. We define the governance processes and standard operating procedures (such as incident management process, change request process) and security controls (such as security conformance standards such as ISO, SOC etc.) that can be used for other projects within the organization.

Digital Factory Dimensions

The digital factory dimensions define the main aspects that need to be considered for digital factory. The main dimensions of digital factory are predictability and standardization, agility and scalability as defined in Figure 6.2.

Predictability and Standardization

The main dimension of digital factory is predictability and standardization wherein we use the tools, processes and methodologies that standardizes the product build and release processes. We apply consistent prioritization processes, validation processes and design processes and development processes across the product life cycle. The process standardization produces the software product predictably.

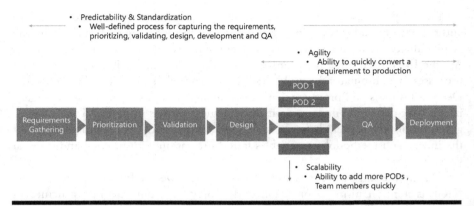

Figure 6.2   Digital factory dimensions.

Agility

The digital factory processes should be able to quickly convert a requirement use case into an MVP (minimum viable product). This can be achieved through agile development methodology wherein we use pods for each of the workstreams that use standardized and automated tools for product development and release. We discuss more about agile delivery in chapter 11.

Scalability

The digital factory should be scalable to accommodate more pods/workstreams and more team members without impacting the delivery quality and the delivery timelines. Scalability can be achieved through automated way of provisioning resources for the new team members and pods and by using a standard set of processes and tools for build and release.

Digital Factory Execution Model

Agile methodology enables the digital factory to become agile and flexible to deliver the products quickly and reliably. We have depicted the digital factory execution model in Figure 6.3.

The operating model consists of agile teams, agile release train team and governance teams. Agile team mainly consist of product teams (product owner, Scrum master, technical leads, data engineers and others) who build and test the product. The agile release train consist of execution team (business and IT teams) who are involved in the design thinking workshops, planning sessions and product backlog planning sessions. The governance teams is mainly responsible for vision and planning of the overall product release and runs various program streams.

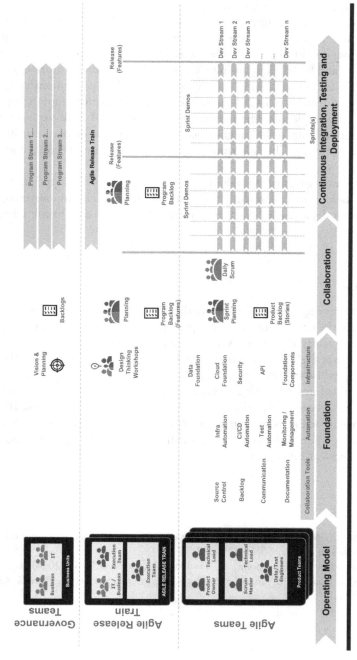

Figure 6.3 Digital factory execution model.

During the foundation phase, the governance team owns the overall program planning and vision and defines the epics and backlog. The agile release train team defines the program backlog and conducts the design thinking workshops to elaborate and refine the features. The agile release train team also defines the roles and responsibilities and RACI (Responsible, Accountable, Consulted, Informed) matrix. The agile team uses various tools, such as communication, continuous integration and continuous delivery (CI/CD) automation, test automation, monitoring, infra automation, and implement the user stories. The technical leads are involved in evangelism and training, technical guidance and align on governance, security, compliance and monitoring. The agile team attends the daily Scrum meetings and sprint planning meetings.

The agile team iteratively builds the product through various sprints through the defined agile practices (including continuous testing, continuous integration and continuous deployment) and performs the sprint demos to finally release the product.

Summary

Digital factory leverages the methods from the manufacturing domain's assembly line delivery where the manufacturing of the products is automated using the assembly line. A digital factory is defined as a set of processes, methods and tools that can be used to deliver high quality software product repeatedly and reliably. The main drivers for digital factory are heterogeneous technologies impacting the integration and delivery timelines, need for automation for faster product release, requirement for a software playbook and the need for standardized tools and processes. The main phases of digital factory phases are planning, design, experience and engagement, build and integration, infrastructure and delivery. Predictability and standardization, agility and scalability are the main dimensions of the digital factory.

References

1. Bracht, U., & Masurat, T. (2005). The digital factory between vision and reality. *Computers in Industry* 56(4), 325–333.
2. Shariatzadeh, N., Lundholm, T., Lindberg, L., & Sivard, G. (2016). Integration of digital factory with smart factory based on Internet of Things. *Procedia Cirp* 50, 512–517.

Chapter 7

First Time Right Methodology in Digital Transformation

Introduction

Software projects have inherent risk involved due to various factors such as improper planning, technical debt of the team members among others. Many software projects fail due to reasons such as such as incomplete requirements, lack of support from the top management, inefficient resource allocation and poor project management (including poor communication leading to decreased turnover), insufficient staff training and inefficient project tracking [1]. The bugs can creep in during any phase of the software development life cycle. The real cost of a software bug can be in billions depending on the type of the software [2]. The damage may cost lives if the software is used in healthcare and government agencies [2].

Digital transformation engagement often involves reimagining the existing business processes, legacy modernization, new development or migration from existing platforms. Due to the complex nature of the digital transformation engagements, the likelihood of errors and risks are high. Hence it is imperative that digital transformation architects and program managers ensure that the digital transformation exercise is planned and designed based on the best practices.

In this chapter we discuss the first time right (FTR) framework that addresses the above issue. FTR framework is a set of guidelines and proven best practices that covers all aspects of digital transformation engagement. FTR framework provides guidelines for various phases of digital transformation engagement including

DOI: 10.1201/9781003390893-10

security, development, DevOps, customer experience and others. In each of these phases, we discuss the proven best practices, metrics and methodologies that needs to be implemented.

First Time Right Framework

FTR framework is a set of categorized best practices and recommendations to enable digital organizations implement digital transformation with lesser risk and optimal cost reliably. We have identified the main categories, such as technology, operations, security and customer experience, that form core elements of majority of the digital transformation engagements.

We start by discussing the key pillars of the FTR framework and then discuss each of the elements within the pillars in detail.

Pillars of FTR Framework

Pillars of the FTR framework are essentially the key categories of concerns that are part of digital transformation engagements. We have identified four key pillars of the FTR framework as depicted in Figure 7.1.

Technology pillar covers the core technology-related concerns such as architecture and design-related optimizations (to ensure that the digital transformation uses right-fit of technologies), testing-related optimizations (to ensure that quality issues are addressed at the source), development-related optimizations (to ensure

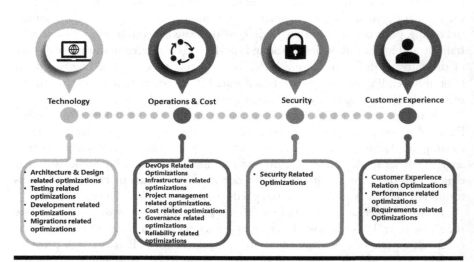

Figure 7.1   Pillars of the FTR framework.

best practices–based approach is used for product build) and migration-related optimization (to ensure the smooth and error free migration).

Operations and Cost pillar covers the operational processes and cost-related concerns such as DevOps-related optimizations (to automate the build and release management), Infrastructure-related optimizations (to provide the right-size infrastructure), project management–related optimizations (to manage the resource, timelines optimally), cost-related optimizations (to use the optimal cost for the digital transformation exercise), governance-related optimizations (processes related to change management, defect fix, review and others) and reliability-related optimizations (to ensure high resilience and high availability).

Security pillar is mainly focused on security-related optimizations that covers security at various layers.

Customer experience pillar covers the customer experience–related concerns such as core customer experience–related optimizations (to ensure the optimal end-user experience), performance-related optimizations (to provide optimal performance and response times for the end users.) and requirements-related optimizations (to minimize the requirements-related gaps).

In the next section, we discuss each of these pillars and deep dive into the concerns addressed in each of the pillar.

Elements of FTR Framework

Each pillar of the FTR framework addresses various concerns of its respective category. We now discuss the best practices, metrics and guidelines for each of the FTR framework pillars.

We have elaborated the elements of FTR framework in Figure 7.2.

Technology Pillar

We discuss the technology-related concerns such as architecture and design, testing, development and migration in this section.

Architecture and Design-Related Optimizations

The architecture and design phase involves identifying the core solution architecture principles, evaluating various solution components, identifying the standards required for the solution and defining the detail solution roadmap.

During the architecture and design phase, the solution architect has to ensure the following for delivering the FTR design and architecture:

Patterns and best practices–based design: The architect has to identify all the application architecture patterns, industry best practices and design patterns applicable for the solution. As part of this exercise, the solution architect has to identify various layers, components and the responsibilities.

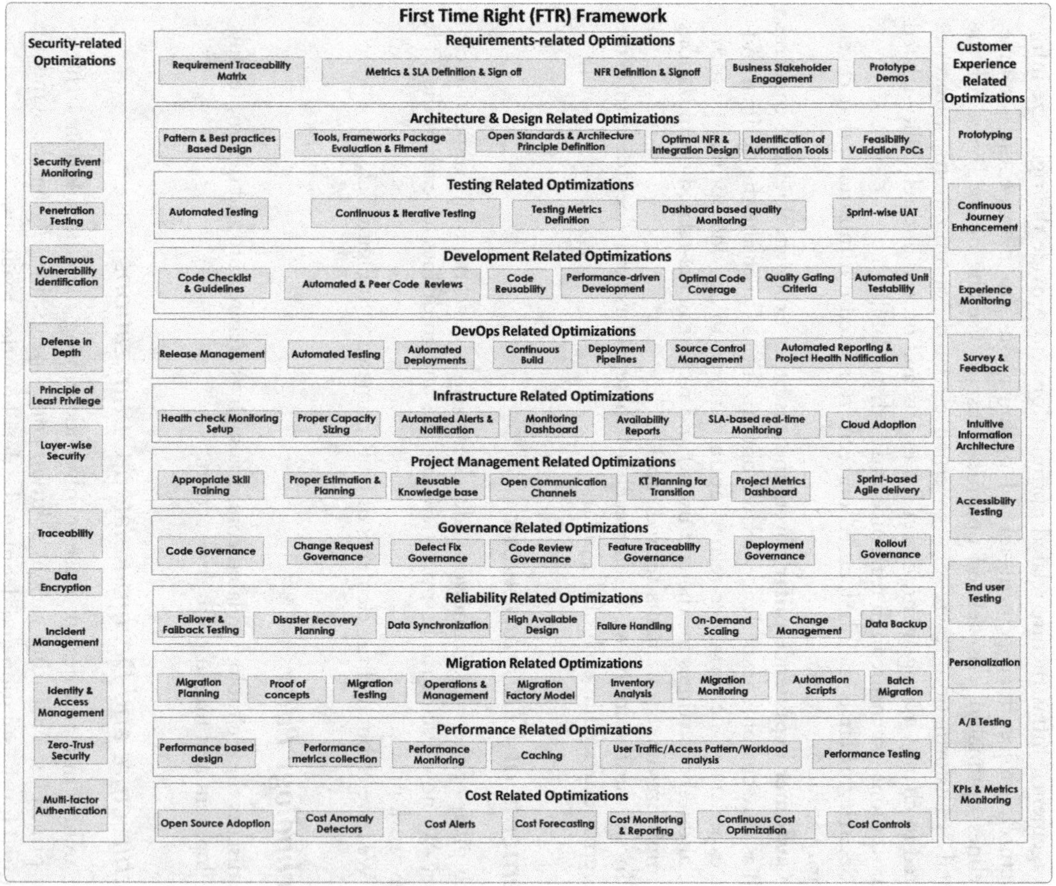

First Time Right (FTR) Framework

Requirements-related Optimizations
- Requirement Traceability Matrix
- Metrics & SLA Definition & Sign off
- NFR Definition & Signoff
- Business Stakeholder Engagement
- Prototype Demos

Architecture & Design Related Optimizations
- Pattern & Best practices Based Design
- Tools, frameworks Package Evaluation & Fitment
- Open Standards & Architecture Principle Definition
- Optimal NFR & Integration Design
- Identification of Automation Tools
- Feasibility Validation PoCs

Testing Related Optimizations
- Automated Testing
- Continuous & Iterative Testing
- Testing Metrics Definition
- Dashboard based quality Monitoring
- Sprint-wise UAT

Development Related Optimizations
- Code Checklist & Guidelines
- Automated & Peer Code Reviews
- Code Reusability
- Performance-driven Development
- Optimal Code Coverage
- Quality Gating Criteria
- Automated Unit Testability

DevOps Related Optimizations
- Release Management
- Automated Testing
- Automated Deployments
- Continuous Build
- Deployment Pipelines
- Source Control Management
- Automated Reporting & Project Health Notification

Infrastructure Related Optimizations
- Health check Monitoring Setup
- Proper Capacity Sizing
- Automated Alerts & Notification
- Monitoring Dashboard
- Availability Reports
- SLA-based real-time Monitoring
- Cloud Adoption

Project Management Related Optimizations
- Appropriate Skill Training
- Proper Estimation & Planning
- Reusable Knowledge base
- Open Communication Channels
- KT Planning for Transition
- Project Metrics Dashboard
- Sprint-based Agile delivery

Governance Related Optimizations
- Code Governance
- Change Request Governance
- Defect Fix Governance
- Code Review Governance
- Feature Traceability Governance
- Deployment Governance
- Rollout Governance

Reliability Related Optimizations
- Failover & Fallback Testing
- Disaster Recovery Planning
- Data Synchronization
- High Available Design
- Failure Handling
- On-Demand Scaling
- Change Management
- Data Backup

Migration Related Optimizations
- Migration Planning
- Proof of concepts
- Migration Testing
- Migration Factory Model
- Operations & Management
- Migration Inventory Analysis
- Migration Monitoring
- Automation Scripts
- Batch Migration

Performance Related Optimizations
- Performance based design
- Performance metrics collection
- Performance Monitoring
- Caching
- User Traffic/Access Pattern/Workload analysis
- Performance Testing

Cost Related Optimizations
- Open Source Adoption
- Cost Anomaly Detectors
- Cost Alerts
- Cost Forecasting
- User Traffic/Access Pattern/Workload analysis
- Cost Monitoring & Reporting
- Continuous Cost Optimization
- Cost Controls

Security-related Optimizations
- Security Event Monitoring
- Penetration Testing
- Continuous Vulnerability Identification
- Defense in Depth
- Principle of Least Privilege
- Layer-wise Security
- Traceability
- Data Encryption
- Incident Management
- Identity & Access Management
- Zero-Trust Security
- Multi-factor Authentication

Customer Experience Related Optimizations
- Prototyping
- Continuous Journey Enhancement
- Experience Monitoring
- Survey & Feedback
- Intuitive Information Architecture
- Accessibility Testing
- End user Testing
- Personalization
- A/B Testing
- KPIs & Metrics Monitoring

Figure 7.2 First Time Right framework.

Given below are the key architecture patterns that are applicable in the modern application platforms:

- Microservices pattern wherein we design modular, fine-grained, independently scalable services.
- Responsive design pattern wherein the presentation components seamlessly render on all devices.
- Loosely coupled layers wherein each layer handles a distinct responsibility as per separation of concerns principle.
- Stateless communication across internal and external systems.
- Containerization of services to provide on-demand scalability.

Tools, frameworks, package evaluation and fitment: The architect has to evaluate the market leading products, frameworks, open source libraries that are best fit for the requirements. Leveraging proven frameworks, tools and open source libraries greatly contribute to the improved productivity, turnaround time and improved quality. For example, as part of the architecture phase, the architect has to critically evaluate technologies such as Angular vs. React vs. Vue for UI; Spring Boot vs. Serverless services; SQL vs. NoSQL; mobile web vs. hybrid app vs. native app; PaaS vs. IaaS vs. SaaS etc.

Standards and architecture principles definition: The architect has to define the applicable standards for the solution and for the business domain. At this stage the architect has to define the architecture principles such as headless design, stateless integration, token-based security etc. Few application domains need to implement specific standards for regulatory compliance (such as HIPAA for healthcare domain).

The main architecture principles for developing a modern platform are given below:

- Stateless design across all layers for seamless integration and extensibility.
- On-demand scalability to provide optimal performance during peak loads.
- Open standards-based integration to ensure extensibility.
- Modular design for flexible integration and to future proof the solution.
- Omni-channel, self-service and consistent experience across users.
- APIfication and token-based security for secure and seamless integrations.
- Embrace microservices architecture with stateless communication.
- Process automation to improve the productivity and overall delivery time.
- Achieve business agility, faster launch of products and services with DevOps, CI-CD/Agile.
- Adopt cloud-based multi-tenancy containerization.
- Use multi-speed integration model to cater to fast-changing presentation needs.

| Lightweight:
Client side MVC
and Responsive
Design | Modular:
Ability to upgrade
components
without re-
deployment | Intuitive, Efficient:
Visual Cues, Self-
service | Reactive:
Highly engaging
event driven pages | Contextual:
Facilitate current
task, inherently
multi-tenant |

Figure 7.3   Presentation layer design principles.

We need to define the design principles for each of the layers. For instance Figure 7.3 provides a generic design principles for presentation layer.

- Lightweight client-side model view controller (MVC) components
- Responsive design for omni-channel support
- Reusable styles, cascading style sheet (CSS) and navigation components
- Reusable and pluggable user interface (UI) modules
- Inbuilt user management, personalization, pages, layouts, multi-tenancy
- Modular, standards-based and extensible UI components
- React/Angular-based modern web-reactive, intuitive and contextual and event-driven components that supports Single Page Application (SPA), client-side MVC, Progressive Web App (PWA) and offline mode
- Modular, extensible and reusable UI widgets

Given below are design principles for services layer:

- Independent and stateless services that can be exposed to external systems
- Modular, scalable and logically decoupled centralized business logic
- Dependency injection and contract-driven services
- Ability to scale independently

Optimal non-functional requirements (NFR) and integration design: The architect has to design the application to satisfy all the specified NFR (performance, scalability, availability and such) and the integration service level agreements (SLAs).

Identification of automation tools: The architect has to identify all the automation tools that can be used for the project. This includes automation tools for code review, IDE, functional testing and such.

Feasibility validation proof-of-concepts **(PoCs):** For complex requirements, we need to carry out the feasibility assessment through PoCs. This helps us to finalize the tool, technology, integration method, performance and assess the scalability and performance of the method.

Testing-Related Optimizations

A comprehensive validation is one of the key success factors for delivering the FTR deliverable. The validation team needs to follow the below given optimizations.

Automated testing: The testing team has to use the automated tools, such as Apache JMeter or Selenium, to automate the regression scenarios and other functional test scenarios to improve the overall productivity.

Continuous iterative testing: The testing has to be a continuous and iterative process across all sprints. This helps us to discover the defects in the early stage.

Testing metrics definition: The testing team has to define the quality metrics, such as defect rate, defect slippage rate and defect density, and track the metrics with each sprint.

Dashboard-based quality monitoring: The test lead should proactively monitor all the testing metrics in a dashboard and notify the project manager in case of any critical violations.

Sprint-wise early user acceptance testing (UAT): Involving the business stakeholders with each sprint delivery in the UAT phase helps us to uncover any business-related gaps early in the game. Additionally the team can incorporate the feedback in the next sprint.

We have depicted the sample end-to-end testing plan along with deliverable in Figure 7.4.

Development-Related Optimizations

The big chunk of responsibility for FTR deliverable lies with the development team. Given below are the optimizations that needs to be done during development stage:

Code checklist and guidelines: Developers should use the code guidelines, naming conventions and coding best practices in a checklist format. Before the start of the project, the architect along with project manager has to create the checklist, naming conventions, best practices and such. Some of the most common code checklist are as follows:

- Language-specific coding best practices
- Performance checklist
- Security coding checklist
- Code naming conventions
- Design checklist

Automated and peer review process: Developers should use automated static code analyzers such as PMD/SonarQube to ensure the code quality. The developers should also get their code reviewed by their peers and leads on a frequent basis.

Code reusability: Developers should actively explore the code reusability opportunities in the following order:

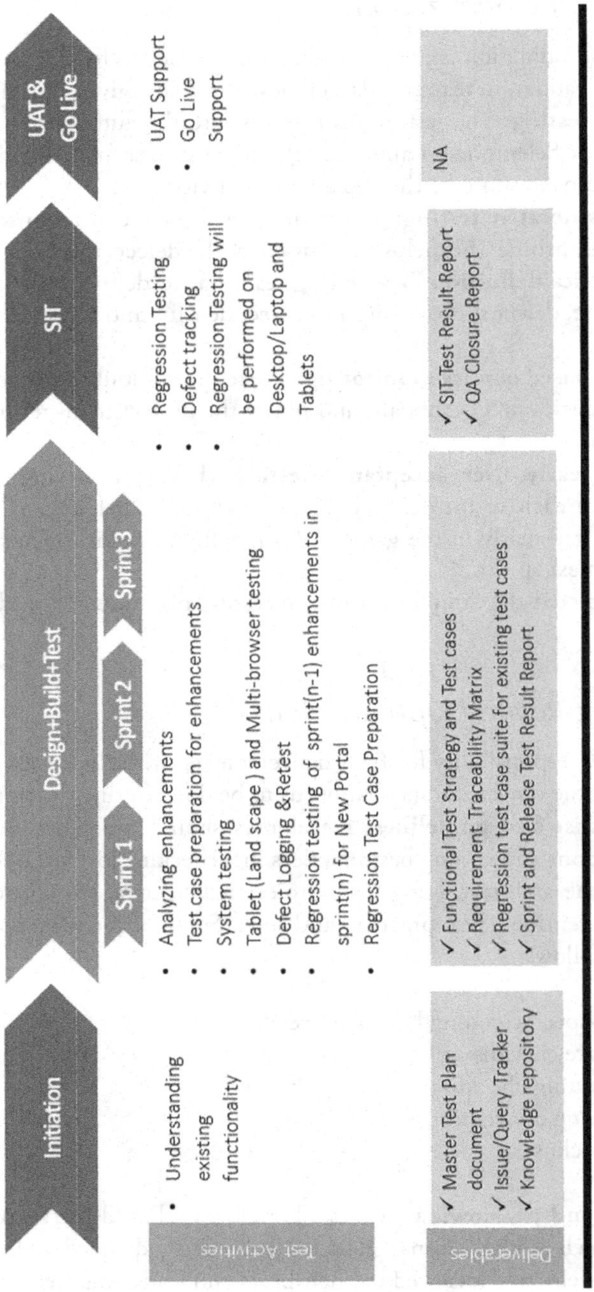

Initiation	Design+Build+Test			SIT	UAT & Go Live
	Sprint 1	Sprint 2	Sprint 3		

Test Activities

- Understanding existing functionality

- Analyzing enhancements
- Test case preparation for enhancements
- System testing
- Tablet (Land scape) and Multi-browser testing
- Defect Logging &Retest
- Regression testing of sprint(n-1) enhancements in sprint(n) for New Portal
- Regression Test Case Preparation

- Regression Testing
- Defect tracking
- Regression Testing will be performed on Desktop/Laptop and Tablets

- UAT Support
- Go Live Support

Deliverables

- ✓ Master Test Plan document
- ✓ Issue/Query Tracker
- ✓ Knowledge repository

- ✓ Functional Test Strategy and Test cases
- ✓ Requirement Traceability Matrix
- ✓ Regression test case suite for existing test cases
- ✓ Sprint and Release Test Result Report

- ✓ SIT Test Result Report
- ✓ QA Closure Report

NA

Figure 7.4 Sample end-to-end testing plans.

- Look for reusable libraries, code modules and components offered by the underlying platform/product/framework/accelerators.
- Explore the availability of reusable libraries, code modules and components at the organization level.
- Look for approved open-source libraries that satisfies the functionality.
- If nothing is available, develop the code in a modular way so that it can be reused.

Performance-driven development: Performance should not be an afterthought but it must be implemented from the very early stages. Developers need to pro-actively carry out the performance testing of the integrated code to ensure that their code is free of memory leaks, integration bottlenecks and others.

Optimal code coverage: Developers should ensure that their unit test cases provide more than 90% code coverage. This ensures high code quality with minimal defects. Developers should also try to use an automated tool for generating unit test cases.

Quality gating criteria: We need to define multi-level code quality gating criteria as follows (this could also go in as code check-in checklist):

- **Developer-level code quality**: The developer has to use the defined coding checklist and naming conventions to adhere to those guidelines. The developer can also use the IDE for the same.
- **Automated local code quality analyzer**: The developer has to use the static code analyzers such as, PMD or SonarQube, to analyze all coding issues and fix the major and critical issues.
- **Manual code review**: The developers can request for peer review and lead review of the code. Once all of the above is completed, the developers can check in the code to the source control system.
- **Integrated code review**: We could setup a Jenkins job with SonarQube to continuously review the integrated code and generate the report. The Jenkins job can notify the developers and project managers for major and critical violations.
- **Automated unit testability**: Developers should use automated unit test generators (such as EvoSuite, Veracode) to improve the quality and productivity of the developer.

Migrations-Related Optimizations

During many digital transformation engagements we migrate the existing platform to the new digital platforms. Hence best practices in the migration stage is key to successful digital transformation.

Figure 7.5 depicts various activities in the end-to-end migration exercise.

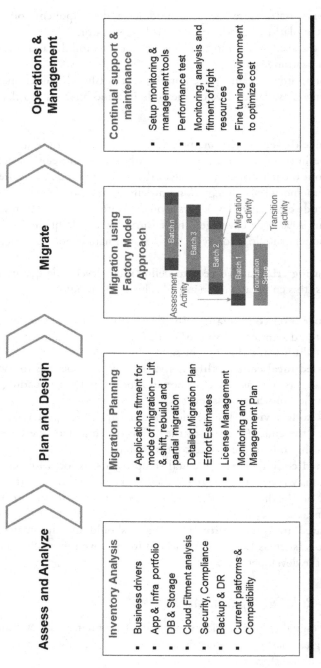

Figure 7.5 Migration exercise.

Given below are migration-related optimizations:

Inventory analysis phase identifies the key business drivers and compiles the inventory of the applications and data to be migrated. We understand the portfolio of services, applications, data and its dependencies. We also identify the backup, disaster recovery (DR) and compliance requirements of the application and data. In order to right size the capacity of servers on the target environment, we also collect the utilization metrics (such as CPU, memory, storage, network) for the current applications. We use application and data discovery tools to automate this process.

Migration planning is carried out for each of the identified applications and data and we analyze if the application is to be retained (lift and shift to the target environment) or refactored (consolidate and redesign) or retired (sunset the application) or replatformed (build in target environment using new platform). Once the migration plan is finalized, we use the appropriate migration strategy for the migration. For example, for the applications that need to be migrated as-is we use lift-and-shift migration methodology retaining the existing application and data and hosting it on a similar capacity server on the target environment. If the application has to be refactored, we redesign the specific solution components (such as modernizing the monolith services layer to microservices). For replatform use cases, we re-develop the application in the new platform (for instance rewrite the Java Server Page application in Angular). We plan the timelines, resources and the cost involved for the migration.

Table 7.1 describes various migration strategies that can be used for migration use cases.

PoC is a commonly adopted strategy to check the feasibility of the complex use cases such as third-party integration, security configuration and migration across

Table 7.1   Migration Use Cases and Strategies

Migration Use case	Migration Strategy	Migration Methodology
Migrate packaged applications that has hard dependency on platform,	Lift and shift	Application—Export the machine image and import in the target environment Data—Use native database tools for export and import of data
Modernize legacy application partially	Refactor	Identify layers and solution components that needs to be refactored. Use conversion tools for refactoring
Revamp complete legacy application	Replatform	Rewrite the application in modern platform and technologies
Applications that are not used	Retire	Stop the application

heterogeneous data sources. The learnings from the PoC are leveraged to plan and automate the actual migration scripts.

Migration using factory model defines the steps to incrementally migrate the application and data in batches. First we setup the foundation (in sprint 0) to develop the basic building blocks in the target environment (such as security, initializing the servers and so on). We then migrate the application in batches. Automation scripts are used to automate the migration in the factory model.

Migration testing involves testing the target application and doing the data integrity testing in the target environment. Based on the type of application and data, we carry out different types of testing.

Migration operations and management involves continuous monitoring of the migration and iterative testing. We automate the migration steps wherever possible to improve the quality and migration time.

Operations and Cost Pillar

In this pillar we discuss the optimizations in DevOps, infrastructure, project management and governance processes.

DevOps-Related Optimizations

DevOps defines a set of tools and processes to ensure the proper delivery and release of the application. Given below are the key optimizations from DevOps standpoint:

- **Release management**: DevOps setup provides an opportunity for setting up automated release management system. We can leverage tools, such as Jenkins, AWS CodePipeline to build the release management pipeline and automate the release management process.
- **Automated testing**: We can configure unit test jobs (using Apache JUnits) and functional testing jobs (such as Selenium) to test the code from source control system.
- **Automated deployment**: We can use Jenkins pipelines and deployment jobs to automate the deployment.
- **Continuous build**: We can enable the continuous build to catch any errors with integrated code.
- **Deployment pipelines**: The pipelines enable and automate the code deployment.
- **Source control management**: As part of the DevOps process we also define the source control management processes related to pull request, approval, code check-in, code merge and such. BitBucket, AWS CodeCommit and GitLabs are the popular source control management systems.
- **Automated reporting and project health notification**: We setup the project monitoring and notification mechanisms to continuously monitor the key metrics such as build failures, test failures, test coverage percentage, code quality and such. The monitoring tools trigger a notification when any

monitored metric falls below the configured threshold (for instance if the recently checked in code causes the build failure, the monitoring system sends out an email to the administrator).

Infrastructure-Related Optimizations

A right-sized infrastructure is critical for the optimal application delivery. In order to deliver the FTR solution, given below are the infrastructure-related optimizations:

- **Health check monitoring setup**: We need to setup the proactive health check/heartbeat monitoring infrastructure to continuously monitor the availability of the servers.
- **Proper capacity sizing**: All the server and network capacity should be sized based on the user load and related NFR (such as scalability, availability, performance). Based on the availability requirements, we should also setup the DR and the corresponding synchronization jobs.
- **Automated alerts and notification**: We should be able to configure notification triggers and the monitoring setup should notify the administrators in case of SLA violation.
- **Monitoring dashboard**: The monitoring dashboard should provide the details of all key parameters such as availability percentage, performance, CPU/memory/network utilization, request rate and such.
- **Availability reports**: The monitoring setup should be able to generate on-demand monitoring reports for various infra-related parameters.
- **SLA-based real-time monitoring**: We should also setup the real-time application monitoring infrastructure across various geographies to understand the performance and availability issues.
- **Single point of failure (SPOF) avoidance**: Ensure that none of the systems in the end-to-end request processing pipeline form the bottleneck leading to SPOF. We can ensure high availability through multi-node cluster setup, redundancy setup, DR setup, regular backup and by other means.
- **Cloud adoption:** As cloud platforms provide elastic scalability and security at optimal cost, we can leverage cloud for customer-facing applications that expect spiky/unpredictable traffic.

Additionally we should setup the automatic elastic scalability, optimal load balancing, content delivery network (CDN)-based caching based on the application requirements.

Project Management–Related Optimizations

Project managers shoulder greater responsibility in defining and enforcing the processes to implement FTR deliverable. Given below are the key optimizations from project management standpoint:

- **Project planning:** The project manager has to allocate the resources and plan the project timelines based on the user stories planned for the sprint. The project manager also has to maintain a risk mitigation plan to handle the risk.
- **Appropriate skill training:** The project manager has to train the project team members to equip them with suitable technology skills. It is recommended to have right mix of skill set (such as technology lead to developer ratio) in the team to ensure timely delivery and high-quality deliverable.
- **Proper estimation and staffing:** The project manager has to do the proper effort estimates and staff resources accordingly. The project manager has to define proper risk management plan for all known contingencies.
- **Reusable knowledge base:** The project manager has to maintain the best practices, standard operating procedures (SOPs), key design decisions (KDD), how-to documents, troubleshooting documents, learnings, process documents, knowledge documents and others in a centralized knowledge base. This helps the team members to build upon the collective knowledge and leverage it for faster and better deliverable.
- **Open communication channels:** In order to avoid information silos, the project manager has to establish open communication channels across all tracks. Various tools, such as Slack or MS Teams, can be leveraged for this.
- **Knowledge Transition (KT) planning:** If the team takes over any new engagement from an incumbent, we need to plan for proper KT from the incumbent.
- **Project metrics dashboard:** The project manager has to track the overall project health in the metrics dashboard. Typically a project dashboard consists of burn rate, code quality score, open defect count, average defect fix time, sprint run rate and such. This helps the project manager to get a holistic view of all open issues and prioritize them accordingly.
- **Sprint-based agile delivery:** Modern digital projects are complex and are end-user focused. Hence the project manager has to plan for sprint-based agile delivery so that we can mitigate the risk and get the early user feedback.
- **Continuous Improvement model:** The project manager has to constantly seek to improve the overall productivity and quality using the learnings, metrics from earlier sprints. The project manager has to continuously look out for automation opportunities.

The project manager also has to proactively understand the regulatory and compliance requirements (such as accessibility standards), browser and device compatibility (browsers and mobile devices that need to be supported) and multi-lingual requirements (list of left-to-right and right-to-left languages) that need to be supported and accordingly plan for the same.

Governance-Related Optimizations

Project governance broadly details the well-defined processes to streamline the complex project activities. Given below are the governance-related optimizations:

- **Code governance** defines the code management-related processes such as code merging, code check-in, code versioning and such. The code governance processes should be built into source control system (for instance, the DevOps engineers should create the required code branches in the code repository and the code pipeline should force developer to complete the peer review prior to the code check-in).
- **Change request governance** broadly defines the scope creep management process. It defines the criteria for change request management, its prioritization and impact management and implementation plan.
- **Defect fix governance** defines the processes related to defect prioritization, SLAs and such. Each of the identified defects should be prioritized and accordingly should be added to the sprint backlog.
- **Review governance** defines the processes related to code review and approval.
- **Feature traceability governance** defines the process to trace the requirement to the final release.
- **Deployment governance** provides the deployment plan for code artefacts.
- **Rollout governance** defines the rollout plan across various geographies, features, languages, rollback plan and such.

Cost-Related Optimizations

Total cost of ownership (TCO) is one of the key factors and helps in the long-term success of the platform. We discuss some of the prominent factors from cost optimization standpoint.

Open-source adoption helps in reducing the license cost of the proprietary software. We can leverage managed open source platforms offered by the cloud vendors to save the cost. During architecture phase, we can identify the relevant open-source platforms for the relevant use cases.

We should plan for the overall solution cost through **cost forecasting** tools. The cost forecasting helps the organizations to allot the suitable budget for the solution.

As part of cost control and cost optimization we adopt various methods on continuous basis. Some of the key cost controls are as follows:

- Move appropriate tiered storage device and move the archival data to the cold storage device to lower the storage cost.
- Use containers to handle the peak demand that provides on-demand scalability.
- Use cost anomaly detectors that identifies any cost anomalies using historical data.
- Explore public cloud platforms that optimize the cost through economies of scale
- Explore Linux platform for implementing the use cases

Cost reporting enables the business stakeholders to get timely alerts and take corrective actions wherever required. We need to setup the cost monitoring and reporting tools to continuously monitor the cost in real time and report it to the relevant stakeholders.

Cost optimization is a continuous journey. We need to iteratively identify the major cost contributors and explore cost-optimal alternatives.

Security Pillar

The book [3] discusses the security testing methodology to design for robust security the first time. For a robust security, it is essential to cover the security concerns such as trust management, client-side security and others [3]. In this section we describe various security related optimizations.

Security-Related Optimizations

On the security front, we need to continuously monitor and audit for critical security events (such as failed login attempts, password change events, impersonation events, role change events etc.) and setup a notification infrastructure for the same.

Given below are the core security-related controls that should be implemented:

- **Continuous vulnerability identification** using VAPT (Vulnerability Assessment and Penetration Testing) tools is essential to continuously monitor the servers for known vulnerabilities and report them for taking the appropriate action.
- **Defense in depth** strategy involves enforcing security policies at each layer starting with infrastructure layer and then using appropriate security controls at network layer (using intrusion detection system, threat intelligence system and network layer encryption), perimeter (using perimeter firewall), application layer (using web application firewalls, authentication and authorization and access list), server layer (using host firewall) and data layer (using database access monitoring tools and encryption at rest).
- **Principle of least privilege** states that access should be granted to users only for essential activities. In order to enforce this we need to start with minimal access (such as no-access) to all users and provide the required permissions that is essential for users to perform their activities. We should also continuously monitor the permission usage of these users and remove the permission wherever it is not required.
- **Traceability** should be enforced through auditing mechanism. All the main events, such as login, password change, failed login attempts, role change events and data access events, should be audited.
- **Data security** should be enforced through key-based encryption at rest.
- **Incident management** ensures that SOPs are in place to do the root cause analysis of an incident and take the corrective action in case of any security incident.

- **Zero trust security** ensures that all users and services are continuously authenticated and authorized and validated for security posture before the access is granted.
- **Multi-factor authentication (MFA)** is used to challenge the user with multiple verification factors to gain access to the system. MFA is used for access to privilege resources.

We should also carry out the penetration testing and vulnerability testing iteratively to discover the security vulnerabilities early.

As many enterprises are reimagining their digital transformation journey on cloud platforms, we have given a comprehensive security checklist for the cloud deployments.

Customer Experience Pillar

The customer experience pillar covers the factors that influence the customer experience such as user requirements, performance and core customer experience–related optimizations.

Customer Experience–Related Optimizations

The overall experience of the end customer is an important success factor for the digital transformation initiative. Responsive user interface, sub second response times, intuitive design all influence the overall customer experience. Customer experience optimizations need to be done as part of the design phase of the product.

We have detailed below the core proven best practices to optimize the customer experience.

- **Prototyping** provides the visual design, navigation, user interface of the planned platform. We can design and validate the prototype with the relevant internal stakeholders, design agencies as well as few of the target end users.
- **Continuous user journey enhancement** is a method to map and fine-tune the end-user journey. User journey mapping identifies the user's path to complete a task, current pain points that are useful in improving all the user touchpoints with the application.
- **Intuitive information architecture** plays a major role in maintaining consistent navigation experience and improves the searchability of the user information. It is recommended to improve the search experience to enable customer find the accurate information quickly.
- **Survey and feedback** is a mechanism wherein the users can actively influence the future sprints and the features by providing the improvement feedback.
- The book [4] stresses on evaluating the progress through KPIs and metrics. We can monitor the user experience through the **key performance indicators (KPIs) and metrics** such as page response time, exit rate, conversion rate and such.

- **Accessibility testing** validates various accessibility features, such as keyboard access and alternate text for images, for the web platforms.
- **Personalization** is one of the key levers to improve the end-user engagement. Based on the end user's interest and the past interactions, we can provide the relevant content and recommend the useful products resulting in improved end-user satisfaction.
- **A/B testing (Alpha/Beta testing)** is a mechanism to experiment different variants of the platform to understand the more impactful version.
- **End-user testing** engages the actual target audience to test the application and provide the feedback.

Performance-Related Optimizations

Performance optimizations need to be done at various layers across different stages of the project.

Performance-based design involves using performance-first approach while designing the solution layers and the solution components. For instance lightweight component design, stateless API calls, containerization of microservices are some of the core tenets of performance-based design. Given below are some of the solution patterns that optimizes the end-to-end solution performance:

- Command and Query Responsibility Segregation (CQRS) pattern that separates the data read and data write operations to optimize the read and write. For data read we use a cached version of read replica and for data write we use the master database.
- Backend for frontend pattern defines a client-specific backend service to manage the channel specific content optimally.
- Event sourcing pattern wherein the data operations are stored as sequence of immutable events and the interested consumers can subscribe to the event store.
- Asynchronous loading pattern wherein we load the content and service response asynchronously.
- Layer-wise decoupling that segregates the solution into various layers such as web server layer, application server layer, database server layer with each layer handling a distinct responsibility.

Merging and minification of the static assets of the web page, HTML compression, content pre-fetching, lightweight components are other key best practices that we follow as part of performance-based design.

For data management, we use the most appropriate data store for the use case. Financial use cases that handle structured data with strict schema requirements need relational databases such as MySQL or PostgreSQL. Reporting use cases that need aggregated data can use denormalized data. Analytical and Online Analytics Processing (OLAP) use cases need a data warehouse system. The use cases that need to manage key-value data can use NoSQL database such as Amazon DynamoDB. Content management systems (CMS) that rely heavily on documents can use MongoDB. Recommendations engines that aim to establish relationship across data can use graph database such as Amazon Neptune.

We analyze the **user access patterns and user traffic** to understand the average load and peak load numbers. The metrics collected are baselined and used for performance testing.

The key **performance metrics** are used during performance testing and for performance monitoring. We have given below few of the key performance metrics that needs to be monitored:

- Page response times provide the average time taken for page load. We measure this at average and peak load
- Conversion rate (which is the ratio of number of visitors who ordered to total number of unique visitors), error rate, bounce rate (number of visitors who exit the platform after single visit/total number of unique visitors). Time to first byte indicates the overall time to receive the first byte response from the server.
- Perceived response time indicates the response time perceived by the user.
- Page size indicates the overall size of the page including the images and the overall content on the page.
- Asset load time indicates the time taken for loading all page assets.
- Time on site indicates the total time spent by the end user on the web page.

Performance monitoring is a continuous real-time monitoring of the platform to understand the performance behavior of the application. We use application monitoring tools, synthetic monitoring tools and real user monitoring tools. We have listed some of the tools in Table 7.2.

Caching is one of the key methods to improve the performance. Frequently used data, query responses, service response, look up lists can be cached. Caching can be done at each of the layers (presentation layer, service layer, database layer and others) for optimal performance. Content can also be cached at the end user's web browser and at the CDN end.

Performance testing involves carrying out various performance validations such as response time testing at average load and peak load, stress testing, multi-geo testing, browser testing. We monitor the metrics, such as throughput, resource utilization, response times and other parameters, during performance testing.

Requirements-Related Optimizations

In many scenarios the requirement gaps snowball into production issues. Hence it is crucial to plug all the gaps in the requirements stage. Below given are the optimizations during requirements elaboration stage:

Table 7.2 FTR Tools

Tool Category	Open-Source/ Commercial Tool(s)
Web page analysis tools (HTML analysis, performance benchmarking, improvement guidelines)	Yahoo YSlow, Google PageSpeed, HTTPWatch, Dynatrace AJAX Edition
Page development tools (analysis of page load times, asset size, asset load times and such)	Firebug, Google Chrome Developer toolbar, Fiddler, HTTP Archive WEB PAGEiddle, CSSLint, JSLint, W3 CSS Validator, W3 HTML validator
Asset merging and minification tools (JS/CSS minification)	JSMin, JSMini, JSCompress
Page performance testing tools (load simulation)	JMeter, LoadUI, Grinder, Selenium
Image compression tools	PNGCrush, Smush It, Img min, JPEG Mini
Web server plugins (for automatic compression, minification, merging, placement, caching etc.)	Mod_pageSpeed, mod_cache, mod_SPDY mod_expiry, mod_gzip
Website performance testing	GTMetrix, Pingdom
Synthetic monitoring (transactions simulation and performance statistics)	Web Page test, DynaTrace Synthetic monitoring
CDN	Akamai, CloudFlare, KeyCDN,
Web analytics (track user behavior, performance reporting)	Google Web Analytics, Omniture, Piwik
CSS optimization tools	CSS Sprites, SpriteMe, SpritePad
Bottleneck Analysis (dependency and bottleneck analysis)	WebProphet, WProf
Real user monitoring (RUM) (monitoring and bottleneck analysis)	New Relic, Dynatrace, Gomez
Network analysis (network traffic, HTTP headers, request/responses, protocol analysis)	Wireshark, Charles Proxy
Application performance monitoring (APM) (layer-wise monitoring of application code)	New Relic, Dyna Trace Monitoring, Nagios

Requirement traceability matrix: The business analysts and the project manager should jointly own the requirement traceability matrix that maps each use case/Jira story to the corresponding test case, code artefact and the release details to ensure that there are no gaps in the delivery.

Metrics and SLA definition and sign-off: We need to quantify the functional and NFR with accurate metrics and SLAs. For instance, a requirement like "*performance should be good*" is vague and ambiguous; we should formally quantity it as "*the total page load time for the home page should be less than 2 second with the maximum concurrent user load of 100 users in the North American geography*". We need to define the metrics related to application response time, availability, scalability, security and get a formal signoff from business stakeholders.

NFR definition and sign-off: All the NFR, such as *security, performance, scalability, accessibility, multi-lingual capability* and such, should be properly defined and signed off by the business.

Business stakeholder engagement: The business stakeholders should be actively engaged throughout the requirement elaboration phase. Without active stakeholder engagement we would miss the requirements and we would face challenges in getting the sign-off.

Prototype demos: We should prepare the mockups/prototypes iteratively and should do frequent demos to showcase the design, user journeys and multi-device experience. This helps us to proactively solicit the feedback comments from all the stakeholders and incorporate them.

Requirements Best Practices

Given below are the main requirements-related best practices:

- Collaborate with internal and external teams to clarify the requirements.
- Have interaction sessions with client to clarify questions and for the demos. This helps us to understand the client's thought process and provides us with crucial insights about the cost and other solution expectations. We can accordingly fine tune our solution to meet their expectations.
- Articulate the design principles for the integration.
- Model all the core flows and how the proposed solution fulfils the solution that was well received.
- Demo the User Experience (UX) design that visually articulated our thought process on the overall journey.
- Analyze and identify the automation and shift left opportunities and articulate the effort savings.
- In case of support engagements, define the ticket reduction architecture to avoid the tickets at the source using code quality controls, root cause analysis and other automation measures.

Tools

We have given various tools that can be used for implementing the FTR framework in Table 7.2.

Summary

In this chapter we explored various aspects of using FTR methodologies in the digital transformation projects. FTR framework is a set of guidelines, proven best practices that covers all aspects of digital transformation engagement. The key pillars of FTR are technology pillar that covers architecture and design, testing, development and migration-related elements; operations and cost pillar that cover DevOps, infrastructure, project management, governance and cost-related elements; security pillar that covers the core security concerns and customer experience pillar that covers customer experience–related elements, performance-related elements and requirements-related elements. Architecture and design-related optimizations identify and provide guidelines to patterns, tools, frameworks, standards, architecture principles and best practices. Testing-related optimizations focus on automation and iterative testing. Development-related optimizations uses various code quality best practices such as code checklists, code reviews and others. Migration-related best practices de-risk the migration through proof of concepts, migration planning, automation scripts and others. DevOps-related optimizations streamline the build, deployment and release management activities through DevOps philosophy. Infrastructure-related optimizations include appropriate capacity planning, monitoring and notifications and health check setup. Project management optimizations involve enabling the team with required skills through training, project planning and estimation and others. Cost optimizations need appropriate cost planning through cost forecasting tools, cost anomaly detection tools and continuous cost control tools. Security can be optimized through various security best practices such as encryption, identity and access management and multi-factor authentication. Customer experience can be optimized through accessibility testing, end-user testing, A/B testing, intuitive information architecture and customer journey enhancement.

References

1. Charette, R. N. (2005). Why software fails [software failure]. *IEEE Spectrum* 42(9), 42–49.
2. Zhivich, M., & Cunningham, R. K. (2009). The real cost of software errors. *IEEE Security & Privacy* 7(2), 87–90.
3. Viega, J., & McGraw, G. R. (2001). *Building Secure Software: How to Avoid Security Problems the Right Way, Portable Documents*. Pearson Education.
4. Morrison, D. (2003). *E-Learning Strategies: How to Get Implementation and Delivery Right First Time*. John Wiley & Sons.

Chapter 8

Experience Transformation

Introduction

A digital experience defines the interaction of the user with an organization through digital technologies (such as web, mobile and others) [1]. Organizations strive to provide superior digital experiences to their customers to establish their brand identity. Digital experience design directly impacts the end user's engagement with the digital platform. Hence it is imperative to deliver engaging, contextual and meaningful experiences to the user. The user experience design involves various disciplines such as information architecture, psychology, accessibility, branding, usability, interaction design, visual design and others. We have depicted various elements of digital experience in Figure 8.1.

Figure 8.1 depicts multiple elements that shape digital experience. Human–screen interaction depicts digital platform touchpoints, such as websites, mobile apps and kiosk apps, where the end-user interacts with the platform. Interaction design depicts the system behavior such as navigations, call-to-action buttons and such. Visual design involves the user interface element such as screen, page layout, color scheme, font style and such. Accessibility design covers the accessibility elements such as text alternatives for image, keyboard navigation and such. Information architecture represents the navigational hierarchy and the way information is organized within the platform. All these elements come together to define the overall experience for the user.

DOI: 10.1201/9781003390893-11

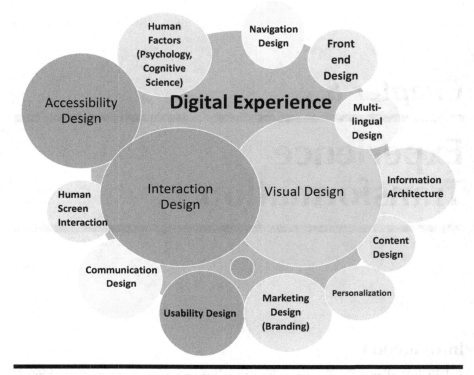

Figure 8.1 Elements of digital experience.

Key Tenets of Digital Experience Design

Designing digital experiences for modern applications should provide engaging and high-performance experience for the users. The key digital experience trends are artificial intelligence (AI)-based conversational user interface (UI), multi-experience (voice, gesture, touch), facial recognition payment and inclusive design [2]. In this section we have detailed the primary tenets of modern digital experience design as depicted in Figure 8.2.

Before we start implementing the tenets of digital experience design, we should carry out the user research to understand the user personas, user goals, user behavior and user challenges. We should create the user journey maps. We discuss the user persona and journey maps in the next section.

The digital experiences need to be user centric that should enable users to achieve their goals seamlessly and quickly. The digital platform should reflect the mental model of the user. The design should reflect the mental model of the end user's requirements.

Frictionless experiences improve the overall user engagement on the platform. Design thinking is one of the key methods to design human-centered experience.

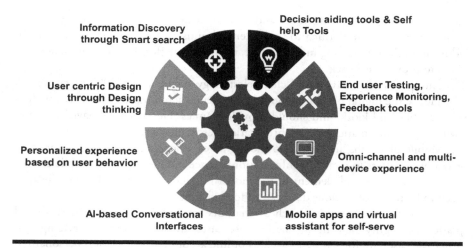

Figure 8.2 Tenets of digital experience design.

Design thinking uses techniques, such as problem identification (by asking right set of questions), prototyping and ideation, to iteratively arrive at the solution. An expert design thinker should factor in how humans will respond to the design and should be able to work visually; design thinkers evaluate multiple solutions while keeping the big picture in mind to come up with the final solution [3]. Organizations should be willing to experiment with novel technologies to provide compelling digital experience.

The digital experience should enable easier, faster and relevant information discovery through smart search. The smart search feature provides a personalized and contextual content by using implicit filters such as user preferences (such as user language, geography, topics of interest) and also provides explicit filters for users to filter the content.

Users should be able to find easy-to-use self-service tools (such as product comparators, calculators, knowledge base, guided navigation tools) that enable them to make data-driven and informed decisions quickly. Automation is another key enabler for improving response time and productivity. Workflow automation, ticket automation are some of the mechanisms that we can use to automate the most frequently used features. Modern digital technologies such as Augmented Reality (AR)/ Virtual Reality (VR) should be used for use cases such as training and education and learning as AR is widely used for job/skill training [4].

We should conduct usability testing to assess the usability of the digital platform by the end users. Modern digital platforms should use analytical tools and should continuously collect the monitoring metrics (such as platform performance, availability, conversions, error rate, bounce rate and such). The monitoring tools should monitor the user's interactions along with success/failure metrics and business KPIs using real-time monitoring tools and system health check tools. The generated monitoring alerts are notified to the system administrators for corrective action. In addition to the monitoring infrastructure, the digital platforms should also allow the users to provide feedback.

Enterprises who have omni-channel strategy retain about 89% of customers [5]. Hence the digital platforms should be available across various channels, such as web, mobile and kiosk, and should provide seamless cross-channel navigation and switching by automatic data synchronization across all channels.

Mobile platforms are central to the digital experiences [6] and are the primary gateways for users to consume information. Hence mobile apps and mobile experience is a quintessential element of the modern digital experience. The mobile apps need to be tested on various devices and form factors.

Conversational interfaces such as chatbots are widely used in modern digital platforms. Eighty percent of chatbot use cases are for customer servicing and other use cases are for use cases such as online account access (31%), personalized guidance (25%) and online appointment (15%) [4]. Hence the modern digital experience should provide instant access to conversational interfaces across all screens and pages. We have detailed the conversational interface case study at the end of this chapter.

Personalizing the user experience and content based on user preferences and user's behavior highly improves the user engagement. Hence we need to provide hyper personalized applications. Using the customer 360-degree data and analytics, we can personalize the user experience in real time. Using the cross-channel user data, we can proactively initiate the conversations with the user and help them resolve any pending issues or provide them with relevant content or surface relevant recommendations. We can start with segment-based personalization (where the user experience, content, features and services are personalized based on the user's segment) and then evolve into individual user-level personalization (where the user experience, content, features and services are personalized based on the individual user's preferences and interests).

Digital Experience Maturity Model

As enterprises embark on digital transformation of the experience, they implement processes, use best practices and tools to achieve higher engagement with the end users. We have mapped the main stage of the digital experience maturity model and have mapped the processes, best practices and tools in each of the stages as depicted in Figure 8.3. The digital maturity model serves as a guideline for the organizations to improve their digital experience.

In the "basic" stage, the enterprises have basic web platform that predominantly uses static content (such as FAQs, common static content for all users). The digital experience provides consistent brand experience across all the channels. Rendering

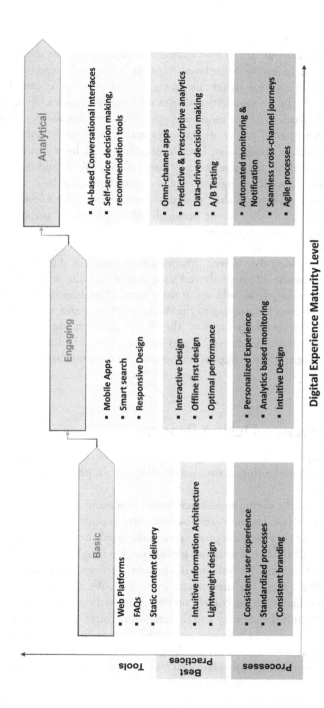

Figure 8.3 Digital experience maturity model.

intuitive information architecture (with predictable navigation, consistent menus) and using lightweight design are recommended best practices in this stage.

For organizations to evolve from basic stage to "engaging" stage, they should provide native mobile apps for richer and engaging user experience. Search should be enabled to provide the personalized and relevant information quickly to the user. Mobile apps should work in offline mode to engage the users in network-constrained locations. The performance of the digital interfaces should be in sub-second to improve the overall user satisfaction. User interfaces should have intuitive design and should be personalized for increased user engagement. We should continuously monitor the KPIs and metrics using analytical and monitoring tools.

Digital enterprises can reach the "analytical" stage, the highest level of digital experience maturity when they adopt personalization, AI-driven automation and data-driven analytics. AI-driven conversational interfaces are used for engaging users and providing the relevant information quickly. Self-service decision-making tools also enable users in taking data-driven informed decisions. The digital applications should be available across all channels and user should be able to seamlessly navigate across the channels. We should setup the analytical and monitoring tools for continuous and real-time monitoring of the digital platforms and notify the system administrators for taking timely actions. The digital platform should harness the data to provide predictive guidance (such as system patching schedule) and prescriptive guidance (recommending products and services for the users based on their past behavior).

Digital Experience Design Process

The experience design process aims to translate the user expectations and requirements into user-centric design. In this section we detail the main phases of digital experience design process.

We have depicted the digital experience design process in Figure 8.4.

In the discovery phase, we interview the end users to understand their goals and requirements. During the interview process we understand the main customer goals, desired outcomes, customer interests and gather insights into the current challenges and pain points of the users. We validate the insights gathered from user interviews with the user feedback from the surveys and interviews. We also model the current user experience to understand the current user journey, friction points, current information architecture and the security and integration requirements. Once we understand the current context and challenges, we model the expected user experience. We model the journey map to address the challenges and friction points.

While analyzing existing web platforms, we perform the competitive analysis of existing web platform to identify areas of improvements. We can compare the existing user experience with that of most popular web platforms in the same domain

Figure 8.4   Digital experience design process.

and same business function to identify areas of improvement. During user research, we also gain user behavior-related insights into the commonly used channels (web or mobile), device preferences (iOS or Android device), browser preferences and so on. We identify the user personas (distinct user groups who share similar goals and needs) and define the journey map (the path traversed by the web user for achieving a goal). We have detailed user persona in the next section.

Based on the insights gathered from the discovery phase, we create the visual design iteratively. We create wireframes and sketches (low fidelity visual elements that communicate the elements like page layout) and mockups and clickable prototypes (high-fidelity visual elements that depict the visual design, interactions, color scheme, font scheme and others). Mockups and prototypes are used to communicate the finalized design to all the stakeholders. We also create interaction design (that includes human interaction elements such as call-to-action buttons, sound design and others), user interface design (that depicts the user interface elements like forms, page layouts and others), navigational design (that includes navigational elements such as menus) accessibility design and other design elements. We iteratively execute ideate-design-test cycle to refine the design based on the user feedback. We formulate hypothesis for user goals, opportunities and validate it. We conduct usability testing to validate the effectiveness of visual design.

Finally in the deliver stage, we build the final mockups and prototypes based on the feedback gathered in the previous phases. The design team delivers visual tool kit (consisting of reusable libraries, icons, stylesheet and others), brand guidelines and visual patterns and libraries. The visual tool kit and the visual libraries can be reused across the platform to build a uniform and consistent brand experience. We build a minimum viable product (MVP) that can be released.

User Research and Hypothesis Testing

User interviews are important aspect of the user research. We ask open-ended questions as given below to understand the users' goals, behavior, current challenges and expectations.

- *"When do you exit the current web platform and why?"*
- *"What are the common goals you want to achieve with the web platform? How often do you achieve it?"*
- *"Tell me about the challenges you face while navigating the current web platform."*
- *"Please provide step by step process steps to complete the order flow in the current system."*

During the user interviews we gather information related to user facts, user goals, user behavior and user challenges as depicted in Figure 8.5.

To understand facts about user, we seek the main characteristics of the web users. For instance we seek to understand the commonly used mobile devices and browsers most frequently used by the users, accessibility, geographic and language requirements, skill level of users and other details. The facts about the users help us to model the user personas and help us in modeling the user journey map.

User goals indicate the main expectations from the platform. We ask probing questions to understand user's goals and wants. We also seek to understand tools, features, services, personalization requirements and expectations from the user.

User behavior indicates the main tasks users perform in the platform to achieve their goals. We also understand the navigation path, strategies, workarounds, hacks and solutions users follow to complete a task using the platform. We also seek to

Figure 8.5   User research dimensions.

understand the current challenges faced by the users. We ask questions to understand the difference in goals across user groups and geographies.

We interview users to understand their existing pain points that prevent them from achieving their goals. The interview throws light on user pain points such as confusing navigation, irrelevant search results, accessibility issues, performance issues, availability challenges and such.

Once we understand the user facts, user goals, user behavior and user pain points, we formulate hypothesis and validate it. Given below are some of the sample hypothesis we formulate during the design phase for e-commerce platform users:

- User behavior hypothesis example—*Customers aged between 20 and 30 mainly read fiction books.*
- User goal hypothesis example—*Customers want instant delivery of books.*
- User challenges example—*Customers face challenge in searching for relevant books.*
- Based on the above, we can formulate the below given testable hypothesis:

Customers aged between 20 and 30 read fiction books and want instant delivery of book and face challenges while searching for relevant books.

We ideate the solution options to address the challenges and we formulate the solution hypothesis as given below:

Personalized search helps customers in finding relevant books eliminating the relevancy issues in the search tool.

We conduct the user interviews and test the hypothesis with sample user population. Based on the feedback, we create low-fidelity wireframes, storyboards that we demo to the sample user population to get the feedback.

User Persona Definition

User persona represents a group of users who share similar characteristics (facts, goals, behavior and pain points). Based on the user research, we model user personas and define the journey map for each of the persona.

Let us look at an example of user persona of an e-commerce platform. Based on the user interviews we have identified two primary user personas:

- Tech-savvy young shopper who represent shoppers between 20 and 30 years of age
- E-commerce admin who represent all the users who manage the e-commerce platform.

We now discuss the tech-savvy young shopper persona.

Tech-Savvy Young Shopper

This user persona represents significant chunk of the e-commerce platform users who contribute to majority of the platform revenue. We have gathered the facts, goals, behavior and challenges of the person as given below.

User Facts

The tech-savvy young shopper is aged between 20 and 30 years and is skilled in using modern technology gadgets like smart phones and the mobile apps. The tech-savvy young shopper uses the e-commerce mobile app for shopping books and expects interactive and responsive user interfaces.

User Goals

The tech-savvy young shopper wants to find the relevant books that suit the user's taste. The user expects the system to understand the book genres based on past purchases and provide personalized book recommendations based on past purchases and book ratings. The tech-savvy young shopper values the search experience and checkout experience on the e-commerce platform.

User Behavior

The tech-savvy young shopper spends majority of the time searching for books based on genre and purchasing the books that interests the user.

User Challenges

Listed below are the main challenges faced by the tech-savvy young shopper in the current e-commerce platform:

- Keyword-based search does not show relevant results.
- Product checkout process has too many steps resulting in delays.
- The book delivery takes a week's time

User Journey Map

We have modeled the to-be user journey map based on the user expectations and to reduce the current friction and current pain points. The journey map depicted in Figure 8.6 addresses the main challenges of the tech-savvy young shopper.

The journey of the tech-savvy young shopper starts when the user receives a personalized notification about the release of a new book. Based on the previous

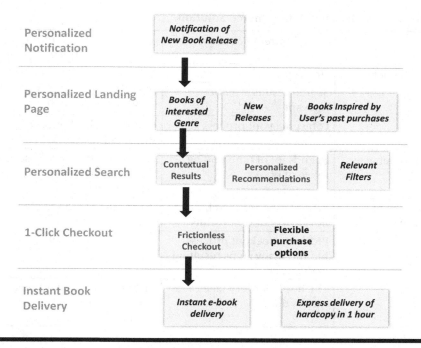

Figure 8.6   Journey map of tech-savvy user persona.

purchases, the e-commerce platform proactively notifies the user when a new book belonging to the genre of user's interest is released.

The user follows the book link in the notification and lands on the newly designed personalized landing page of the e-commerce platform. The personalized landing page provides details of the newly released book and also displays other new releases as well as books belonging the user's genre of interest. The user can select the book for a one-click checkout.

If the user wishes to search for other book titles, the personalized search contextualizes the search by adding the relevant filters (such as language, genre, author etc.) based on the user's past purchases. Additionally the personalized search feature also provides the personalized recommendations that are likely of interest to the user.

The one-click checkout feature offers frictionless checkout. User can instantly checkout the selected book with a single click. The system uses the delivery address, payment method from the user's profile to facilitate the one-click checkout. The system instantly delivers the e-book to the user and delivers the hard copy within one hour.

Table 8.1 pain point to the solution elements in the proposed system.

Table 8.1 Redesigned E-Commerce Solution

	Current Scenario	*Proposed Solution Components*
User's goals	Find relevant books	Personalized search to provide relevant book based on user's past purchase
	Search results are not relevant	
	Long checkout process	One-click checkout using the saved values
User's behavior	Spends lot of time finding relevant books	Personalized search to save the user's time through relevant results
User's pain points	Keyword-based search does not show relevant results	Personalized search with improved relevancy
	Product checkout process has too many steps resulting in delays	One-click checkout
	The book delivery takes a week's time	Instant delivery of e-book and one-hour delivery of hard copy

Case Study Conversational Interface Design

Conversational interfaces or chatbots are one of the most popular self-service tools used in various industries such as financial services, retail and commerce. In this case study we discuss various phases of designing digital experience of a banking conversational interface.

As depicted in Figure 8.4, we go over the discover and design phases of the case study.

Discover Phase

Currently the customers of XYZ bank use the phone banking to contact customer care. Long wait times is one of the common problems that is impacting the customer experience. The current web portal of XYZ bank does not provide self-service tools. The bank customers want a simple yet easy-to-use interface to complete common tasks such as request for a statement, transfer money to another account, report a lost card and others.

Majority of the XYZ bank customers access the Internet through mobile device. The customers expect a smart chatbot that can provide the relevant information and help them complete their tasks.

Main Use Cases

The key use cases for the chatbot are given below:

- The users should be able to access the chatbot instantly from anywhere.
- The users should be able to type a command or should be able to speak the commands over microphone.
- The chatbot should be able to provide multiple options (such as quick reply buttons) for the users to choose.

Design Phase

In this section we discuss the main design elements based on the requirements.

Conversational Interface

The conversational interface is accessible using floating action button available on all screens so that users can access the chatbot instantly from anywhere within the platform.

The conversational interface provides a personalized greeting to the user and provides quick reply buttons on how the chatbot can help the user. The chatbot interface is depicted in Figure 8.7. The chatbot provides various actions (such as "*show transaction I made yesterday*", "*transfer money*", "*report lost card*") as shown in Figure 8.7. The user can select quick reply buttons and the chatbot performs action corresponding to the selected option.

Users can also speak to the chatbot using microphone to get the support from the chatbot as depicted in Figure 8.7.

Service Options Available in Conversational Interface

The chatbot provides options related to payments, account and transaction as depicted in Figure 8.8.

Users can select the required options under Payments, Account or Transactions headings to initiate the transaction.

Summary

A digital experience defines the interaction of the user with an organization through digital technologies. Information architecture, visual design, psychology, accessibility, branding, usability, interaction design, visual design and others elements shape the final digital experience. The main tenets of digital experience are user-centric design,

Figure 8.7 Main chatbot interface.

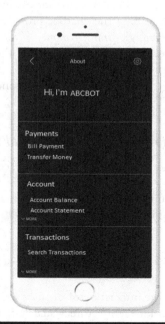

Figure 8.8 Service options of the chatbot.

smart search, decision-aiding tools, end-user testing and monitoring and feedback tools, omni-channel and multi-device experience, mobile apps and virtual assistants, conversational interfaces and personalized experience. Design thinking is one of the key methods to design human-centered experience and uses problem finding methodology to evaluate multiple solution alternatives. Modern digital experiences enable relevant and faster information discovery through smart search. Self-service tools enable users to make data-driven and informed decisions quickly. Personalizing the user experience, content based on user preferences and user's behavior highly improves the user engagement. The main stages of digital experience maturity model are basic, engaging and analytical. In the basic stage, the organization has a static content-based web platform that provides consistent brand experience. In the "engaging" stage, we provide mobile apps that provides personalized, engaging and interactive user experience. In the "analytical" stage, the platform uses AI-based automation and data-driven decision-making and provide seamless omni-channel experience. Digital experience design process consists of discover, design and deliver phases. In the discovery phase, we conduct user interviews to get the context and define the user persona and user journey map. In the design phase, we iteratively design the low-fidelity wireframe and high-fidelity prototypes. In the deliver phase, we iteratively build the MVP. During user research we ask open-ended questions to understand users' goals, behavior, current challenges and expectations. User persona represents a group of users who share similar characteristics (facts, goals, behavior and pain points).

References

1. Gentile, C., Spiller, N., & Noci, G. (2007). How to sustain the customer experience: an overview of experience components that co-create value with the customer. *European Management Journal* 25(5), 395–410.
2. Gartner identifies Top Digital Experience Trends for 2020. Gartner. (n.d.). Retrieved January 28, 2023, from www.gartner.com/en/newsroom/press-releases/2019-10-29-gartner-identifies-top-digital-experience-trends-for-
3. Razzouk, R., & Shute, V. (2012). What is design thinking and why is it important?. *Review of Educational Research* 82(3), 330–348.
4. 2022 consumer innovation survey insights. CapTech. (n.d.). Retrieved January 28, 2023, from www.captechconsulting.com/articles/2022-consumer-innovation-survey-insights
5. Demery, P. (February 20, 2017). Why an omnichannel strategy matters. Digital Commerce 360. Retrieved January 28, 2023, from www.digitalcommerce360.com/2013/12/31/why-omnichannel-strategy-matters/
6. The future of digital experiences. Forrester. (n.d.). Retrieved January 28, 2023, from www.forrester.com/report/The-Future-Of-Digital-Experiences/RES120364

## Chapter 9

Transforming the Platform Performance

Introduction

The performance of the digital platform has the greatest impact on the end-user experience. Hence organizations plan to improve the overall performance of the digital platform as part of the digital transformation.

Web performance impacts the success of digital strategy in multiple ways. Optimal web performance increases revenue [1,2] and improves search engine ranking [3]. Web performance also has positive impact on user traffic [4,5] as good performing web pages increase perceived success on the end users [6]. As far as the response time is concerned, most users expect the web page to load within 2 seconds [7] and a sub 2 second performance improve the conversion rate [11]. On the contrary the users are more likely to abandon the slower web pages [8–10] and page abandonment rate increase if page takes more than 3 seconds to load [12].

For comprehensive performance optimization we leverage various methods such as performance-based design, performance patterns, performance testing, performance monitoring and such. Web performance patterns provide guidance in implementing the best practices–based solution.

In this chapter, we discuss the performance-based design to implement the performance best practices at all the SDLC phases. We also discuss the main performance patterns and anti-patterns.

DOI: 10.1201/9781003390893-12

Performance-Based Design

A performance-based design incorporates the performance best practices in all phases of the Software Development Life Cycle (SDLC) across all layers of the platform. We have depicted various performance optimizations that can be done through the SDLC phases in Figure 9.1.

During the design and architecture phase, we adopt performance-based design. This includes defining performance design principles and developing a performance checklist and performance patterns that could be used during the development and testing phases. We will also finalize the performance SLAs related to response time, throughput, and resource utilization, and such. We design performance test cases and setup right sized infrastructure. Performance modeling and user load modeling of the application are done using peak loads, peak usage hours, application usage patterns and identifying key performance scenarios and performance objectives and metrics.

During the development phase, a performance-based development methodology is adopted using iterative performance code reviews. Application code, server configurations, and web pages are fine-tuned from a performance standpoint. The development team also uses the performance design checklist and architecture principles defined in the design and architecture phase. The multi-layer caching system is developed. Asset, service and content optimization techniques are implemented for page modules.

Performance validation phase involves iterative performance testing and measures all the identified performance metrics and SLAs for end-to-end performance scenarios. We conduct various types of performance testing such as peak load testing, infrastructure testing, endurance testing and volume testing. During the performance testing and analysis phase, we would identify performance bottlenecks and fine-tune components and systems to address the bottleneck. Performance testing is conducted on all supported browsers and mobile devices.

In post-production phase, we mainly conduct performance monitoring activities such as server health check monitoring, real-time application monitoring and automated performance testing. SLA violations are reported and notified proactively to system administrators to take corrective actions.

Horizontal components, such as performance tools and accelerators, are used in all phases for enhanced productivity. Web performance governance spans all phases of web performance optimization. The web performance is optimized at various phases of the web request processing pipeline.

Web Performance Anti-Patterns and best practices

Insights into performance anti-patterns helps us to avoid the anti-patterns during design time and during the review time. In this section, we identify the key performance anti-patterns and look at the best practices to address the anti-patterns.

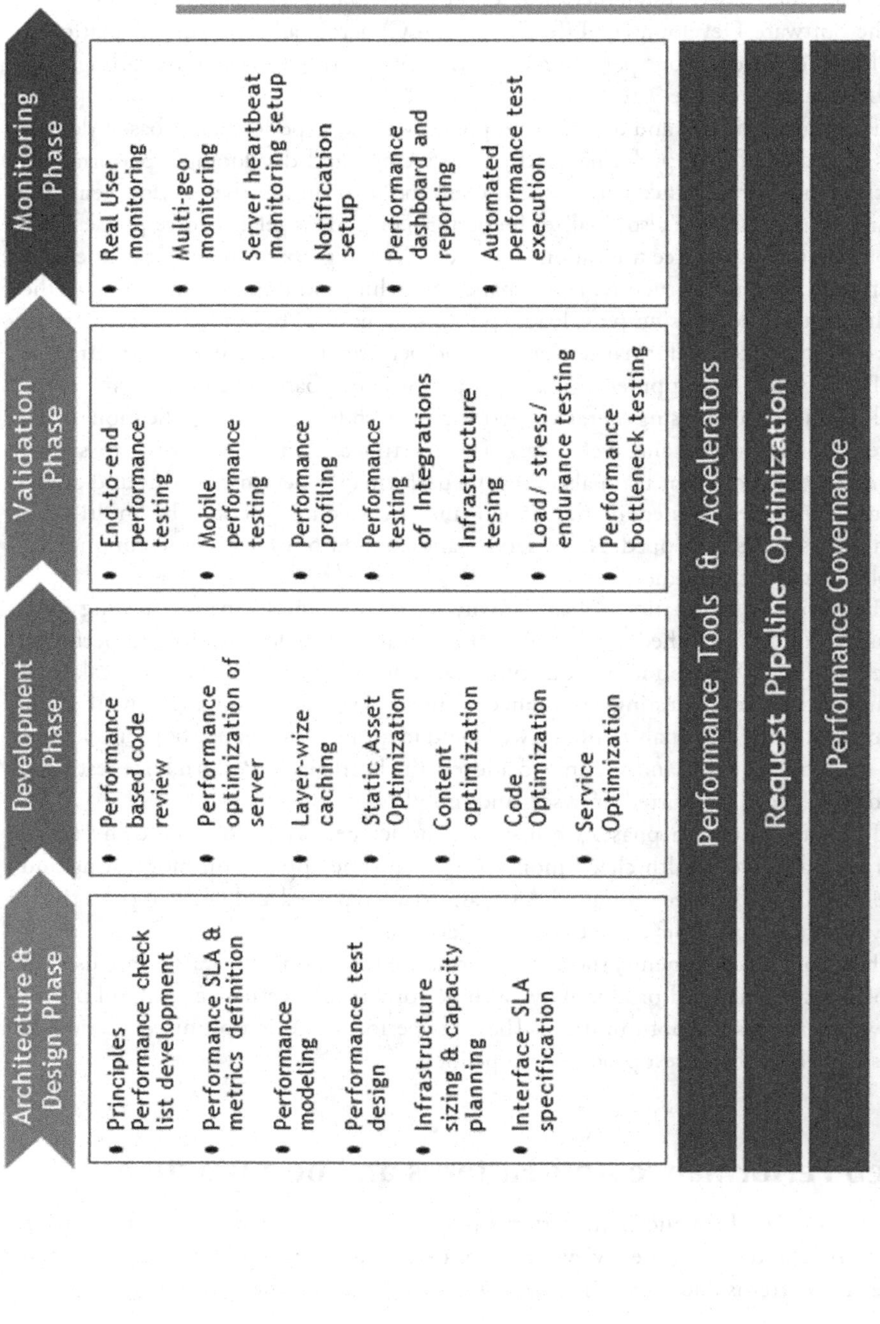

Architecture & Design Phase	Development Phase	Validation Phase	Monitoring Phase
• Principles Performance check list development	• Performance based code review	• End-to-end performance testing	• Real User monitoring
• Performance SLA & metrics definition	• Performance optimization of server	• Mobile performance testing	• Multi-geo monitoring
• Performance modeling	• Layer-wize caching	• Performance profiling	• Server heartbeat monitoring setup
• Performance test design	• Static Asset Optimization	• Performance testing of Integrations	• Notification setup
• Infrastructure sizing & capacity planning	• Content optimization	• Infrastructure tesing	• Performance dashboard and reporting
• Interface SLA specification	• Code Optimization	• Load/ stress/ endurance testing	• Automated performance test execution
	• Service Optimization	• Performance bottleneck testing	

Performance Tools & Accelerators

Request Pipeline Optimization

Performance Governance

Figure 9.1 Performance optimizations across SDLC phases.

Web Page Design Anti-Patterns

Given below is the list of common anti-patterns in web page design that leads to sub-optimal web page performance.

- Bad design of key pages (such as gateway pages, homepages, or landing pages) by including numerous images, entry popups, heavy banners, banner ads, and presentation components.
- Cluttered and heavy landing pages that are not targeted for user personas and complex page design without unified interface. Using a huge number of resource requests impacting parallel downloads and having banner ads, entry popups, and too many calls to actions and clickable links in landing pages.
- The absence of real-time performance monitoring and notification infrastructure and absence of layer-wise caching strategy.
- Using uncompressed images and scripts on the pages.
- Bad integration design.
    - Third party component integration without proper SLA framework.
    - Improper handling of timeouts and exceptions in the services.
- Having front-end Single Point Of Failure (SPOF) such as blocking third-party script, synchronous load, delayed/long-running blocking JavaScript, in-lined font-face, in-lined scripts, and in-lined images that prevent browser caching, edge caching, and on-demand loading and increased load time.
- Huge white space in HTML document that increases page size.
- Absence of omni-channel strategy.
    - Absence of mobility-enabled sites or lack of multi-device testing.
    - Absence of cross-browser testing.
- Absence of early and iterative performance testing.
- Other common issues with page performance are as follows:
    - Numerous JS/CSS includes.
    - Duplicate calls.
    - Broken links.
    - Unnecessary calls.
    - Placement of JS/CSS calls.
    - Bloated size of web page.
    - Frequent resource requests with huge payload.
    - Inline styles and JS logic.

Page Design Best Practices

Given below are the performance best practices and performance design patterns that are applicable in the design phase of the project:

- Avoiding extraneous content such as advertisements reduces the number of objects per page and improves latency.
- Adopting user-centric design approach addresses challenges related to usability, information discovery, accessibility and task completion.
- Conducting iterative performance testing assesses the page performance across geography and omni-channel testing for all pages.
- Adopting user-friendly and intuitive information architecture and minimizing pages/links needed to find the information or to reach the correct page. Creating information architecture and page flows based on user goals and personas so that users can reach the information quickly and complete the intended task.
- Keeping the key pages simple in design. This involves using only necessary user interface (UI) components. Complex page design and page cluttering should be avoided. Optimizing the landing page through techniques such as eyeball tracking, uncluttering, targeted and useful information, and A-B Split testing/multivariate testing analysis. The right pane elements can load late as its performance is less critical.
- Use Responsive Web Design (RWD) technique to cater to multiple devices and form factors. RWD consists of fluid grids, media queries that can auto-adjust based on the target device specifications. Users perceive instantaneous response time (0.1–0.2 seconds), and they feel that that information interaction time is 1–5 seconds; hence it is important to adopt the responsive design to create interactive and highly performing UI elements.
- Minimizing page weight. Preferably the overall page size should be between 100KB and 400KB for home pages and landing pages. Minimize session size and cookie size.
- Business-critical processes should be optimized. This includes business process optimization, page design optimization, search optimization, check out/shopping process optimization, user registration optimization and such.
- Removing known performance blockers such as numerous unnecessary links, iframes, numerous pages, and non-intuitive information architecture.
- AJAX-enable the web applications to fetch the resources and to load the page data. It results in more responsive and shorter response times.
- Making web components lighter, moving them closer to the layer where it is used, caching them longer, and loading them more intelligently.
- Layer-wise caching at all layers in the request processing pipeline for optimal performance.
- Progressive enhancement technique that uses layers of standards such as XHTML, CSS JavaScript to overlay dynamic content with CSS, JavaScript to provide cross-browser accessible content. The technique mainly consists of the behavior layer (implemented through unobtrusive JavaScripts), presentation layer (implemented through CSS), structure layer (implemented

through HTML standards) and core content layer and these layers are selectively added based on the device capability to maximize usability and accessibility.

■ Minimal round trips: The web page should minimize the server calls to the extent possible. Wherever possible, the calls should be batched to minimize the calls.

■ Asynchronous loading pattern: All the page assets should be loaded asynchronously and resource requests should adopt asynchronous communication.

■ Lazy loading pattern: The page assets should be loaded when required and on-demand.

■ Lightweight design: The page should adopt a lean model using Web-Oriented Architecture (WOA) and use lightweight integration technique.

■ Device specific rendition: The page content, assets should be optimized for the rendition device.

■ Responsive page content: Responsive design for HTML elements and adaptive design for content should be followed.

Design of Server Calls

Given below are the main best practices that needs to be adopted during the backend call or services design.

■ Explore ways to load the page content asynchronously. We can leverage AJAX requests to load the page sections, which provide non-blocking page loads.

■ Ensure the page data is loaded only on demand and in lazy mode. For instance, the list data or results data can be shown in paginated view and can be loaded only on user navigation.

■ Use asynchronous scripts and AJAX gets requests.

■ Specify design goals for external and third-party scripts. The main design goals for the external scripts are small size, readable, unobtrusive, and easy to copy-paste to the host page and asynchronous support.

Web Performance Patterns

In this section we define the main performance patterns and web architecture patterns. The patterns can be used while designing the application and web services during the design phase.

The Model-View-Controller Architecture

The model-view-controller (MVC) architecture style is the widely used architecture pattern that creates loosely coupled flexible web applications with modular components. From the performance viewpoint, interactional styles, such as event observation and notification, publish/subscribe and asynchronous communication, can be added as features for MVC applications. Most modern web applications heavily use the Representational State Transfer (REST) architecture style that provides lightweight and asynchronous methods for requesting and updating web resources.

Microservices Architecture

The microservices architecture allows us to build a web application as a composition of multiple independently scalable services. The architecture uses lightweight communication mechanism and functional model for building services. Since each of the microservices are individually scalable, we could build a highly scalable and performing system using microservices.

Web-Oriented Architecture (WOA)

WOA involves lightweight pluggable client-side widgets. WOA architecture is lightweight in design and we can easily implement the web performance best practices. AJAX-based client-side MVC and Model–View–View Model (MVVM) architectures are used to build rich, interactive and responsive web applications.

Single Responsibility Principle (SRP)

According to the SRP principle, modules should only do one task. The SRP makes it simpler to maintain, modularize, test, and extend the code by applying it to components and services. The following are some SRP best practices:

- Each service should address just one issue. The context ought to encompass the services.
- Only logic associated with the view should be handled by a component. Every additional logic should be handled by the services.
- Create reusable services with straightforward, reusable components.
- Create more compact, modular, and reusable functions.
- Business logic and presentation logic should not be combined.
- Observe the DRY principle (don't repeat yourself). Reusability, maintainability, testability, and complexity are all ensured by the DRY method.
- Adaptive Design
- To support various devices and browsers, responsive design should be used. To render the web page optimally across different browsers and devices, the responsive design makes use of HTML 5, CSS 3, and media queries.

- Use a tool that employs a single code base for both the web and different mobile devices to develop the web platform. Applications that are isomorphic employ a same code base on both the client and server sides. For example, we can use a single source code for both iOS and Android mobile apps when developing hybrid cross-platform apps. A single code base enhances maintainability and reduces implementation, support, and maintenance costs significantly. Moreover, the one code base reduces time to market.

Separation of Concerns

To handle data, UI rendering logic, business logic, and communication logic, create individual modules and components each handling a specific concern. The testability, reuse, and extensibility of the code are all enhanced by this design.

Testability

The SRP, which segregates concerns, should be used for development of the modules and components. This makes it simple to test the code.

Plug-and-Play Architecture

The server APIs must be adaptable enough to support a wide range of clients (including browsers, mobile apps, tablets, wearables, watches, kiosks etc.), deployment models (including on-premise, cloud, or serverless architecture), protocols (including HTTP, HTTPS, REST, SMTP etc.), and platforms (including on-premise, cloud, and serverless architecture) (across cloud, database, UI framework etc.).

Extensibility

The APIs ought to be divided up based on how businesses use them. API-driven design ought to make it possible to gradually add business features.

Service Governance

Typically, the service governance is provided via integration middleware systems. Service governance should handle the below given best practices:

- Parsing incoming requests to match patterns for malicious pattern. We can leverage the web application firewall (WAF) to protect the application against the web vulnerabilities. For instance, we may parse the HTTP request using body-parser middleware.

- Prior to processing, requests must be authenticated. For instance, we might handle numerous authentication schemes using passport (such as OAuth, Email, AD, third-party authentication etc.). Using headers, middleware like Helmet can secure APIs.
- Recording requests and answers.
- Controlling CORS (Cross Origin Resource Sharing).
- Requests being proxied using middleware like http-proxy.
- Error management by graciously addressing data, network, and application problems.
- Reduce the HTTP response's size. Compression middleware, for instance, can be used to compress HTTP responses.
- Cache the static data that is needed.
- Carry out any necessary data transformations.

Middleware can organize system-specific requests and hide the details from the caller by employing the API façade design.

Asynchronous API Calls

The majority of contemporary online platforms use asynchronous server API calls. These asynchronous calls allow us to run the jobs concurrently and prevent delays in the processing of requests.

Handling Performance Bottlenecks

In Table 9.1 we have defined various performance bottleneck scenarios and web performance optimization patterns to avoid the bottleneck scenarios.

Performance Validation

During performance testing, we must imitate the user load and comprehend how the resources are used. We carry out numerous types of performance testing depending on the requirements of the application and performance SLAs. The typical types of performance testing are given below:

Load testing: Calculate the system performance for a specific concurrent user load under pre-defined load circumstances. Keep track of how the load has changed the system's behavior and performance. Throughout the load testing, keep an eye on the usage of the system's resources, including the CPU, RAM and network.

Stress testing: Evaluate the system's performance and behavior under pressure. As part of this testing, the system will be put through peak loads, unexpected

Table 9.1 **Performance Bottleneck and Patterns**

Component Causing Bottleneck	Bottleneck Scenario at High Load	Web Performance Optimization Pattern
User-Agent Layer		
Page level web objects	Large number of objects per page impact page size and page load times.	Minimize objects per page and load resources asynchronously.
Resource requests	Higher synchronous resource requests per page impact page load time.	Minimal HTTP requests. Avoid long-running scripts. Minify and merge resources to minimize resource requests.
Inline image and inline script	Inline image and inline script increase page load time.	Externalize images and scripts. Avoid inline scripts and images.
Web objects in critical path	HTML Parsing and JS execution forms 35% of critical path and creates bottleneck.	Avoid long-running scripts. Use asynchronous scripts.
Web server layer		
Third party script/ external object	Creates front-end SPOF for long running scripts.	Use async scripts and test third-party objects. Use time-out to avoid blocking.
Scripts	Synchronous request of long-running scripts/files blocks the page and creates a single point of failure.	Asynchronous resource request and on-demand loading. Use the iframe of the third-party scripts. Real user monitoring of performance metrics.
Application server layer		
Server response	Impacts Time to first byte (TTFB) and latency and page load time.	CDN usage and connection caching
Server configuration	Improper connection pool size, connection pool setting, threads' pool size impacts performance at heavy load.	Fine-tune and test the application server settings.
Network layer		
DNS lookup	DNS lookup impacts the critical path.	DNS caching and connection caching.

spikes, and prolonged high load situations. We will determine the application's breaking point and the highest load the system can support without experiencing performance degradation. Keep in mind that during this testing, the system will experience resource depletion. The following metrics are monitored and validated during stress testing:

■ Determine peak limits, such as the maximum number of concurrent users, transactions and availability.
■ How many concurrent users at peak and average load?
■ How many transactions were active concurrently at peak and average load?
■ Endurance testing: To evaluate the system's performance and behavior, a prolonged load test will be performed on it (often for 48–72 hours). During this testing, we can find any potential memory leaks, buffer overflow problems, and hardware-related problems.
■ Testing for scalability: Using different workloads depending on the workload model we will evaluate the system. We iteratively raise the number of concurrent users during this testing while monitoring the system's performance. The main workload must be determined, and bottlenecks that prevent application scalability must be eliminated. We start with 10% of data, then ramp up to maximum with increasing data volume frequently.
■ Reliability and availability testing: During load testing and stress testing we will assess the system's dependability and availability. We will also examine the system's MTTF (Mean Time Between Failures).
■ Performance benchmarking testing: We assess the application's performance in comparison to that of prior iterations. We also evaluate the application's performance in comparison to applications from the same category and applications from rival categories.
■ Data volume testing: To test the system effectively, production-like data volume and content must be used.

Performance Metrics

We can track the overall performance of the system using the performance metrics. We have given the key performance as follows:

Response time—We assess how quickly pages, transactions, and business operations respond overall. Testing the response time under varying user loads is required for this. The key metrics in this category are round trip time (RTT), page response time, time to first byte, asset load time and others.

System scalability—Using different workloads depending on the workload model, we test the system. We gradually raise the number of concurrent users and test the system's scalability under varied demands. The key metrics in this category

Table 9.2 Performance Tools

Category	Sample Tools
Performance monitoring and visualization	Prometheus and Grafana
Synthetic monitoring	• DynaTrace (Commercial) • Selenium • Lighthouse • Webpagetest.org
Log monitoring	• Splunk • Fluentd • DataDog
Container monitoring	• Node exporter • Docker stats • cAdvisor • Prometheus
Web page monitoring (page size, page response time, number of requests, asset load time etc.)	• Webpagetest.org • Site speed (https://www.sitespeed.io/) • Google page speed insights • (https://developers.google.com/speed/pagespeed/insights/) • Pingdom (commercial) • Silk performance manager (commercial) • Uptrends (commercial) • https://web.dev/measure/

Development tools/ page auditing	• Google Chrome developer tools
	• Test my site
	  - (www.thinkwithgoogle.com/feature/testmysite/)
	• Google Chrome lighthouse
	• HTTP Watch
	  - https://blog.speedrank.app/
	• Fiddler
	• Firebug
	• Web tracing framework
	  - http://google.github.io/tracing-framework/
	• Timeline tool
	  - https://developer.chrome.com/docs/devtools/performance/timeline-reference/

Cloud monitoring	Amazon CloudWatch
Website speed test	https://tools.keycdn.com/speed
Load testing	• BlazeMeter • Apache JMeter
Website latency test	• Ping test (https://tools.keycdn.com/ping)
Real user monitoring (RUM)	• New relic • SpeedCurve (https://speedcurve.com/)

are transactions per second, throughput, resource utilization metrics during average and peak loads.

Availability—During load testing and stress testing, we evaluate the system's dependability and accessibility. We also examine the system's MTTF.

Resource utilization—During varied loads, we keep an eye on the system's resources, including the CPU, RAM, network bandwidth and input/output activity. The main metrics in this category are average CPU utilization, average RAM utilization and such. During varying loads, we assess whether resource consumption is sound and within predetermined limits. For instance, we keep an eye on whether CPU usage stays within 80% for the whole load testing period.

Resilience—We evaluate the system's ability to tolerate component failures and recover from errors and manage them graciously.

Performance Tools

We have detailed the tools that can be used for performance monitoring and performance testing in Table 9.2.

Summary

A performance-based design incorporates the performance best practices in all phases of the SDLC. During the design and architecture phase, we define the performance design principles and develop a performance checklist and performance patterns that could be used during the development and testing phases. During the development phase, a performance-based development methodology would be adopted using iterative performance code reviews. We perform iterative performance testing and measuring all the identified performance metrics and SLAs for end-to-end performance scenarios during the validation phase. During post production we conduct performance monitoring activities. The main performance anti-patterns are bad design of key pages, heavy landing page, absence of performance monitoring and bad integration design. The main page design best practices are adopting user-centric design, conducting iterative performance testing, adopting user-friendly and intuitive information architecture, using RWD, light weight design and others. The main web performance patterns are MVC architecture, microservices architecture, WOA, SRP, adaptive design, single code base, separation of concerns, testability, plug-and-play architecture, extensibility and service governance. Load testing and stress testing are main performance validations to assess the overall performance of the application. The main performance metrics are response time, system scalability, availability, resource utilization and resilience

References

1. Galletta, D. F., Henry, R., McCoy, S., & Polak, P. (2004). Web site delays: how tolerant are users? *Journal of the Association for Information Systems* 5(1), 5–6.
2. Shopzilla: faster page load time = 12% revenue increase. Available from: www.stra ngeloopnetworks.com/resources/infographics/web-performanceand-ecommerce/shopzilla-fasterpages-12-revenue-increase/
3. Google. (April 9, 2010). Using site speed in web search ranking. Available from: http://googlewebmastercentral.blogspot.com/2010/04/using-sitespeed-in-web-search-ranking.html
4. Lohr, S. (March, 2012). For Impatient Web Users, an Eye Blink Is Just Too Long to Wait. Available from: www.nytimes.com/2012/03/01/technology/impatient-web-users-flee-slow-loading-sites.html
5. Souders, S. (July, 2009). Velocity and the Bottom Line. Available from: http://radar.oreilly.com/2009/07/velocity-making-your-site-fast.html
6. Palmer, J. W. (2002). Web site usability, design, and performance metrics. *Information Systems Research* 13(2), 151–167.
7. For Impatient Web Users, an Eye Blink Is Just Too Long to Wait: Available from: www.nytimes.com/2012/03/01/technology/impatient-web-users-flee-slow-loading-sites.html?_r=2
8. Rempel, G. (2015). Defining standards for web page performance in business applications. *Proceedings of the 6th ACM/SPEC International Conference on Performance Engineering – ICPE '15*, 4–5.
9. Galletta, D. F., Henry, R., McCoy, S., & Polak, P. (2004) Web site delays: How tolerant are users? *Journal of the Association for Information Systems*, 5(1), 1.
10. Hoxmeier, J. A., & DiCesare, C. (2000). System response time and user satisfaction: an experimental study of browser based applications. Proceedings of the Americas Conference on Information Systems, Association for Information Systems, Long Beach, CA, USA., 140–145.
11. Available from: www.compuware.com/application-performance-management/performance-index-faq.html
12. Available from: www.akamai.com/html/about/press/releases/2009/press_091409.html

Chapter 10

AI and Digital Transformation

Introduction

We are living in an era where most of the tasks, processes and day-to-day activities are getting increasingly automated by machines. Automation brings in productivity, convenience, time savings, cost savings that allow humans to invest their time and energy in more valuable and complex tasks. Machine-led automation is revolutionizing the way we live, communicate, work and do business. Artificial Intelligence (AI)-led systems are becoming ubiquitous, impacting modern human civilization in numerous forms and redefining the daily tasks in our lives.

AI is the guiding force behind the automation revolution. AI helps machines "learn", "understand" like the way humans do. AI is an interdisciplinary science that uses various methods such as natural language processing (NLP), machine learning (ML), knowledge processing, reasoning, predicting and such.

In simple terms AI includes methods and systems to make the machine perform intelligent and cognitive tasks that humans are good at performing. Tasks such as game playing, language translation, recognition patterns, identifying images, coming up with a rationale decision, problem-solving, reasoning and such.

AI and ML are key tools in digital transformation process. ML enables many digital transformation of processes such as forecasting of sales and inventory, computer vision–based auto checkout, customer churn prediction, fraud detection and such. In this chapter we discuss history, foundations and applications of AI.

DOI: 10.1201/9781003390893-13

Definition

The term "intelligence" means many things. Let us look at some of the definitions of it:

- "The capacity to acquire and apply knowledge especially toward a purposeful goal".
- "An individual's relative standing on two quantitative indices, namely measured intelligence, as expressed by an intelligence quotient, and effectiveness of adaptive behavior" (*The American Heritage® Stedman's Medical Dictionary*).
- "The ability to learn or understand or to deal with new or trying situations".
- "The ability to apply knowledge to manipulate one's environment or to think abstractly as measured by objective criteria (as tests) (*Merriam-Webster's Medical Dictionary*).
- "The ability to comprehend; to understand and profit from experience".
- "The ability to learn and solve problems" (Webster's Dictionary).

Essentially intelligence incorporates three core attributes:

- **Knowledge acquisition/learning/adaptation:** An intelligent entity should be able to acquire knowledge through understanding, observation, inference, experience, learning, reading and such. An intelligent entity should be able to continuously learn from its experience and adapt to the new or never-seen-before scenarios.
- **Reasoning with knowledge:** An intelligent entity should be able to leverage knowledge to arrive at the most optimal outcome, decide between various options, planning, and perform tasks efficiently and such. An intelligent entity should be able to deal with uncertainties and unexpected problems.
- **Understanding and perception:** An intelligent entity must be able to understand and perceive the world through speech, vision and pattern recognition.

Broadly speaking, AI is an area concerned with making the machines "intelligent". AI involves methods for machines to acquire knowledge, reason with acquired knowledge and help machines understand and synthesize the real world.
The common attributes of AI in all the definitions are as follows:

- Human-like qualities such as thinking, learning, decision-making, reasoning and such.
- Rational behavior by arriving at the most optimal outcome for given inputs or solve the problems optimally.
- Exhibit human-like intelligence in processing knowledge, understanding and making intelligent decisions.

AI Methods

Knowledge acquisition, reasoning with knowledge and understanding and perception are the key tenets of an AI system. Knowledge takes many forms (such as knowledge in written text, images, and visuals), many formats (such as structured or unstructured and such), is constantly changing, and high volume in nature. Hence in order to acquire knowledge, an AI system should possess these properties:

- Identify and extract the key elements/entities of the knowledge.
- Identify common patterns or group similar elements in the knowledge.
- Extrapolate the acquired knowledge to unseen or exception scenarios.
- Ability to work with inaccurate or ambiguous knowledge content.
- Ability to reduce the knowledge by eliminating the unnecessary knowledge content.

In order to achieve the above, the key methods AI methods commonly used are as follows:

- Search: Employ the search method to solve the problem through usage of heuristic and other search methods.
- Knowledge usage: Leverage the structure of the knowledge to solve complex problems.
- Abstraction: Extract the important and key features of the knowledge from the unimportant ones.

The relationship among the key AI methods is given in Figure 10.1:

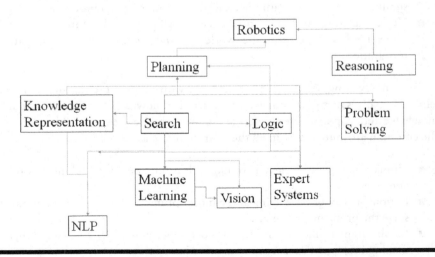

Figure 10.1 Relationship among AI Methods.

Foundations of AI

AI uses the methods and techniques from various fields of science. We have given the list of fields that has contributed to the AI in Figure 10.2

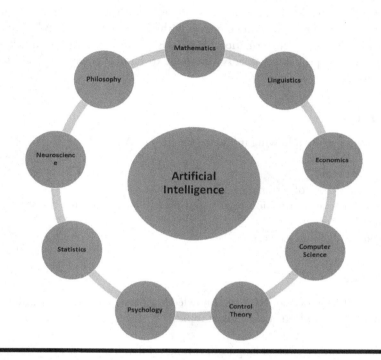

Figure 10.2   Fields of science that have contributed to AI.

Philosophy

Concepts such as logical reasoning and theory of rationality, theory of language, reasoning are part of philosophy. Laws of rationality define the laws and rules that govern the mind and dualism (describing dual forms of reality material/physical and immaterial/spiritual and mind and body are separate from each other), materialism (mind and body and other entities in the world are adhering to physical laws), principle of induction (rules are based on association sensory exposure to the elements) and others. The key ideas of philosophy that has influenced AI are as follows:

- Logic and methods of reasoning
- Mind as physical system
- Foundations of learning
- Language
- Rationality

Mathematics

Concepts such as probability, logic (such as propositional logic and predicate logic), algorithms, decidability and formal representation and proof algorithms, automated reasoning, formal logic and knowledge representation are parts of mathematics that has influenced AI. Historically the concepts such as intractability (time for solving the problem exponentially increases with the input size such as NP complete problems), reduction (transformation of one class of problems to another class with known solution), probability theory (methods to handle uncertainty) are used in decision-making.

Economics

Concepts such as the following influence the field of AI:

■ Game theory
■ Formal theory of rational decisions
■ Combination of decision theory and probability theory for decision making under uncertainty
■ Markov decision processes

Linguistics

Concepts such as grammar, NLP and knowledge representation are key influences to the AI field along with the below given topics:

■ Understanding natural languages through different approaches
■ Formal languages
■ Syntactic and semantic analysis
■ Knowledge representation
■ Relationship between language and thought process

Statistics

Topics such as regression models, learning from data, modeling uncertainty are used in artificial intelligence.

Neuroscience

The key ideas influenced by neuroscience are:

■ Neurons as information processing units used in artificial neural networks
■ Study of brain functioning

Psychology

Concepts related to behaviorism and cognitive psychology (the study of information processing by brain) are areas of interest in psychology. The key factors of psychology influencing the AI are:

- Phenomena of perception and motor control
- Human adaptation analysis
- Human behavior analysis, (how people think and act)
- The study of human reasoning and acting
- How do humans learn and process knowledge
- Study of learning, memory and thinking
- Provides reasoning models for AI
- Human brain as an information processing machine.

Computer Science

Most of the core concepts of the computer science (such as programming, algorithms, design patterns, parallel computing, data structure, large scale computing, Machine Learning (ML), pattern detection, grid computing and such) are used in logical reasoning and decision-making.

Control Theory

The main concepts influenced by control theory are as follows:

- Stability of systems
- Simple optimal agent design (systems that maximize objective function over time)
- How can artifacts operate under their own control?
- Optimal agents receiving feedback from the environment.

Problem-Solving

AI programs are often used for solving structured problems with well-defined structure and rules.

In this section we will list the main steps for problem-solving. We have depicted the key steps in problem-solving as given in Figure 10.3:

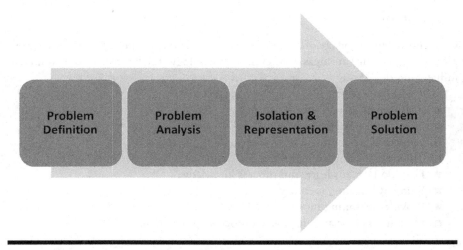

Figure 10.3   Steps for problem solving.

Given below are the key steps in problem-solving:

- **Problem definition**: During this stage we must provide precise problem specifications with initial solution and final solution. We should also define the acceptable solution criteria.
- **Problem analysis**: In this stage we need to shortlist the main features and select the most important features that has high impact and the ones that are appropriate for problem-solution techniques.
- **Isolation and representation**: In this stage we convert the selected features and task knowledge into knowledge representation.
- **Problem-solving technique(s)**: In this stage we choose the most optimal technique that can be applied to the problem.

Key Considerations

Given below are main problem considerations:

- Solution guarantee: We need to ensure problem solver can guarantee a solution.
- Termination guarantee: We need to ensure that the system always terminate or never be caught in an infinite loop.
- Optimality: The selected solution should be optimal.
- Search complexity: The complexity of the searching process is also one of the key considerations.
- Reducing search complexity: We need to reduce searching complexity.

Problem-Solving Using State Space Search

Search is one of the main problem-solving methods adopted by AI programs. A problem-solving AI agent solves the problem by finding a solution in the problem space (overall problem statement that needs solution). The search strategy provides the overall strategy to find the optimal solution.

State space formally represents the problem definition that provides conversion of one state to solution state using operations. We can navigate the state space through the problem space applying solution techniques till we reach the goal state. The solution is represented by a path from initial state to one of the goal states.

The key components of state space model–based problem-solving are:

- **Search space**: This represents the set of all states reachable from the initial state. In graph representation, each state is the node in graph and actions are represented by arc between nodes. The path is represented by sequence of states connected by sequence of actions.
- **Search tree** provides tree representation of all the possible from initial state.
- **State**: The state represents all the problem elements at a given moment. In graphical representation, state is represented by a graph node.
- **Operators/actions**: An operator is represented by a directed arc from one node to another. Operator denotes a legal action that an agent can take to move from one node to another.
- **Initial state** represents the start for the search process.
- **Goal state** represents the set of desired end states of the searching process. The goal states satisfy the search goal.
- **Solution**: A solution is represented by a path from initial state to the goal state.

In the traveling salesman problem, the initial state is the start city, goal state is the end city, action/operator is the movement from one city to another city and solution will be sequence of actions from start city to end city with minimal cost.

A state space search is **represented by a four-tuple [*N, A, S, GD*], where:**

- *N* represents the problem space.
- *A* is the set of arcs (operators) between nodes.
- *S* represents the start state(s) of the problem. S is a nonempty subset of N.
- *GD* represents the goal state(s) of the problem. GD is a nonempty subset of N.

We represent a solution as a path from node *S* to a node in *GD*.

Problem Characteristics

In order to provide optimal solution to the problem we need to understand and analyze the problem from various dimensions. We need to identify the problem characteristics so that we can identify and choose the solution strategy, operators and arrive at the most appropriate solution.

Given below are some of the problem characteristics:

■ Decomposability: We need to check if the given problem can be decomposed into smaller sub-problems. If the main problem can be decomposed into smaller sub-problems, we could independently solve the smaller sub-problems in parallel. For example a string search problem can be decomposed by using binary search method wherein we recursively split the string array and search for the required string.

■ Ignorable/recoverable/irrecoverable: The solution steps used for solving a problem can be classified as ignorable (the solution steps that can be safely ignored without any impact to the overall solution), recoverable (sub-optimal solution steps can be changed/corrected through backtracking), irrecoverable (solution steps that cannot be changed having direct impact on final solution). For instance a validation step at the end of the solution is an optional feature; even if the validation is ignored, it does not impact the solution approach. In some of the solutions such as n queen, subset sum, the solution steps can be backtracked if it does not lead to optimal solution. In case of problems such as a chess game, the solution steps are final cannot be backtracked. The understanding of problem characteristic (ignorable/recoverable/irrecoverable) helps us to design appropriate control structure. For ignorable section of problems, there is no need for backtracking; for recoverable we can design backtracking and for irrecoverable problems, we need to make robust decision-making process as there is no backtracking.

■ Solution predictability: Some of the problems have a predictable solution (such as water jug problem) whereas few other problems have an unpredictable solution (such as playing cards). For problems with predictable solution, we can design the solution steps to arrive at the solution and avoid all the unnecessary solution steps. In case of unpredictable solution, we can design solution steps that has good probability leading to the solution.

■ Solution optimality: In this category we have two classes of problems: any path problem and best path problem. In any path problem, we can arrive at an optimal solution taking any solution path. For instance for water jug problem we can arrive at the fixed solution through various solution paths. In second set of problems, we have multiple solution paths leading to a solution and the best solution path is the preferred solution. For instance in the traveling salesman problem, we have multiple solution paths to travel from source city to destination but the solution path with minimal cost is the preferred solution.

■ Knowledge dependency: Few problems have heavy dependency on knowledge and need good amount of training data. For instance the game of chess not just needs the knowledge of legal moves but the machine also needs vast knowledge of various game strategies and the machine needs to be trained with numerous games. Game strategies help machine to narrow the search space and arrive at the optimal solution in a quick time.

■ Interactiveness: Few problems need machine interaction with humans and few other problems can be solved in isolation. For instance search problems, water jug problems can be solved in isolation whereas conversational interface systems (such as chatbot) or medical diagnosis problems need interaction with humans.

Constraint Satisfaction

Constraint satisfaction involves a search in the space of constraint sets. During the initial state the constraint set includes the explicitly specified constraints. The goal state is a state that satisfies the given set of constraints. The AI program has to discover the goal state that satisfies all the constraints.

By applying constraints we can eliminate numerous branches of a search space. After making a decision, propagate any new constraints that come into existence. Constraint satisfaction can also be applied to planning where a certain partial plan may exceed specified constraints and so can be eliminated. There are mainly two kinds of rules:

■ Rules that define valid constraint propagation.
■ Rules that suggest guesses when necessary.

The two-step process of constraint satisfaction problem (CSP) is as follows:

■ All the constraints are identified/discovered and propagated throughout the system.
■ Search is done at each step by guessing and adding a new constraint to the system.

CSPs are mainly used for scheduling problems, map coloring problems, timetabling problems, assignment problems, cryptarithmetic problem and others.

Applications of AI

AI is becoming more popular and powerful with the improvisations in learning algorithms and with the advent of information processing methods. AI is continuously becoming effective in solving new problems, handling complex information relieving humans from information/cognitive overload. AI is effectively complimenting humans in all cognitive tasks.

Broadly we can classify the AI applications into the below categories:

- Knowledge representation: This category includes expert systems.
- Machine Learning (ML): This category includes deep learning applications, pattern recognition, recommendations systems and automatic classification.
- Reasoning and problem-solving: In this category we have theorem provers and gaming applications.

Digital Transformation Use Cases Enabled by AI

In this section we have detailed various digital transformation use cases enabled by AI and ML across various industries.

Financial industries: AI and ML models are heavily used in the below given use cases:

- Credit decisioning: AI and ML models can help in credit/loan decisioning based on various data points related to customer's credit history, repayment history, bureau data and so on.
- Credit underwriting: We can leverage AI and ML models for deciding the appropriate credit amount based on the credit score of the AI and ML models.
- Predictive analytics: Financial institutions mainly use AI and ML models for predictive analytics for use case such as up-sell and cross-sell of financial products, propensity models for product renewal, default prediction, non-performing asset forecast, spend enhancements, customer segmentation and others.
- Fraud detection: AI and ML models can efficiently identify potential frauds in credit card transactions based on customer spend patterns and historical data.
- Document processing: Many of the document processing use cases such as claims processing (for insurance industries), automated loan processing, digitization of physical forms into digital forms through OCR (optical character recognition) can be efficiently done by AI and ML.
- Call center intelligence: We can use AI/ML to transcribe the call center voice data in real time and analyze the customer sentiment, customer satisfaction level and interfere to enhance customer experience.
- Digital banking: Financial institutions can enable a range of digital banking services such as mobile banking, internet banking with features such as video Know Your Customer (KYC), digital branch, virtual assistant, chatbots and so on.

Besides these AI/ML can be employed in wide variety of use cases such as antimoney laundering, credit card frauds, cyber attack detection, document classification, speech to text use case, and text to speech use case.

Retail and e-commerce: Given below are popular use cases for AI/ML in retail and e-commerce industry

- Personalized recommendations: AI/ML can recommend the products based on its learning from customer's interests, preferences and the other data points.
- Customer experience: AI/ML models provide seamless onboarding and search experience for the customers. AI/ML can also automate many of the activities such as ticket logging, search and others.
- Conversational interfaces and Chatbots: Chatbots and virtual assistants powered by AI/ML can help customers by providing a faster first response and help in resolution of queries and performing tasks.
- Customer onboarding: Using video KYC, automated data validation AI/ML solution can seamlessly onboard the customer quickly.
- Product bundling: AI/ML can recommend the products that can be packaged/bundled along with other products based on customer's interests, product affinity and other attributes.
- Sentiment analysis: The advanced NLP capabilities of the AI/ML models can be leveraged to assess the overall customer sentiment in product reviews, comments, social media feeds and such. This helps in providing a feedback loop to the product teams and to address any complaints in quick time.
- Image analytics: Enterprises can offer image analytics feature such as image search, documenting the image, image matching and other capabilities using AI/ML.
- Inventory management: AI/ML models are used for analyzing and forecasting inventory so that we can ensure that items are available in the inventory during peak sales.

Capital markets

- Portfolio management and portfolio optimization - We can optimize the customer portfolio based on the long term goals
- Algorithmic trading - AI models can be leveraged for algo-trading to take advantage of rapidly changing stock prices.

Automotive industry

- Shipping/delivery optimization and prediction, autonomous driving.
- Manufacturing
- Routing optimization, predictive machine maintenance, remote equipment manufacturing, remote surveillance.

Healthcare and pharma
Automating claims processing, accelerate drug discovery, patient health prediction.

Agriculture
Generate Crop insights.

Media and entertainment
Personalized content recommendation, content moderation.

Education
Learning bots, personalized learning content recommendation.

Generative AI
The new breed of Generative AI built on large language models (LLMs) are trained on massive volumes of data and hence can be used for variety of use cases. The foundational models of generative AI are pre-trained on massive volume of data and generates new content (such as text content, image, music and such). Foundational models can be used for variety of use cases. Given below are high-level digital transformation use cases for Gen AI:

1. Conversational interfaces that can help customers by providing human-like conversation experience.
2. Generate blogs, articles, product documentation, marketing campaign emails.
3. Summarize and extract key insights from documents and vast amount of data.
4. Generate images based on text prompts to help the marketing and creative teams.
5. Generate learning content and decrease cognitive burden on knowledge workers.
6. Create Q&A bots to answer customer's questions from internal enterprise data.
7. Translate one language to another.
8. Generate report based on vast amount of data.
9. Generate code and use Gen-AI as coding assistants.
   We have discussed various use cases for generative AI across various industry domain in subsequent sections.

Digital Transformation Trends in AI

AI is playing a key role in digital transformation journey of enterprises. AI is redefining the ways to automate the structured activities and help enterprises to engage customer actively through advanced NLP tasks. We have defined the key digital transformations powered by AI below:

■ Computer vision: AI and ML provide advanced object detection capabilities that are used in digital applications such as remote monitoring, video KYC, digital banking, digital branches, facial recognition and so on.

- Conversational interfaces: AI-powered applications can converse with humans in natural language. Enterprises deploy the conversational interfaces as chatbots, voice bots, virtual assistants, digital personas to help customers resolve their queries faster.
- Contextual search: Enterprises use AI to perform semantic search to provide the most relevant content to its customers. AI-powered semantic search engines index the enterprise data and can provide the personalized and relevant results for the customers.
- Recommendations: AI-powered applications can use the historical purchase data of the customer and employ methods to match the interests and preferences of the current customer with other customers to provide relevant product recommendations. Enterprises use the AI-powered recommendation applications to implement cross-sell and up-sell strategies.
- Forecasting systems: AI-powered systems can use various methods to forecast inventory, sales helping enterprises to fine tune the marketing strategy and stock their inventory.
- Anamoly detection: Enterprises can identify the anamolies in the sales trends and reports using AI methods.
- Content generation: Generative AI based on LLMs are capable of generating content based on the input prompts. Generative AI models are trained on vast volume of data and can be used for variety of use cases such as content creation (marketing content, product manuals etc.), image generation (such as creative images), video creation, question and answers, logical reasoning, content summarization, call analytics (such as post call analytics), document summarization, conversational interfaces and so on.

Digital Transformation Using AI

Modern enterprises rely on AI and ML models to scale their complex tasks, automate the activities and scale to process large volumes of data. AI-enabled applications drastically reduce the processing time thereby enhancing the customer experience. In this section we deep-dive on couple of use cases where we use AI for digital transformation of legacy processes.

AI-Powered Customer Onboarding

AI and ML models enable enterprises to seamlessly onboard customers. Digitization of customer onboarding is one of the most common digital transformation use cases. In this section we describe the ways to digitize the customer onboarding process.

Legacy Customer Onboarding Process

Many of the enterprises such as banks and other financial institutions use offline channels to onboard the customers. The customers need to visit the bank branches, fill up the application form and submit the identity documents to the branch executives. The branch executives will then verify the documents and enter the customer details into the bank's systems. As much of these processes are manual, the overall time for customer onboarding is anywhere between 3 days to 1 week.

Speeding up the onboarding process enables organizations to quickly onboard the customer thereby impacting the overall customer experience.

Digital transformation of customer onboarding process

Modern enterprises heavily rely on digital processes to quickly onboard the customer. We have depicted a digital onboarding process in Figure 10.4.

The detailed steps of the AI-enabled digital customer onboarding process are given below:

1. The customer visits the AI-enabled digital banking mobile app.
2. Customer will be ready with the identity proof and address proof documents required by the mobile app.
3. When the onboarding process is initiated the mobile app captures the customer's photo and detects the liveliness.
4. In the next step, the mobile app takes the picture of the identity and the address proof documents.
5. The AI-powered mobile app extracts the key details from the documents. The key details include customer's full name, customer address, customer's identity number and others.
6. If any of the details is missing, the mobile app requests for the additional information (such as current phone number, current email address etc.).
7. Customer can use the mobile app and provide the additional information.
8. AI-powered mobile app now compares the information given by customer with information extracted from the documents. For instance, the mobile app matches the customer photo captured during the live-session with the pictures extracted from the identity documents. If the images match above a configured threshold, the customer's onboarding is completed.
9. Verified customer's details are added to the enterprise database.
10. Customer can login to the system using the mobile phone or email address.
11. The onboarding process is marked as complete.

As we can see in the above process, all the steps are digital and many of the tasks such as photo match and document extraction are automated and driven by AI. Hence we can complete the entire process within an hour leading to quicker onboarding of the customer.

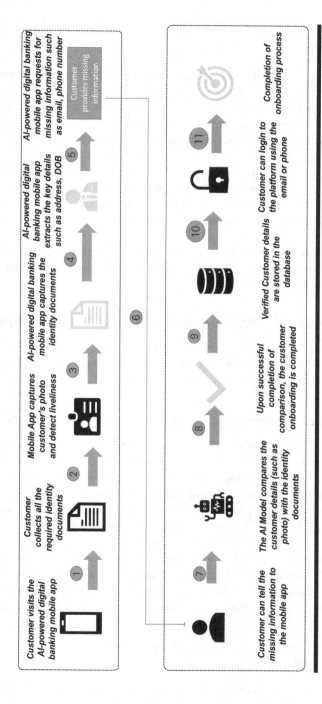

Figure 10.4 AI-enabled digital customer onboarding.

We have listed the key AI and ML services using the digital customer onboarding below:

1. **Computer vision:** We use image recognition ML models to detect the customer's face. We also use the image recognition models to detect the liveliness of the person, and during the verification stage, we match the face from the live session to the customer's image extracted from the identity document. If the match percentage exceeds a configured threshold (like 98%) we can confirm the customer's details.
2. **Intelligent document processing:** We use the ML models related to intelligent document processing to extract the key details from the identity document. The ML models are trained to identify the key details such as name, address, photo and other details, and the models can extract the text information from the image.
3. **Speech to text:** When the customer provides the missing information by speaking, the speech-to-text ML models translate the audio to the text and process the information.

AI-Powered Credit Decisioning and Credit Underwriting

Credit processing is a key business activity for the financial institutions. In this section we detail how AI and ML models redefine the way credit decisioning and credit underwriting are done.

Legacy Credit Decisioning and Credit Underwriting Process

In the legacy credit decisioning and credit underwriting process, a customer visits the bank branch and applies for a loan. The customer will fill up the loan application form and provide the supporting documents such as bank statements and identity documents. The bank's credit team will then start processing the loan application. The credit team will use a pre-defined set of criteria (such as income value, past default history etc.) and the customer's credit score which is received from the bureaus. Once the credit decisioning is done, the underwriting process kicks in. The credit underwriters look at various parameters such as existing loans, current liabilities, customer's payment history and others paramters to arrive at the total loan amount that can be sanctioned. This entire manual process takes anywhere between 2 and 4 weeks depending on the amount of loan and the number of decision points.

Digital Transformation of Credit Decisioning and Credit Underwriting Process

When we do the digital transformation of the credit decisioning and credit underwriting process, we use AI and ML models to automate the key process steps so that

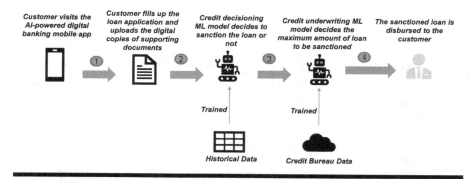

Figure 10.5 AI-enabled credit decisioning and credit underwriting process.

we can scale the process to large number of applications. We have depicted the AI-enabled credit decisioning and credit underwriting process in Figure 10.5.

The detailed steps of the AI-enabled credit decisioning and credit underwriting process is as follows:

1. The customer visits the AI-enabled digital banking mobile app.
2. The customer fills up the digital loan application form and provides the digital copy of the supporting documents.
3. The credit decisioning ML model is trained on the historical data related to credit decisioning. This includes the historical credit decisioning data, delinquency data and so on. Based on the training the ML model can arrive at the credit decision given the key attributes (such as customer's income, open loans and so on). Hence the credit decisioning model uses the data from the customer's loan application and makes the decision.
4. Once the customer's loan application is approved, the credit underwriting ML Model will be used to decide the maximum loanable amount to the customer. The credit underwriting ML model will use the historical data as well as the data from the credit bureaus to decide the maximum sanctionable loan amount which will be disbursed to the customer.

AI-Powered Surveillance, Monitoring and Anomaly Detection

We can leverage computer vision AI models for identifying the events of interest. In financial services we can use the computer vision models to remotely monitor the events at ATM centers and alert in case of any anomalies. In the manufacturing plants we can remotely monitor the machines to proactively identify the maintenance opportunities.

In this section we detail the digital transformation of remote surveillance and monitoring systems.

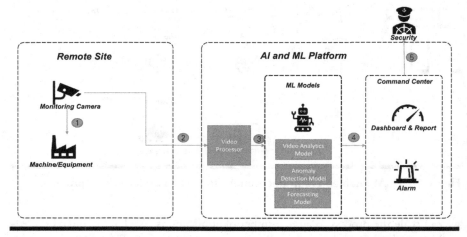

Figure 10.6 Digital transformation of remote monitoring and surveillance.

Legacy Remote Monitoring and Surveillance Process

The legacy remote monitoring and surveillance process are predominantly manual processes wherein the video feeds are continually monitored in real time by security personnel. This process is prone to security incidents and also impacts the incidence response time.

Digital Transformation of Remote Monitoring and Surveillance Process

We leverage the AI and ML models in remote monitoring in real time. We have depicted the key process steps in Figure 10.6.

The key steps in the AI-driven remote monitoring and surveillance process are given below:

1. The monitoring camera continuously monitors the machine or equipment in real time.
2. The camera sends the video feed in real time to the AI and ML Platform. Additionally we can also send the sensor data from the machine to the ML models. Upon ingestion of video feed in real time, we perform the video processing. The video processing steps involves identification of time-based frames (for instance, one frame for every 30 seconds) and the frame resizing so that it can be fed to the ML models.
3. The ML models are trained on image data to detect the anomalies. For instance, the ML model is trained to detect events such as any smoke from

the equipment, high temperature from the sensor as anomalies. Based on the sensor data, the forecasting ML models also can forecast and predict potential failures in the future.

4. The anomalies are fed into the command center which displays the events in dashboards and alerts.
5. The critical events are notified to the security personnel who can respond to the incident in real time.

Digital Transformation Using Generative AI

Generative AI is backed by LLMs also known as foundational models (FMs) which is pretrained on large corpus of data. Gen AI models can be used for variety of use cases such as content generation, chatbots, logical reasoning, image generation, music generation, video creation and so on. Gen AI is used to automate the activities, optimize the cost and reduce the response time.

In this section we have defined the Gen AI use cases across various industries.

Financial Services Industry

Financial institutions such as banks can leverage the power of Gen AI for the below given use cases:

- Develop conversational interfaces that leverage the enterprise data to respond to the queries from employees, customers and partners.
- Analyze a call-center conversation in real time to understand the customer sentiment, customer satisfaction levels and so on. This helps organizations to interfere in real time to effectively engage customer and reduce the customer churn. We can also summarize the customer conversations and send to leadership team for their review.
- Generate emails to respond to customer complaints.
- We can develop financial virtual assistants, digital relationship managers and digital personas powered by Gen AI models to effectively engage customers.
- We can ensure compliance to legal and regulatory policies using Gen AI models.
- Automatic claim processing in insurance industry can leverage the Gen AI models.
- Use language translation capabilities of Gen AI to serve customers across various languages.
- Automate business processes such as document processing and build new products.

Manufacturing

Given below are the Gen AI use cases for manufacturing industry:

- Employee chatbot: Help employees to complete the tasks and get information quickly through Gen AI.
- Report generation and insights gathering: Use Gen AI to generate reports or generate insights from vast data (such as sales data).
- Learning and training: Use the Gen AI to generate training content based on enterprise data.
- Image documentation: Leverage Gen AI with remote equipment monitoring ML models to detect any anomalies in real time.
- Image generation: Generate creatives from image generation Gen AI models to assist design/marketing teams.
- Product design: Leverage Gen AI models to rapidly prototype product designs.
- Supply chain analysis: Feed the supply chain data to the Gen AI model to identify any anomalies related to sales or products or regions.
- Safety and compliance insights: Ensure safety and compliance by feeding the product and operational manuals to the Gen AI which can validate the content against defined SOP (standard operating procedures) and safety guidelines.
- Predictive maintenance of equipments.

Lifescience and Healthcare

Given below are the key Gen AI use cases in healthcare and pharma industries:

- Use Gen AI to adhere to SOPs and regulations and compliance guidelines
- Summarize the patient medical records and history for the physicians.
- Automate the discharge summary for the patients. Enhances drug discovery and research and improve operational efficiency.
- Enhance patient support and experience.

Given below are Gen AI use cases across various functional domains within an organization.

Automotive

- Create digital twin models in 2D/3D using Generative AI.
- Generate personalized videos for marketing and sales.
- Create product specifications and validate the adherence of the automobiles to the specified regulatory guidelines.
- Create conversational interfaces to answer queries from customers, field agents based on product manuals.
- Use Generative AI for call center analytics to understand the customer sentiment, customer satisfaction and improve the overall user experience.
- Create personalized training for the employees.

Energy

- Generate operational report.
- Create safety videos for field training.
- Create training audio and content for factory worker training.
- Use generative AI to create executive summaries from the data.

Marketing and Sales

Given below are the marketing and sales use cases which can leverage Gen AI:

- Marketing campaigns: Create personalized email and video campaign by leveraging the content generation capability of Gen AI to effectively engage customers.
- Automatic database query generation: Use Gen AI to translate the natural language queries into SQL queries against the database to democratize the database access.
- Article creation: Gen AI models can be used to create blogs and articles about the products and services.
- Sentiment analysis: We can analyze the customer feedback and customers' social feeds to assess the overall customer sentiment and take appropriate responses.
- Create effective advertisements/creatives needed for the campaigns using Gen AI.
- Automate generation of images and videos from storyboards.

Product Development

Given below are the main Gen AI use cases in product development:

- Code generation: Leverage Gen AI to generate the code to improve the developer productivity.
- Code reviews and testing: Gen AI can be used to perform the security review of the code to make the code more secure. Generative AI models can also be used to identify potential security issues with the code.

Summary

Intelligence mainly has three core attributes: knowledge acquisition/learning/adaptation, reasoning with knowledge and Understanding and perception. AI involves methods and systems to develop human-like abilities such as learning, decision-making and rationalizing for machines. The four categories of AI are thinking humanely, thinking rationally, acting humanely and acting rationally. The machine needs to exhibit cognitive capabilities to mimic human behavior to pass the Turing test. Knowledge acquisition, reasoning with knowledge and understanding and perception are the key tenets of an AI system. The main AI methods are search, knowledge usage and abstraction. The main foundations of AI are philosophy, linguistics, mathematics, computer science, economics, philosophy, neuroscience, statistics, control theory and psychology. The key AI applications are in the field of Knowledge representation, ML, reasoning and problem-solving. Artificial Intelligence (AI) is an essential part of digital transformation. The Machine learning models are leveraged in various industries such as financial industries (for use cases such as credit decisioning, predictive analytics, credit underwriting, fraud detection, document processing, digital banking etc.), capital markets (for use cases such as portfolio management, algorithmic trading), automotive industry (for use cases such as shipping delivery, routing optimization), healthcare and pharma (for use cases such as automated claim processing, drug discovery). Generative AI is built on large language models (LLMs) are trained on massive volumes of data and hence can be used for variety of use cases such as Conversational interfaces, blog creation, article creation, image generation, report generation, code generation and such.

DIGITAL TRANSFORMATION OF PROCESS

IV

Chapter 11

Agile Delivery in Digital Transformation

Introduction

During the digital transformation journey, enterprises strive to become lean, agile and responsive to the customer expectations. Agile delivery model is best suited to achieve the goals of rapid innovation and higher customer engagement. Organizations often face challenges in aligning the delivery processes with the business goals and outcomes. The delivery and release management processes should be agile and should be streamlined for the organization to quickly respond to changes.

Legacy delivery processes used development models like waterfall that took a big-bang approach to deliver the product. The release timelines spanned anywhere between six months to two years based on the complexity of the project. As a result, the delivery risks were higher and time to market was high. Any change request took lot of time to implement and turnaround. Larger team size further increased the collaboration challenges, governance challenges and quality challenges.

The expectations from the modern platforms are unique—faster release velocity, flexibility in accommodating the change request, faster turnaround time, enhanced quality, reduced maintenance, reduced risk, reduced cost and increased collaboration. In order to increase the overall agility of the delivery and release management process, agile delivery model is the most popular choice.

As part of digital transformation of delivery process, the project managers switch from the traditional waterfall-type of delivery models to the agile execution models.

DOI: 10.1201/9781003390893-15

In this chapter we dive deep into the agile delivery concepts and best practices with examples.

Agile Introduction

Agile is a project management and software development approach that delivers value incrementally in iterations (called sprints). Agile delivery teams follow plan-build-test-release cycle for each sprint to quickly deliver a product. Specific tasks are defined for each sprint and they are time boxed (normally spanning two to four weeks). The agile teams are organized as two-pizza team (the team size that can be fed with two pizzas normally consisting of 6–8 team members) who own the end-to-end delivery of the product. The sprint team plans the release in sprint planning session and define the requirements as part of user stories. The team then takes the complete ownership of building the product, testing it and releasing it.

Agile model is well suited for modern products with evolving requirements. Some of the key business drivers for agile model are to improve the customer engagement, to enhance product quality, to increase the release velocity, to increase flexibility, to reduce risk and for continuous improvement and improved collaboration.

Agile Manifesto

Agility is the principle focus of the agile model. The agile values are designed to foster the agility in the overall delivery. The four key values proposed in agile manifesto [1] are as follows:

Individuals and interactions over processes and tools—The agile methodology focuses on close collaboration between team members to accelerate the development. Traditional process-oriented approach is given low priority. The fluid communication and team member collaboration is facilitated by daily standup meetings, retrospective meetings and backlog meetings.

Working software over comprehensive documentation—For each sprint a working version of the software is delivered and working software is the measure of the progress. The initial sprint delivers the minimum viable product and each subsequent sprint delivers an enhanced/incremental version of the software in iterations. The continuous feedback cycle from the previous sprint and based on the results of experiments, the Scrum team iteratively adds value in each sprint.

Customer collaboration over contract negotiation—The delivery team collaborates with end customer often to improve the product. Customer is involved in testing the product and the customer feedback received during the initial phases are added to the sprint backlog for the implementation in the subsequent sprints.

Responding to change over following a plan—The change requests are encouraged in the agile delivery model. The change requests coming from customer or due to market dynamics are taken up as for development based on the priority.

Agile Principles

The twelve agile principles are given below.

Customer satisfaction—The overall satisfaction of customer is the prime focus of agile model. Hence the customer requirements, customer feedback and customer experience with the product are prioritized in the agile model. Customer satisfaction is one of the key success factors for the product and assumes higher priority.

Welcome change—The agile model embraces change requested by customers or resulting from the market dynamics. The adaptability and flexibility to accommodate the change makes the agile model effective in delivering the value to customers. The change coming even late in the project phase is encouraged to provide differentiated experience to the customers.

Frequent delivery—Agile model uses continuous delivery and DevSecOps processes to iteratively and frequently delivery the product. The frequent delivery reduces the overall risk and provides an opportunity to incorporate the customer feedback early.

Working together—Collaboration among team members is facilitated through daily standup meetings where the team member discusses their tasks and roadblocks. Team members are training on cross-functional skills to effectively deliver the product. The technical and business teams work together for a successful delivery.

Motivated team—The agile teams are autonomous and self-organized and have the complete ownership of the product leading to a motivated team. The leaders empower the team members with required resources, tools and provide necessary support to work independently.

Face-to-face interaction—The team members are encouraged to interact face to face among themselves and with cross-functional teams to effectively collaborate and deliver. Face-to-face meetings are encouraged for sprint planning meetings, daily standup meetings, product demos and for sprint retrospective meetings.

Working software—Each sprint aims to release a working version of the software. The product is iteratively enhanced with each release based on the feedback and backlog.

Constant pace—All the teams involved in the product delivery should be able to maintain the constant pace of delivery to ensure high degree of customer satisfaction.

Good design—The industry best practices, past learnings and proven design patterns are used for building the product.

Simplicity—The simplicity mantra is followed in designing the user experience, integration contracts, services and other aspects of the product.

Self-organization—The teams involved in product delivery are self-organizing and take the end-to-end ownership of the product delivery.

Reflect and adjust—The team frequently reflects on the ways to improve the delivery quality and speed. The lessons learnt and best practices are discussed in the sprint retrospective meeting.

Agile Glossary

Given below are main terms used in an agile model.

Scrum—The agile approach that delivers business value through iterative sprints. In each sprint a self-organizing sprint team delivers a working software that delivers the prioritized set of requirements in 2–4 weeks' intervals.

Epic/Use case—The high-level scenario that can be broken down into user stories. For example, an epic can be defined as— *as a retail organization, I would like to provide a digital commerce for my company.*

User stories—The requirements are written from the end-user view in user stories that can be completed in one- or two-weeks' time. Each user story delivers incremental business value. Example—*as a buyer I would like to search for the product by using its name.*

Acceptance criteria—Each user story needs to satisfy the acceptance criteria in order to be approved. For instance, *given a buyer wants to look for a product, when he/she searches for the product using the product name, then the system should show the products matching the product name.*

Definition of ready—The criteria a user story has to meet before being accepted by the development team for development.

Definition of done—The set of validation criteria that the deliverable of a user story has to meet before being released.

Task—The set of activities that is required to implement the user story.

Sprint—Time-boxed iterations in which the team completes the planned user stories.

Product backlog—The prioritized list of requirements taken from the product roadmap.

Sprint backlog—The requirements that are derived from the product backlog.

Scrum master—The lead person who facilitates the Scrum meetings, manages the sprints and sprint backlogs, assigns the tasks to the team members and supports the team.

Sprint review—The sprint review meeting happens at the end of the sprint to review the progress of the sprint and to adjust the backlog if required.

Product owner—The product owner (PO) is responsible for prioritizing and collaborating with the team to deliver the product features and product increments. The PO signs off on the requirements and validates the final deliverable.

Agile vs. Traditional waterfall model

Agile delivery model shines in quickly delivering the business value through iterative sprints. Let us look at the use cases where the project managers can evaluate agile delivery model against the traditional waterfall delivery model.

We have depicted the scenarios for agile vs. traditional waterfall model in Table 11.1.

Scrum in Action

The Scrum execution is organized into various sprints. Each sprint is time boxed for 2–4 weeks. We have depicted various activities in a Scrum-based release in Figures 11.1 and 11.2.

We do sprint planning in sprint 0 wherein we reassess the product backlog and evaluate the sprint backlog and we discuss the use cases and create user stories from it. The cross-functional teams come together to the epic/user story grooming sessions to discuss the requirements and to clarify the user stories. The Scrum master prioritizes the user stories for the sprint and defines the sprint plan for the release. The Scrum master creates and assigns the tasks to the team members. We identify various workstreams (such as testing stream, mobile app development team, web application development team and such) and define the strategy documents for each stream (for instance, overall test strategy document for the test stream). The Scrum master manages the backlog for each sprint based on the priority of the user story. The team members discuss the status of the tasks assigned to them and the blockers (challenges that are blocking their daily tasks) in the daily standup meetings. At the end of each sprint, a sprint retrospective meeting is conducted wherein the team discusses the experiments that worked in that specific sprint and the processes that could be improved along with learnings. The main deliverable from the initial sprint are user stories, sprint plan, roadmap plan, definition of done (acceptance criteria for each user story), backlogs and the training plan for the team members. Based on the product backlog, we develop the release backlog and the Scrum master creates the Scrum backlog from the release backlog.

In the first sprint, the team creates the design for the user stories and develops the user stories. Individual developers perform the unit testing of the user story. Post development, the solution modules are integrated with the external and internal interfaces. The team members demo their respective user story and demonstrate that the assigned task is completed as per the definition of done. Once completed, the team members update the status of the task in the project management tool (such as Jira). The testing team conducts functional and non-functional testing. The DevSecOps processes are implemented to automate the build-test-deploy activities. The tested code is deployed to user acceptance testing (UAT) environment for

Table 11.1   Agile vs. Traditional Delivery Model

Criteria	Agile Delivery Model	Traditional Waterfall Model
Nature of requirements	Best suited when requirements are fluid, evolving or change frequently.	Best suited when requirements are well defined with minimal changes.
Organizational Processes	Best suited when organizational processes are lean.	Best suited when there are rigid processes.
Customer involvement	Best suited when customer is available throughout the project for feedback and testing.	Best suited when customer is involved only during the final testing.
Delivery timelines	Best suited when the timelines are flexible and are of shorter duration (6–12 weeks).	Best suited when timelines are fixed (typically 6–12 months).
Delivery team	Best suited when team size is small and when coordination is required.	Best suited when the team size is large, deliverable contracts are well-defined with lesser team coordination.
Delivery risk	Best suited when the delivery risk is very high. Scrum teams can experiment often to minimize the risk.	Best suited when delivery risk is low.
Technology maturity	Best suited when the development involves experimenting with newer or complex technology stack.	Best suited when the development involves matured and proven technology stack.
Integration and testing	Best suited when we need to continuously test and integrate.	Best suited when testing and integration has to be done post development.
Development	Best suited when the build has to be prioritized based on customer requirements and business value.	Best suited when all the features have to be built to the pre-defined specifications.

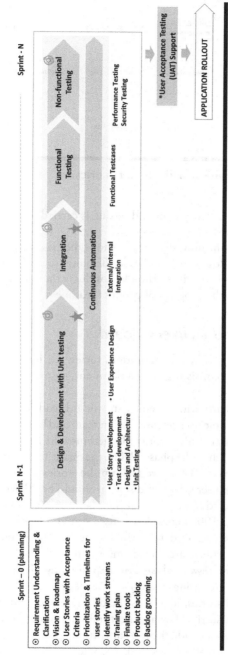

Figure 11.1 Sprint stages.

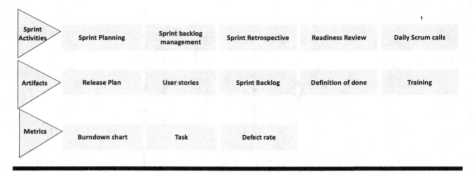

Figure 11.2   Sprint activities, artifacts and metrics.

business validation. The development and testing is carried out in various sprints till all the backlogs are cleared.

The Scrum master continuously tracks various metrics, such as task completion status, defect rate, burndown chart (number of hours spent by team for a project) and others, to respond to any risks. The PO conducts the product readiness review on regular basis to track the progress of product readiness.

Demand Board and Delivery Board

The demand board (consisting of elaboration, review, design and planning phases) and the delivery board (consisting of development, testing phases) is depicted in Figure 11.3.

The sprint journey starts with an epic. An epic is broad, high-level story that we eventually split into multiple user stories. Design team and business analysts (BAs) can elaborate the epic into user stories that get logged into the demand board. The completeness definition for each of the phases define the quantifiable metric values for each of the phases in the journey. Before we pick up the stories for dependency planning and review planning, the user stories and screens should be 90% completed and epic should be 100% completed. At the end of the planning phase, we define the "ready for design" if the epic is 100% completed; user stories are 90% completed; screen designs are 90% completed and data attributes are 100% completed. Requirement stability and change percentage are the key metrics that are tracked at this stage.

During the "**Story review, analysis and dependency planning**" stage, the BAs will conduct the story grooming session to the development team. The development team analyzes the stories, identifies the dependencies and comes up with the technical design for the stories. For architecturally significant use cases (ASU), the development team plans to conduct proof of concept (PoC) to assess the feasibility.

Once the technical low-level design is completed, the development team and the project manager conduct the sprint planning based on the priority; the project manager decides the sprint velocity. The technical team builds the capabilities

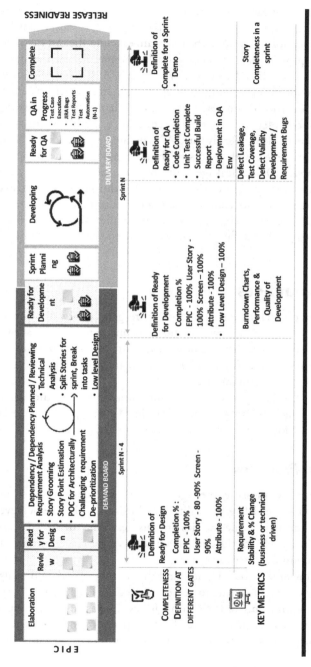

Figure 11.3 Demand board and delivery board.

in iterations. Normally each sprint will be anywhere between two weeks and four weeks. Once the developer-level unit testing is completed, the artefact will be handed over to the QA team for validation. The QA team executes the test cases and prepares test reports. The project manager closely tracks the metrics such as defect leakage, test coverage, defect validity, defect density and such. At the end of design phase, we define the "ready for development" if all epics, user stories, screens, attributes and low-level design are 100% completed. Burndown charts, velocity (average amount of work the team completed in a sprint), performance and quality of deliverable are key metrics that are tracked. "Ready for QA" is defined when code is fully developed, unit testing is completed with successful build report and the build is deployed in QA environment. Defect leakage, test coverage, defect validity, development/requirements bugs are key metrics that are tracked during the QA phase. Finally a sprint is completed when the team provides a demo to the stakeholders. Once the testing is successfully completed, we promote the application to other environments.

We have also given the definitions of gating criteria at different phases.

Agile Best practices

Some of the key obstacles to agile adoption are general organizational resistance to change, lack of leadership participation, inconsistent processes and practices and organizational culture (the values, beliefs of the organization) [2]. Hence organizations should adopt the best practices to implement the agile model and effective change management culture.

The POs and Scrum masters need to continuously improve the delivery quality and the delivery time with every sprint execution. We have provided the proven best practices in this section that forms as a reference for the team.

General Best Practices

Organizations mainly measure the agile success through customer satisfaction, business value, on-time delivery, quality and business objective achievement [2]. Accordingly the top three agile metrics are business value delivered, customer satisfaction and velocity. Hence the agile mechanisms should focus on business value, customer satisfaction and delivery speed.

Business value and goals—Understand the business values and goals and align the user story priority and sprints to achieve the goals. For instance, if the business wants to uniquely differentiate itself through best-in-class user experience, identify the top user stories that impact the overall user experience and prioritize the roll-out of those features. Create a feedback loop that incorporates the key user feedback into the next sprint.

Cross-functional and self-organizing teams—Identify the team with cross-functional skills and support them through the required resources, training, coaching and by providing required tools. Remove any communication or process barriers to foster the collaboration. Empower self-organizing teams to own the end-to-end product responsibility and for quicker decision making. The team that is clearly committed to the goals, with a strong sense of purpose with a shared ownership is a true characteristic of high performing team.

Hyper focus on customer—Listen closely to customer and work backwards to meet the customer expectations. Simple yet intuitive user experience, frictionless processes, quicker enhancements and bug fixes are some of the main focus areas that bring in superior customer experience.

Collaborative commitment—The agile methodology puts main focus on enhanced cooperation between team members. Effective collaboration also enables team members commit to the delivery and to the sprint goals. The quote from famous coach Vince Lombardi "*Individual commitment to a group effort—that is what makes a team work...*" sums up the value of individual commitment to the team's success.

Continuous improvement—The agile team has to constantly find effective ways to continuously improve the process, leveraging tools and collaborate. Leveraging agile mechanisms, such as daily standup, sprint retrospective meetings and constant collaboration, are effective ways to remove impediments and continuously improve.

Best Practices of Scrum Meetings

In this section we detail the best practices to improve the productivity in Scrum meetings.

Sprint Planning Meeting

The sprint planning meeting is to define the overall deliverable of the sprint and define the plan for the same.

Activities

The main goals of sprint planning meeting as follows:

- PO shares the overall objectives and the product backlog items.
- Scrum master facilitates the meeting and defines the sprint goals and priorities the sprint backlog.
- Team members estimate the effort for sprint backlog and commit to the sprint goal.
- Backlog grooming sessions to dive deep into each of the user stories.
- Define various work streams for the sprint. The work streams are formed based on the domain of the work handled by the team members. For instance, we can constitute separate work streams for mobile app development and web application development as each of these teams work on different domains.

- Identify ways of working to achieve the goals. The ways of working define the collaboration process, SLAs, point of contacts and tools and frameworks to be used for various work streams.
- Define the acceptance criteria or definition of done.

Participants

Scrum master, team members, BAs, PO.

Outcome

The main outcome of the sprint planning are as follows:

- Team commits to the delivery of the sprint backlog.
- Time-boxed sprints and the resource capacity for each of the sprints.
- Well-defined sprint goals to enable team implement the sprint backlog.
- Prioritized list of sprint backlog derived from product backlog.
- Detailed sprint plan covering the goals, timelines and workstreams.
- Well-defined acceptance criteria (definition of ready and definition of done) for accepting the product.

The Scrum master also facilitates the grooming session post sprint planning to discuss each of the user stories in detail. The team members can dive deep into the requirements and dependencies for each of the stories.

Daily Standup Meeting

The daily standup meeting is a 15-minute daily meeting to assess the progress of the assigned tasks and discuss the blockers in an all-hands meeting. The team members provide updates in a round-robin way. The daily standup meeting fosters collaboration and performance of the team. The daily standup meeting targets to identify the impediments, improve the communication and enable quicker decision-making. Post the daily standup meeting, the team members collaborate for detailed discussion related to the blockers or to the assigned sprint tasks.

Activities

The main goals of daily standup meeting as follows:

- Team members inspect the progress made in last 24 hours and discuss the planned activities for the day to achieve the sprint goal.
- Team members announce their self-commitment for the day.

- Team members discuss any blockers and seek support from their fellow team members in resolving the blockers.

Participants

Scrum master, team members.

Outcome

The main outcome of the daily standup meeting are as follows:

- Define prioritized work plan for the day.
- Provides the visibility into the sprint progress.
- Promotes the self-organization of the team and builds trust among team members.
- Secure commitment/resolution from team members on the blockers.

Sprint Review Meeting

The sprint review meeting happens at the end of each sprint to inspect the sprint accomplishments and adjust the backlog as required. The team collaborates in this meeting to improve the ways of working for future sprints to deliver the value efficiently. The sprint review meetings helps us in the next sprint planning meeting.

Activities

The main goals of sprint review meeting as follows:

- The team discusses the backlog items that are completed and the ones that are not completed based on the acceptance criteria/definition of done.
- The team members demo the completed user stories.
- The team discusses the key blockers they faced in the sprint and the way those challenges were solved.
- The team discusses the timelines and budget for the subsequent releases.
- The team members also seek feedback on the progress.
- The PO projects the target dates for the release based on the progress made.

Participants

Scrum master, team members, PO.

Outcome

The main outcome of the sprint review meeting are as follows:

- Demo of the completed user stories.
- Review the outcome of the sprint and adjust the backlog for the future sprints.
- Alignment on the overall progress.

Sprint Retrospective Meeting

The sprint retrospective meeting happens after the sprint review and before the next sprint planning. In the sprint retrospective meeting, the team discusses the things that worked and any potential improvements. The team adjusts the ways of working to continuously improve and to add value more efficiently. The sprint retrospective meetings provide opportunity to the team to adapt to the changing conditions.

Activities

The main goals of sprint retrospective meeting as follows:

- Introspect the effectiveness of existing tools and processes.
- Discuss the main blockers of the sprint and the best practices used to overcome the blockers.
- Discuss the improvements that can be made for the existing processes, tools and ways of working.

Participants

Scrum master, team members, BAs, PO.

Outcome

The main outcome of the sprint retrospective meeting are as follows:

- Establish and improve rules of engagement in accordance with continuous improvement spirit.
- Fine tune the processes for the subsequent sprints.
- Leverage the best practices and lessons learnt for the subsequent sprints.
- Well-defined acceptance criteria for accepting the product.

Day wise sprint activities

We have depicted the common day-wise sprint activities in Figure 11.4. During sprint planning the backlogs are analyzed and estimated and the user stories along with its acceptance criteria is defined. Scrum master performs the capacity planning and user story estimation.

In each of the sprints, the development team performs the impact analysis of the user stories. The PO and BA are involved in the grooming and design review sessions for the user stories. Once the development team develops the user stories, the stories are validated based on the defined validation criteria and deployed to the production environment.

Agile Digital transformation Process

We detail an agile-based digital transformation process in this section. Digital transformation process involves elaborate design and groundwork. We need the team consisting of varied skill set such as BAs, experience designers, security architect, solution architect and such. We have depicted the high-level process steps for the discovery and jump start stages in Figure 11.5.

We have detailed each of the steps in the discovery and jumpstart stages below.

Vision

The organization should have a clear vision of the end state of the solution. The senior executives and the business leadership team should define the transformation themes, business goals, branding targets, timelines, KPIs/success metrics and such.

Strategy

The leadership team should clearly articulate the strategy for realizing the overall vision and get business value. Identify and prioritize the goals, releases and timelines. As part of overall strategy we should also design the user adoption strategy and define the collaboration and communication strategy to facilitate better information sharing.

Discovery and User Journey Mapping

We need to elaborate the requirements and business rules in detail for the program. We need to interview the stakeholders and users to identify the information needs, goals, current pain points and challenges. We conduct discovery workshops, focused meetings and surveys to understand the current ecosystem.

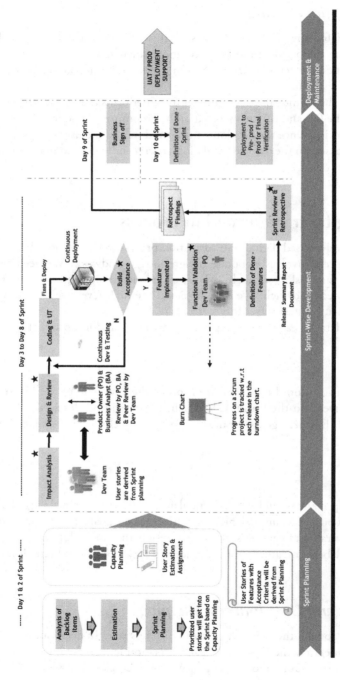

Figure 11.4 Day wise sprint activities.

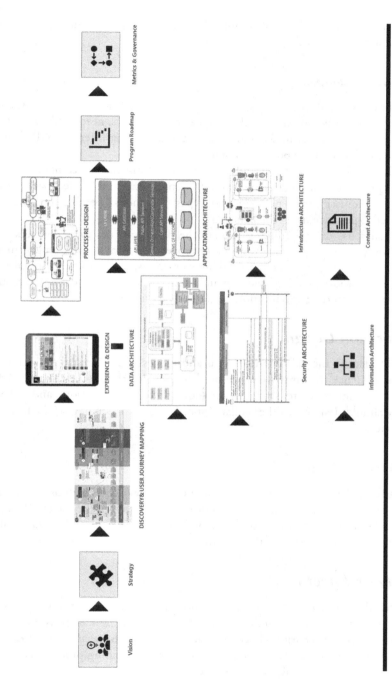

Figure 11.5   Discovery and jumpstart stages of digital transformation.

As part of discovery phase, we should also assess the current state and create an inventory of current tools, technologies and frameworks.

Experience Design

As part of this, we need to define the user personas and map the user journey. The set of all unique personas should cover the unique characteristics, needs and goals of all unique users of the platform. We also need to define the user interface (UI)-related optimizations during the experience design.

Develop clickable prototypes and seek feedback from the stakeholders for the developed prototypes through "show and tell" demos. Based on the feedback, iteratively refine the user experience and prototypes. We should be able to provide a personalized experience using the personas.

We should use design thinking to map the daily activities for employees and simplify the processes and find ways to improve their productivity, engagement and performance. As part of design thinking workshops, we adopt the principles of empathy, co-creation, learning by doing and holistic thinking. We define the visual style guide and branding specifications as part of experience design.

Collaboration Design

We should identify the collaboration tools and processes. As internal social media platforms influence the employees, we need to plan for the internal social media platforms for employees to share information, voice their opinions and collaborate. We should design for other collaboration tools such as blogs, wikis, forums, calendar etc.

Data Architecture

We identify the key data sources and define the data flow across various layers. The data architecture defines the way data is transformed in each of the stages. The data architecture clearly depicts the upstream, downstream systems from data standpoint and details the characteristics of the data that is flown across systems.

Security Architecture

We depict the authentication process, authorization process and single-sign-on (SSO) process in the security architecture. We also depict the standards, protocols and ports needed for security-related communications in the security architecture. Based on the requirements, we also depict the user provisioning process, federated login process, user synchronization and others.

Process Redesign

Based on our analysis from the discovery phase, we need to identify the pain points, challenges and gaps in the existing processes and simplify the processes. We should also seek to optimize the processes wherever possible; this can be done by reducing the process steps, automating the process steps and through other means.

Application Architecture

We identify and define technology stack as the foundation and standardize the technology and integration. During this stage, we also evaluate the products and technologies and explore the feasibility through PoC. The technologies and products should be aligned with the program vision and we should support the implementation of the strategy.

We need to build the capabilities through platform principle. The digital platform should provide the required tools and we should be extensible enough to easily onboard new services and capabilities.

Information Architecture

As part of information architecture, we define the site hierarchy, navigation components (such as menus, left navigation), search design, metadata hierarchy, UI component hierarchy and such. The information architecture should be intuitive for the user so that they can easily find the required information.

Infrastructure Architecture

In this architecture view, we define the key infrastructure elements and cloud components we use for the solution. This includes the high availability design, disaster recovery design and also includes the capacity of each of the infra components. We evaluate various infrastructure components for the requirements and select the best fit components. We design various infrastructure components such as server, virtual machines, network, storage drives, security servers, API gateway, container specification and such.

Content Architecture

As part of the content architecture, we define the content types, content sources, content templates, digital assets, content languages, content transformation design, content translation needs, metadata design, content hierarchy and such. We identify the static and reusable artefacts while defining the content architecture.

Integration Architecture

We should evaluate various integration options that can be easily extended and that provides high performance. We can specify the integration methods, protocols, ports and data exchange formats for the integration.

Program Roadmap

As part of roadmap we define the prioritized releases, action plan, overall program plan, milestones and the overall capability of the onboarding plan. We adopt agile delivery to enable quick, iterative releases and for faster time to market. We experiment with niche technologies, methods and tools through pilot releases and then plan for major releases based on the learnings and findings. We can assess the technology feasibility and impact on the business and organization culture through the pilot releases.

Metrics and Governance

In this stage, we define the key metrics and goals that can be quantified and measured. We should setup suitable tracking and monitoring mechanism to continuously monitor the metrics. As part of governance process, we should define the roles and responsibilities for various team members. We should also define and establish the standard operating procedures (SOP) and various processes such as monitoring process, incident management system, release management process, build process, quality assurance process and such. For each process, we define the ownership and accountability and the access-control matrix. We should also define the process for change management.

Digital Transformation Execution

The discovery and jumpstart phase takes about eight weeks. Once we have the finalized project plan, we can initiate the feature execution.

Feature Execution

Feature execution is the primary build phase of the project wherein we develop the solution components iteratively. We have depicted a sample feature execution in Figure 11.6.

We have categorized the feature execution into four tracks:

■ **Functional and user experience**: In this track we analyze the requirements and the as-is state and develop personas and user journey maps and experience design as part of discovery and jumpstart phase. During the execution phase, we incorporate any feedback, changes and manage these changes.

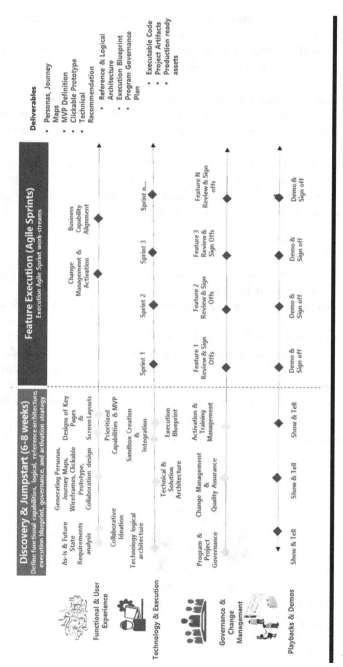

Figure 11.6 Feature execution.

- **Technology and execution**: We define the logical and solution architecture and integration architecture in the discovery and jumpstart phase. We use sprint delivery wherein we deliver the capabilities in iterations. We adopt continuous integration, testing and delivery philosophy for the execution.
- **Governance and change management**: We define the processes related to change management and quality assurance in the discovery and jumpstart phase. During execution phase, the governance team reviews and signs off on the features.
- **Playbacks and demos**: We use "show and tell" philosophy during the discovery phase to demo the changes to the stakeholders. We incorporate the feedback from the stakeholders during the subsequent demos. During the execution phase, we get the sign off on the demos.

Sprint Delivery

As the sprint-based delivery is one of the most important activities during the execution phase, we have elaborated this phase.

We have elaborated the key delivery tenets depicted in Figure 11.7 below:

- **Continuous delivery**: Modern digital platforms are iteratively deployed to the production in shorter sprints. The time to market for each delivery is about 2–4 weeks. We can leverage the continuous integration platforms and continuous delivery platforms for quickly delivering the releases. We can also shorten the feedback loop and incorporate the feedback in the subsequent iterations.

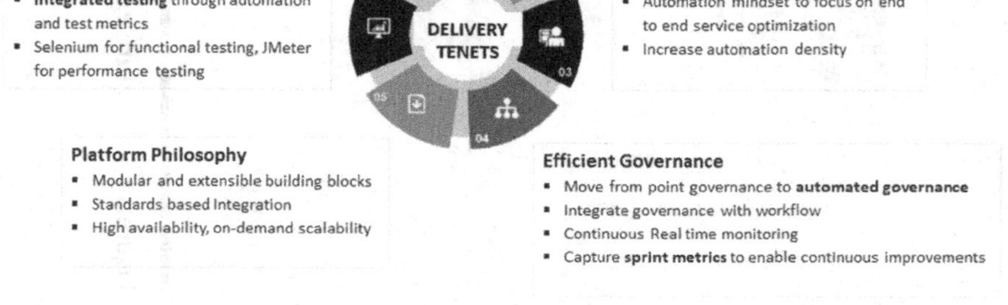

Continuous Delivery
- Increase speed to market and quality of the delivery
- Shorten feedback loop
- Leverage CICD platform

Continuous Integration
- Seamless integration of builds
- **Leverage Jenkins Pipelines** as the CI orchestrator
- Mandate unit testing and code quality scans with SonarQube

Integrated Testing
- **Integrated testing** through automation and test metrics
- Selenium for functional testing, JMeter for performance testing

End to End Automation
- Automation mindset to focus on end to end service optimization
- Increase automation density

Platform Philosophy
- Modular and extensible building blocks
- Standards based Integration
- High availability, on-demand scalability

Efficient Governance
- Move from point governance to **automated governance**
- Integrate governance with workflow
- Continuous Real time monitoring
- Capture **sprint metrics** to enable continuous improvements

Figure 11.7   Delivery tenets.

- **Continuous integration**: We could use Jenkins or cloud-based DevOps platforms for continuous integrations. We can use SonarQube for code quality analysis for every release to manage the quality metrics.
- **Integration testing**: We can achieve the continuous integration testing and automate the testing using tools such as Selenium, Apache JMeter and such.
- **End-to-end automation**: Explore and identify the automation opportunities for the project. We could automate structured and routine activities such as regression testing, release management, monitoring, static code analysis, data synchronization and such.
- **Platform philosophy**: We should focus on using the modular, extensible and scalable building blocks to develop the application. The digital platform should support on-demand scalability and high availability.
- **Efficient governance**: Define the processes for quality assurance, release management, deployment, monitoring, sprint-based continuous improvements and other core project concerns.

Summary

Agile is a project management and software development approach that delivers value incrementally in sprints. The agile teams are organized as two-pizza team (the team size that can be fed with two pizzas) who own the end-to-end delivery of the product. The four key values proposed in agile manifesto are individuals and interactions over processes and tools, working software over comprehensive documentation, customer collaboration over contract negotiation and responding to change over following a plan. The 12 agile principles are customer satisfaction, welcome change, frequent delivery, working together, motivated team, face-to-face interaction, working software, constant pace, good design, simplicity, self-organization and reflect and adjust. Scrum is an agile approach that delivers business value through iterative sprints. The Scrum execution is organized into various sprints time-boxed for 2–4 weeks. The main agile best practices are business value and goals, cross-functional and self-organizing teams, hyper focus on customer, collaborative commitment and continuous improvement. The sprint planning meeting is to define the overall deliverable of the sprint and define the plan for the same. The daily standup meeting is a 15-minute meeting to assess the progress of the assigned tasks and discuss the blockers in an all-hands meeting. The sprint review meeting happens at the end of each sprint to inspect the sprint accomplishments and adjust the backlog as required. The sprint retrospective meeting happens after the sprint review and before the next sprint planning.

Appendix
Agility Assessment Checklist

Dimension	Sub Dimension	Checklist Item
Culture	Skill	Are technical teams trained on agile concepts?
	Skill	Are business teams trained on agile concepts?
	Skill	Are Scrum masters trained on agile concepts?
	Skill	Are product owners trained on agile concepts?
	Skill	Are development team members trained on cross-functional skills like build, test, deploy?
	Self-organized	Is a dedicated product owner assigned to the team?
	Behavior	Is team using the retrospective improvement for continuous improvement?
	Behavior	Are teams trained on cross-functional skills?
	Behavior	Is team aware of iterative and sprint releases?
Methodology	PO Methodology	Is the product owner facilitating the user story analysis, story prioritization?
	SM Methodology	Is the Scrum master helping the team to practice agile behavior and helping the team to address challenges?
	Methodology	Is the team using Kanban for managing the flow?
	Methodology	Is the team qualifying the user stories used in the iteration?
	Methodology	Is team estimating the effort required for user stories?
	Methodology	Is the team following the plan-build-test cycle for each of the user stories?
	Methodology	Is the acceptance criteria/definition of done well defined?
	Methodology	Is the team sharing the design responsibility?

Dimension	Sub Dimension	Checklist Item
	Agile events	Does the team perform the sprint planning during the beginning of each spring?
	Agile events	Does the team conduct daily Scrum meeting?
	Agile events	Does the team conduct Scrum review meeting?
	Agile events	Does the team conduct Scrum retrospective?
		Does the team conduct Scrum refinement?
	Behavior	Does the Scrum master prioritize the feature backlog?
		Does the team follow the continuous integration and continuous deployment?
		Does the team follow pair programming?
		Does the team perform automated testing?
		Are the code reviews automated?
	Continuous Improvement	Are the continuous integration and automated tested in place?
Deliverables	Backlog	Does the team iteratively reduce the backlog items?
	Sprint backlog	Does the team define the goals of current sprint and the backlog?
	Metrics	Does the team track the key metrics such as code coverage, release velocity and other code quality metrics?
		Does the team produce the weekly status reports?
		Has the roadmap been created?
		Does the team deliver a product in each sprint?
Tools		Does the team track the backlog in a tool?
		Does the team use a tool for collaboration and for tracking the user story status?
		Is the team comfortable adding/editing user stories in the backlog?
		Does the team track the metrics related to effort burn rate, project financials, burndown metrics and others?

References

1. Fowler, M., & Highsmith, J. (2001). The agile manifesto. *Software Development* 9(8), 28–35.
2. State of Agile. (n.d.). State of Agile. https://stateofagile.com/#ufh-i-615706098-14th-annual-state-of-agile-report/702749

Chapter 12

Digital Transformation of Incident Management Process

Introduction

Digital operations and governance of digital transformation projects include the ongoing post production activities. Digital operations ensure that digital platforms operate with optimal performance, minimize outages and ensure appropriate service level agreement (SLA) for the services. Digital operations include activities such as server and application patching, incident management (or ticket management), infrastructure maintenance, infrastructure migration and others.

Incident management (or ticket management) is an important aspect of digital operations. Incident management defines the processes to handle production incidents. System and infrastructure-related incidents include incidents related to production system outage, server performance issues, scheduled server management and such. User-related incidents include tickets logged by end users such as incidents related to application errors, incidents logged due to user calls, user incidents–related to access requests, how-to documents and such.

As part of digital transformation of the incident management process, we need to optimize the incident management process through initiatives such as automation, incident-avoidance design, proactive maintenance and such measures. We can design the incident optimization measures based on deep analysis of the incident resolution process and through insights gathered through the root cause analysis of the historical incidents. Naturally, incident management process optimization reduces the turnaround time, ensures high availability of the application and improves the overall user experience with the digital platform.

In this chapter, we discuss the ways to identify the optimization methods for a retail functional domain. We also deep dive into the incident optimization processes including proactive maintenance, shift left, incident response automation, automated monitoring and alerting system.

Incident Management Optimization Process

Incident management processes can be optimized during the design of the incident response process or based on the deeper understanding of the nature of the logged incidents and the corresponding incident management response.

We shall discuss the incident management optimization process in detail here.

Optimization of Incident Management Based on Pre-defined Responses

The incident management activities that can be optimized based on the pre-defined responses for the incident fall into this category. Maintenance incidents, server restart incidents are few examples for this category.

An enterprise typically needs to define processes for infrastructure maintenance (such as server patching, server upgrades, server hardening and such). The processes for handling majority of the maintenance activities are structured (involving pre-defined sequence of known steps) and hence organizations define the standard operating procedures (SOPs) for maintenance activities. Hence maintenance-related activities become the primary candidates for automation. During the design of the SOPs of the maintenance activities we can identify the steps that can be automated during the maintenance exercise.

Server restart process is also a structured activity wherein we know the scripts and sequence of steps required to restart a server. Hence scheduled server restarts are easy candidates for automation.

Other operational activities, such as patch management, configuration management, data backup, health checks, resource utilization monitoring and billing alarms, have well-defined steps that can be automated. Incident responses related to infrastructure maintenance and server restarts can be readily optimized.

Optimization of Incident Management Based on Historical Data Analysis

End users of the digital platform log incidents that impact their experience. For such incidents, we need to do a deep analysis of the root cause of the incidents. The historical analysis uncover the incident solution patterns, the areas where problems are more concentrated to provide us opportunities to optimize the related incidents. We could take some of the proactive measures such as problem-avoidance design and use automation to optimize the incident management belonging to this category.

Incident Management Optimization Analysis

As part of historical incident analysis, we take a deeper look at the root cause of the historical incidents. We focus more on the recurring incidents that contribute to a larger percentage of the overall issues. We analyze the remediation steps for the commonly occurring incidents and identify the automation opportunities for each of them.

We have depicted the automation opportunities for the common incident requests in Table 12.1.

Table 12.1 Automation Opportunities for Common Incident Requests

#	Common Incident Requests	Remediation Step	Automation Opportunity
1	Server down	Restart server	Server restart script
2	Access request	Provide relevant access	Self-service tool for access provisioning
3	Report generation request	Generate report with required data	Batch job for report generation
4	Publish content request	Publish relevant content	On-demand content publishing
5	Application unavailable	Restart server	Server restart script
6	User creation request	Create the user with required permissions	User creation job
7	Data quality issues	Check for data correctness and completeness	Data reconciliation jobs
8	Recurring application errors (such as HTTP 40X HTTP 500 errors)	Error specific remediation steps	Bot to fix the issue based on the HTTP error code
9	How-to requests	Provide the relevant content (such as how-to article, blog, document)	Smart search to provide the contextual results

Table 12.2   Automation Opportunities for Maintenance Activities

#	Maintenance Activity	Remediation Step	Automation Opportunity
1	Server patching	Apply the latest patch	Scheduled patching script.
2	Application monitoring	Setup the monitoring infrastructure	End-to-end monitoring setup.
3	Server maintenance	Restart server	Housekeeping jobs.
4	User training	Complete the user training using the knowledge base	Training portal based on existing knowledge base. Develop a conversational interface to handle user questions.
5	Data backup	Backup the data at regular intervals	Schedule the backup job.
6	Change management	Implement the change management	Create a bot for each of the change management activities.
7	Configuration management	Implement the configuration management	Create a bot for each of the configuration management activities.

Table 12.2 depicts the automation opportunities for common maintenance activities.

Incident Management Optimization Methods

Once we analyze the optimization opportunities for commonly occurring incidents, we devise the mechanisms (called incident management optimization methods) to optimize the incident management process.

Automation, self-service, proactive maintenance and incident-avoidance design are the most commonly used incident management optimization methods. As part of the automation, we automate the structured repetitive steps using a job or using a bot. Self-service mechanism provides self-service tools such as self-service portals to enable the end users by providing an user experience to users for completing their tasks and by providing the relevant information.

For incidents that has pre-defined responses (such as server maintenance, server restarts and others), we can adopt a mix of automation and problem-avoidance design. For other incidents we adopt a mix of incident-avoidance design, automation and self-service methods.

In the subsequent sections, we discuss the incident management optimization methods and the details of the optimization methods.

Automation Methods

Automation Frameworks

Automation is one of the quintessential elements of incident management optimization. The first step in smart automation is to identify and automate the tickets.

Ticket Automation Framework

We have depicted the ticket automation framework based on sample ticket analysis in Figure 12.1.

Initially we need to identify the ticket categories along with its volume percentage. We have given the sample categories such as external integration, data quality, FTP (file transfer protocol) connectivity and so on. In the sample data we have identified that majority of the historical incidents are related to external integration. Other top category issues are related to data quality, FTP connectivity, HTTP connectivity and so on.

In the next step, we classify the top tickets into their respective categories. In Figure 12.1, we have identified two major categories—connectivity issues and data quality issues. We bucket the ticket categories into one of the major categories.

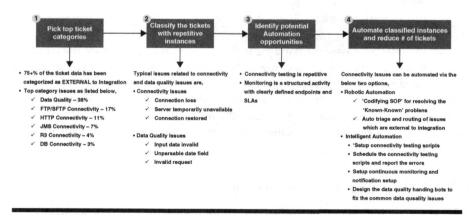

Figure 12.1   Ticket automation framework with sample data.

In the third step, we identify the potential areas of automation that can be implemented. In this example the connectivity testing and monitoring are structured activities that can be automated.

In the final step, we implement the automation to minimize the tickets. Setting up monitoring jobs and connectivity testing scripts and data quality bots reduces the ticket volume.

We have defined the common automation solutions to the recurring problem categories in the Table 12.3.

Automation Bots

In this section, we discuss the bots that can be used for automating the commonly identified problem patterns in the sample use case.

Cognitive Assistant System

The ticket resolution system involves a set of bots and cognitive services that automatically classifies and resolves the common tickets. The detailed steps for ticket management bot is depicted in Figure 12.2.

The cognitive assistant chatbot is the first-line contact for the end-user queries. The cognitive assistant bot uses the trained cognitive services to resolve the common and non-complex queries.

The detailed steps of cognitive assistant system are as follows:

1. User logs the ticket describing the problem or query.
2. The cognitive assistant chatbot is the first-line contact for the end user queries. The cognitive assistant bot uses the trained cognitive services to resolve the common and non-complex queries.
3. The cognitive assistant bot logs the ticket for the queries that cannot be resolved.
4. The cognitive assistant bot assigns the ticket to the appropriate resolver bots which use the pre-defined methods to solve the ticket. Tickets are triaged based on their priority and resolution time.
5. The resolver bots employ various methods such as server restarts, access provisioning and such to automatically resolve the issues.
6. The support team continuously monitors the ticket dashboard to identify the SLAs of various tickets.

Ticket Monitoring and Solver System

The ticket monitoring and solver system continuously monitors the logged tickets and automatically handles the logged tickets using solver bots.

Table 12.3   Automation Solution for Recurring Problems

Category	Problem	Automation Solution
Training	User creating ticket to check the application functionality/ Process/user management questions	Create conversational AI and continuous learning. Use intelligent process automation. Provide a self-service knowledge base with smart search.
Data quality	Due to old migration data being corrupted and duplicate data exists	Implement a rule-based data quality bot to watch and fix the data issue. Create batch monitoring and data reconciliation robotic process automation (RPA) bots.
Data quality	Due to interface issues data is not in sync	Monitor the data flow and data quality. Implement a rule-based bot to watch the dashboard and fix the data issue and publish to downstream system.
User management	User can't change or reset their password. They need to reach out to support team	Create bot for user management and password reset.
User management	Support team is managing the user management manually	Create self-service portal for user management. Create access provisioning bot to provide the system access in batch mode or in real time.
System admin	Manual deployment and monitoring by system admin	Create bot for application deployment and monitoring.
Data access	Need on-demand data access and reports	Create bot that generates on demand filter-based dashboard. Create report bot to provide periodic, criteria specific report.
Maintenance task	Server stop/start/ restart System patching	Create maintenance bots for patching and for server restarts. Develop self-healing scripts for self-recovery and data reconciliation. Health-checks and housekeeping jobs to monitor the availability and performance.

(Continued)

Table 12.3 (Continued)

Category	Problem	Automation Solution
System or network issues	Connectivity failures	**Intelligent classifier:** Use ML models on historical data, NLP and rules for identifying connectivity tickets. **Human in Loop (HIL) approach:** Use HIL approach for Classifier Learning— Tickets with less than 100% accuracy in prediction score. **Robotic automation:** Scripted tasks to check connectivity with application server/database to validate the ticket.
Training	Training the new users	Create conversational AI/chatbot for descriptive user training.

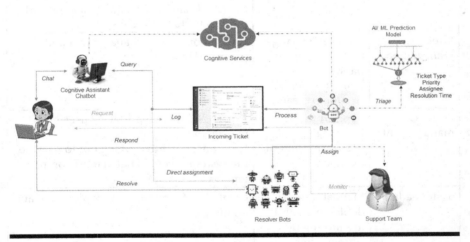

Figure 12.2   Cognitive assistant system.

The detailed steps for monitoring and solver bot is depicted in Figure 12.3. The detailed steps for ticket monitoring and solver system are as follows:

1. The L1 (call desk) or the business and IT teams log the ticket in the ticketing system. Users can also use chatbot to get the first responses and log the ticket.
2. The dispatcher bot uses ML classifier that is trained on the historical ticketing data to classify the tickets into known categories (such as access related, database related and such). The dispatcher bot then sends out an email or a message to the monitoring bot with the details such as ticket category.

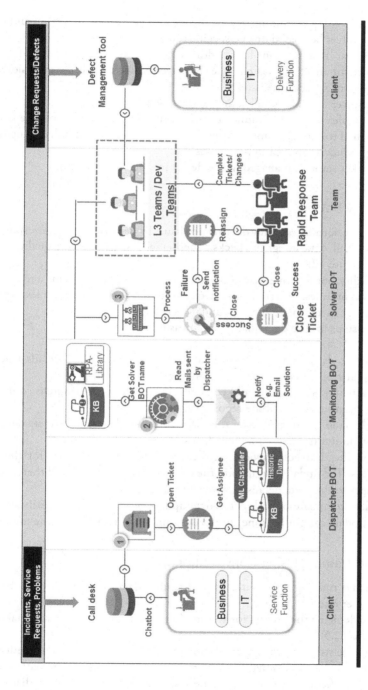

Figure 12.3 Ticket monitoring and solver system.

3. The monitoring bot monitors the message sent by the dispatcher bot and picks up the solver bot based on the specific category.
4. The solver bot is trained on addressing specific category of issues. For instance for an access-related issue the solver bot automatically provisions the permissions to close the issue.
5. If the solver bot successfully handles the ticket the ticket is closed.
6. For complex issues that cannot be solved through the solver bot, the issue is reassigned to the L3 teams. The level 3 team is a specialized in handling complex product or application-related issues.
7. The ticket status is managed in the defect management system.

Data Quality Bot

The data quality bot addresses any data-related issues by performing the corresponding data updates and data integrity checks. The detailed steps for data quality bot is depicted in Figure 12.4.

Data quality bot is a rule-driven bot that identifies source systems and updates the data based on rules. When the user requests for data updates we can leverage the data quality bot to automate the data update activities.

The detailed steps for the data quality bot are as follows:

1. A user sends the data update request with all the required details (such as entity, attribute details) to the demand bot.
2. The demand bot validates and confirms the attributes. Attribute is confirmed from a centralized attribute repository.
3. The demand bot then invokes the verification bot that gets the meta details of the attributes (such as data type, data size, constraints and others).
4. The verification bot provides all the details to the update bot for the final updates. The update bot updates the data and its update rules. If there are any changes to the meta details, the meta database is also updated.
5. Finally the update bot relays the data update confirmation or justification (if data update cannot be done) to the demand bot which notifies the user.

Automated Training Using Conversational Interface/Chatbot

The automated training system uses the structured data in the knowledge base to respond to user queries.

We have depicted the process for automation training using conversational interface in Figure 12.5.

The system consists of knowledge graph that manages the structured knowledge and its hierarchy. The conversational framework consist of various components such as content builder (to retrieve and build the response content), dynamic dialog (for

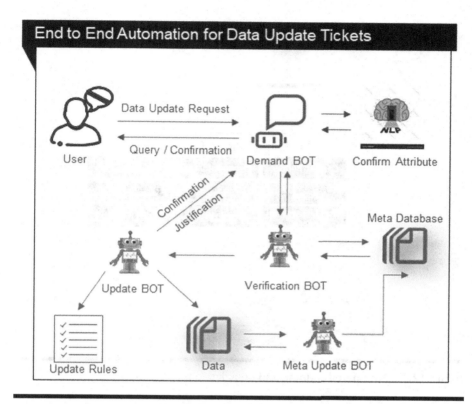

Figure 12.4   Data quality bot setup.

conversing with the user in the natural language), dynamic form (to provide entry options to the user), context (to understand the user context), state, analytics (for measuring the metrics), threshold manager (to identify the confidence score of the response), query history and model manager.

The detailed steps for the training and the knowledge management bot are as follows:

1. The user interacts with demand bot with the queries.
2. The demand bot forwards the query to the conversational framework.
3. The conversational framework interacts with the knowledge graph to get the suitable response. The conversational framework manages the context and the dialog with the user.
4. The demand bot responds to user queries using the conversational framework.

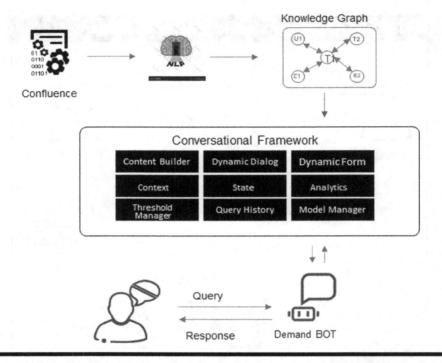

Figure 12.5 Automated training and knowledge management bot.

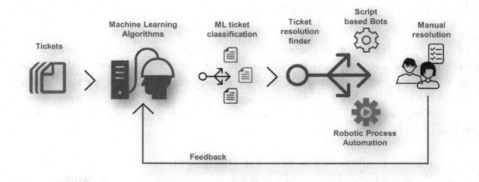

Figure 12.6 User access management bot.

User Management Bot

A user management bot handles the access requests from users. We have detailed the user access management process using a bot in Figure 12.6.

Once the ticket is logged, the machine learning (ML) algorithms classify the ticket based on the historical ticket data. Based on the type of the access request, either a script-based bot or robotic process automation or manual resolution method is used.

The user management bot uses automated scripts to carry out the authorized access actions such as user provisioning, access grants, access revocation and such.

Connectivity Checker Bot

As depicted in Figure 12.1, one of the top incident categories is related to the connectivity. The connectivity checker bot validates the connectivity to the target endpoints.

We have described the system connectivity checking process using a bot in Figure 12.7.

The detailed steps for connectivity checker bot is as follows:

1. The connectivity-related ticket is logged.
2. The ML ticket classifier uses historical data and rules to classify the ticket into sub-category. If the ticket is related to connectivity, then the ML ticket classifier invokes connectivity bot for resolution/re-assignment for manual investigation.
3. Connectivity bot collects the information about the source and destination endpoints from semantic representation. The semantic representation system holds knowledge about the server endpoints, its attributes, characteristics and syntax for connectivity queries.

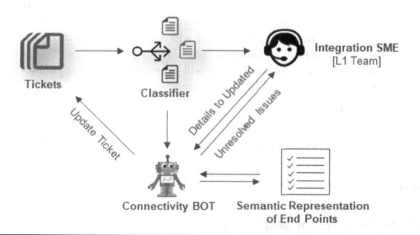

Figure 12.7   Connectivity testing bot.

4. After getting the endpoint details from the semantic representation, the steps for connectivity verification are as follows:
   - Login to the production server with required credentials
   - Perform connectivity test for the relevant server based on the details inferred from semantic representation.
   - Validate session response for success/failure
5. Based on the connectivity testing the bot closes or reassigns the ticket.

Automated Ticket Responder

The automated ticket responder uses the combination of bots to automatically handle the ticket end to end.

We have depicted the main steps and methods of a smart responder in Figure 12.8. The detailed steps for automatic ticket responder are as follows:

1. The users log a ticket describing an error.
2. The error handling framework (EHF) captures the error and uses the logs and to provide the pre-defined solution for the known problem as the selfheal option. If the issue is resolved, the issue is closed. If not the system logs the ticket in the ticketing tool.
3. The service desk can interact with the chatbot ecosystem for the query. The chatbots look up the knowledge base to provide the response.
4. If the issue is not resolved, robotic process automation (RPA) bots take over the issue. RPA bots are designed to handle the specific and well-defined changes. The RPA bots carry out the rules-based structured changes such as user access provisioning, system restarts, data updates, cancelling the process and such.
5. The machine learning process learns from the knowledge base and trains the RPA bots. The trained RPA bots are used for ticket analytics and solution recommendation. The AI/ML-based support uses various methods such as classification, real time prediction to resolve the ticket.
6. If the issue is still not resolved, it will be routed to the support team. The support personnel in the L2/L3 team resolves the ticket.

Self-Service Methods

In this section, we describe various self-service methods that can be used as part of ticket-avoidance framework.

Self Service Portal and Tools

Self-service is an integral part of the incident management optimization. In this category we provide self-service tools, self-service applications and business self-service

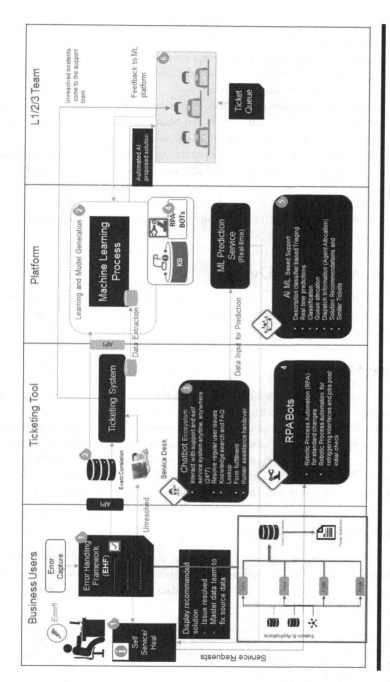

Figure 12.8 Smart responder.

management interfaces for users. Few examples of self service includes but not limited to the following:

Admin tool for business managers improves self-service and interactive user interface help for users. The admin tool users can control various application configuration settings and manage the application.

Customer self-service portals for customer onboarding to enable the easier and faster onboarding of customers. Customers can create account, reset password, purchase the products and search for products in the self-service portals.

Other self-service tools are self-service reports (to generate the reports on demand), self-service calculators (to calculate the product price), product comparators (to compare the product features), search (to search for the), product recommendation tools (to recommend the relevant products and services based on historical data) and productivity improvement tools (such as schedulers, alarms, bill payments and such).

Incident-Avoidance Design

Ticket avoidance and ticket reduction model involves taking many proactive measures to minimize the tickets. We have discussed some of the key measures in this section

Proactive Maintenance

Proactive maintenance tools monitor the application and take proactive corrective steps to avoid a potential incident.

As part of proactive maintenance, a continuous real-time monitoring agent monitors the applications and the servers. Based on the configured thresholds, such as consistent performance time, system health check thresholds (CPU, memory, network utilization) and error rate, the maintenance bot classifies the issues. Table 12.4 provides the sample rules, issue categories and the possible proactive maintenance steps.

Shift left Design

Shift left involves structuring and automating the complex activities involving manual intervention. The shift left aims to enable the L1 support team (the first level on-call support) to handle the incidents earlier managed by L2 (Level 2 team). It includes but not limited to below given steps:

- Create standard operation procedures (SOP) that codifies the knowledge. SOP helps management team to define best practices–based steps for handling a scenario.
- Identify the high-volume issues and transactions and create SOP for them.

Table 12.4 Proactive Maintenance Steps

Problem Symptom	Problem Category	Proactive Maintenance Step
The performance of the application is more than 5 mins consistently for more than 10 mins	Performance issue	Increase the number of service pods to handle high traffic. Log the performance ticket for further debugging.
The heartbeat ping responds with 40x response code	System outage	Attempt auto restart of the system and the related services. Log the production incident ticket with high priority.
The CPU, memory thresholds exceed consistently for more than 10 mins	Resource issue	Increase the number of service pods to handle high traffic. Log the resource ticket for further debugging.

- Create smart search tools to help the L1 team to provide known solutions to common problems.
- Create tools to automate the most frequently used activities or common requests. For instance reporting, content publishing, logging and cache maintenance etc.
- Create admin access tool for server maintenance (server restarts).

Root Cause Analysis and Quality Improvement

The root cause analysis for top category tickets reveal the underlying problem. Based on the underlying root cause, we need to proactively address the issue. For instance if there are frequent code-quality related defects in a solution module, we should improve the code quality and carry out thorough unit testing.

Automation of Maintenance Activities

We already discussed various automation methods for various maintenance activities such as server restarts, patching, data backup, system monitoring, user training and others. We automate these structured maintenance activities through bots, scheduled jobs and scripts to minimize the incidents that are potentially caused by the lack of maintenance.

System Monitoring and Health Checks

We need to setup the end-to-end logging and monitoring infrastructure to monitor the resource metrics, SLAs and key performance indicators (KPIs). Health checks continuously monitor the health of the infrastructure, application and services.

Infrastructure monitoring tools should be setup to monitor the health of the infrastructure resources such as CPU utilization, memory utilization, storage utilization, throughput and others. We need to define the thresholds for each of the resource metrics and trigger a notification when the configured threshold is breached. For instance, when we can configure a CPU utilization threshold of 70% for 5 minutes the monitoring system triggers a notification if any of the monitored resources breach this threshold so that the system administrator can take corrective actions.

Application monitoring services should monitor the health of the deployed application and services. The health checks invoke the application or service endpoint and monitors the response. If the health check tool receives an error or a non-healthy response (such as HTTP 500 status code) it triggers a notification. Application monitoring service checks the availability of the application and service and other dependent third-party services. As part of SLA monitoring, the application monitoring services also check the 95th percentile and 99th percentile response time for the application. Error rates, page traffic, passed and failed transactions, total page hits are some of the key metrics monitored by the application monitoring services.

Enterprises also monitor the business KPIs such as conversion rates, promotion success rate, payment success rates, revenue values, order counts and others.

Summary

Incident management is an important aspect of operations in an enterprise. Incident management defines the processes to handle the production incidents. We can adopt automation for optimization of incidents (such as maintenance incidents, server restart incidents, patch management, configuration management, data backup, health checks, resource utilization monitoring, billing alarms) based on pre-defined responses. We can optimize the incident management based on historical data analysis through deep dive analysis of the root cause of the incidents. Automation opportunities involve scheduled or batch jobs, scripts and bots that automate the activities. We discussed various automation frameworks such as ticket automation, framework and automation bots such as cognitive assistant system, ticket monitoring and solver system, data quality bot, user management bot, connectivity checker bot and automated training using conversational interface/chatbot. In these automation methods, we use ML classifier to analyze the ticket metadata and use the appropriate solver bot to address the incident. Self-service portal and tools are effective ways to reduce the incidents. We can use methods such as proactive maintenance, shift left design, root cause analysis and quality improvement, automation of maintenance activities, system monitoring and health checks as part of an incident-avoidance design.

DIGITAL TRANSFORMATION OF OPERATIONS

V

Chapter 13

Digital Transformation of Operations

Introduction

Digital operations involve managing day-to-day activities of an enterprise. System maintenance, patch management, incident management, logging and monitoring, business continuity, configuration management, change management are some of the key digital operations of the digital enterprise. There should be continuous improvement in the digital operations and the related processes to ensure the business value.

In this chapter, we discuss the digital transformation of the operations and the related processes. The chapter discusses the best practices of patch management process, logging and monitoring framework and look at the sample logging and monitoring setup. We also discuss the change management, configuration management and digital operations best practices. We discuss a sample migration runbook and the post migration testing as part of digital operations best practices.

Patch Management

Product vendors release patches to address the security issues, to fix functional bugs or to add new features to the platform. Patch management defines the processes for applying the patches to the platforms. Patch management covers patches for

DOI: 10.1201/9781003390893-18

operating systems, system software, application software, databases, browsers and other platforms.

A robust patch management is necessary to ensure high security posture and to ensure regulatory and organizational compliance. The key attributes of patch management process are given below.

Centralized management—The patch management infrastructure should provide a single and centralized console for patch management for all environments and platforms.

Automated provisioning and deployment—The patch management infrastructure should provide ways to automate the patch provisioning and deployment across environments to ensure minimal downtime and to minimize manual efforts.

Consolidated view of compliance—The patch management infrastructure should provide a dashboard view of consolidated patch compliance view across all systems and environments. This enables system administrators to address the gaps and ensure compliance.

Prioritization—The patch management system should be able to prioritize the patches based on its criticality and impact. The security hotfixes that address the zero-day bugs should be prioritized with strict deployment timelines.

Testability—The system administrator should be able to test the patches to validate any side effects on existing applications and platforms.

Monitoring—The patch management console should monitor the patch deployment status across all platforms and environments. Any failed deployments should be notified to the system administrator for further analysis and for re-deployment.

Minimal downtime—The patching process should minimize the system downtime and ensure high availability (HA). It should be possible to define the maintenance window for scheduling the patch deployments with minimal impact on existing users.

Digital Transformation of Patch Management Process

We define the process steps for transformed patching process across all environments in this section.

Prerequisites for Patch Management Process

We should setup the governance processes as a prerequisite for the patch management process as given below.

Continuous monitoring of patch releases—The patch management solution should continuously scan the product vendor endpoints for new patch releases.

Automated patch deployment jobs—The patch management solution to automatically deploy the patch across all environments should be in place.

Patch approval process—The patch approval process for manual or automated approvals based on priority should be in place.

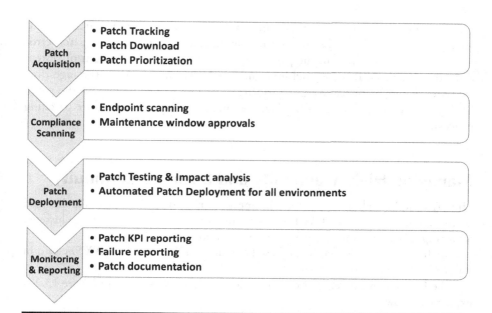

Figure 13.1   Patch management process.

System inventory—The inventory management system should identify the complete inventory of the infrastructure ecosystem. The infrastructure inventory is checked for compliance checks and monitoring.

We have depicted the transformed patch management process in Figure 13.1.

Patch acquisition—The initial step of the patch management process is to track the recently released patches and download them. Based on the criticality of the patch, the patch management tool assigns the priority and the associated deployment timelines for the same.

Compliance scanning—The patch management tool should scan the endpoints of the enterprise infrastructure components (such as laptops, desktops, servers etc.) to check for their compliance level in patching. The endpoint scanning provides the list of endpoints that need to be patched with the recently downloaded patches. Based on the criticality of the patch, the patch deployment has to be approved. Security hotfixes can be auto approved and other severity patches can be manually approved. Post approval, the maintenance window for patching is scheduled.

Patch deployment—The patches are initially tested in the lower environments to assess the impact of the patch on existing applications and platforms. Once the patch testing in lower environment is successfully completed, the patches are automatically deployed across all environments.

Monitoring and reporting—Post patching, the patch management tool monitors the endpoints for patch key performance indicators (KPIs). All patching errors are notified to the system administrator. The patch KPIs are patch compliance (percentage of systems that are in compliance with the patch), patch error rate (percentage of errors in the patching process), downtime (amount of system downtime incurred during patching) and patch deployment time (average time for patch deployment based on its priority). We should also document the patch deployment best practices, findings and learnings to improve the future patching process.

Managing High Availability and Business Continuity

High Availability (HA) ensures that the applications and services are available based on the defined availability SLAs. HA design involves creation of multi-node clustered servers spread across multiple data centers or cloud zones.

We have depicted a HA design based on Amazon Web Services (AWS) cloud in Figure 13.2.

The HA design elements of the three-tier application depicted in Figure 13.2 is explained below.

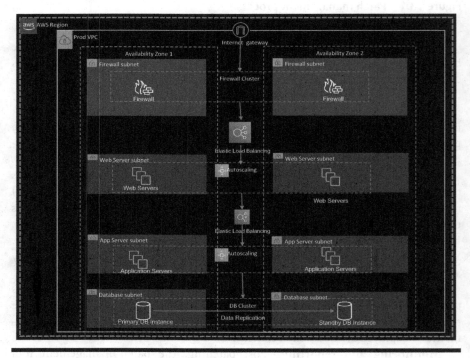

Figure 13.2   High available 3-tier application.

Multi-Instance Multi-Zone Servers

The instances for web servers, application servers and database servers are distributed across multiple availability zones (AZs) of the AWS region. The servers (such as web servers, application servers, database servers) are deployed in active-active setup across multiple availability zones wherein all the server instances are serving traffic. The load balancer distributes the traffic to the server instances.

Health Check Monitoring

The load balancer performs the health checks of the backend server instances at regular intervals. If any of the backend servers is down, the health checker marks the instance as unhealthy and the traffic to the unhealthy server is stopped.

Automated Instance Failure Handling

In the active-active setup, the load balancer uses the health checker to send the traffic only to the healthy instances. As a result, the end user does not experience any disruption even when one of the backend server instances go down.

Data Synchronization

In the HA design, the data is replicated across multiple storage volumes spread across different AZs (or data centers). The database cluster in Figure 13.2 performs synchronous data replication from primary database instance to standby database instance. If the primary database instance goes down, the standby database instance is promoted and will take all the database traffic.

As part of digital operations for HA design, the health checker tool should be configured to continuously check the availability of the server instances. The data backup and data synchronization jobs should replicate the data in real time.

Business Continuity Process through Disaster Recovery

Business continuity process (BCP) defines the operational processes to enable the business continuity in the event of a disaster impacting the primary data center. BCP is managed by disaster recovery (DR) processes that includes handling application DR, database DR, storage DR and other involved components.

DR processes are mainly driven by Recovery Point Objective or RPO that specifies the maximum acceptable data loss and Recovery Time Objective or RTO that specifies the maximum acceptable downtime.

Based on the RPO and RTO, we design the DR setup and the data backup frequency. For achieving DR we mainly use a distant geo-location as the DR site. We then backup the data and deploy standby application instances in the remote DR site.

Table 13.1   DR Process

Solution Component	Disaster Recovery Process
Virtual machine	Copy the machine image to the DR site at a regular frequency based on RPO and RTO.
Database data	Perform synchronous/asynchronous replication of data to the remote DR site.
Storage data	Backup the data on regular basis to the remote DR site based on RPO and RTO.
Volumes	Create the volume snapshot and backup the snapshot on regular basis to the remote DR site based on RPO and RTO.
Infrastructure setup	Use Infrastructure as Code (IaC) to create the mirror replica of the primary infrastructure at the DR site.

Table 13.1 defines the DR process for various solution components. We can automate the data synchronization and replication jobs using scripts and backup jobs.

As the DR process is mainly driven by the RPO and RTO requirements, we have defined the DR methods for specific RPO/RTO needs in Table 13.2.

We have defined the DR process along with the main DR activities and tools used in Figure 13.3.

In the "define" stage, we primarily identify the RPO and RTO requirements and accordingly we design the data backup and data synchronization jobs. We also identify the main DR tools (that handle both fail over and fail back). We then test the DR processes as part of the "test" stage. We use fault simulators to inject the failures and monitor the application resilience. We also simulate the disaster and monitor the RPO and RTO to fail over to the DR site. We mainly use the data backup tools, data synchronization jobs and data replication agents in this stage. During "monitor" stage we use the logging and monitoring tools and health checker tools to monitor the performance and response time of the application in the DR site. Finally in the "failback" stage we use data replication agents to perform the failback from DR site to primary site and test the RPO, RTO and the data correctness.

Logging and Monitoring

Logging and monitoring of the events is crucial for improving the overall health of the platform. This also helps in faster incident response aiding in the root cause analysis and troubleshooting. A centralized logging and monitoring dashboard should be setup to monitor the KPIs in real time and take necessary corrective action.

Monitoring the workload also provides insights into the traffic patterns and component-wise response times in the request processing pipeline.

Table 13.2   DR Process Based on RPO/RTO

RPO/RTO Requirements	*Disaster Recovery Process*
RPO/RTO in real time with zero data loss	• Create an active-active full setup across primary site and the DR site. • Setup real-time continuous replication of data, snapshots and machine images from primary site to the DR site.
RPO/RTO < 30 mins	• Create an active-active reduced capacity setup at the DR site. For instance if there are two web server instances in primary site, setup single web server instance in DR site. • Setup the asynchronous replication of data, snapshots and machine images from primary site to the DR site every 15 mins.
RPO/RTO > 30 mins and < 60 mins	• Define the infrastructure templates to create the DR environment during the DR event. • Setup the asynchronous replication of data, snapshots and machine images from primary site to the DR site every 30 mins.
RPO/RTO > 60 mins	• Setup the data backup jobs between primary site and the DR site on hourly basis. • Setup the DR environment when the DR event happens.

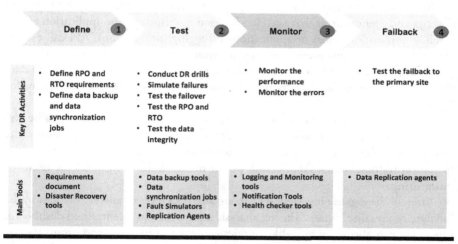

Figure 13.3   DR process.

Logging and Monitoring Framework

The logging and monitoring framework defines the process steps and the best practices to implement a robust logging and monitoring setup for an organization. We identify the sources and define the security policies for the logging and monitoring setup.

We log the crucial events of the application based on the levels such as info, error and debug. The main application errors are logged into the log files. All the log files are collected into a centralized log folder for analysis and reporting.

The centralized log analytics software (such as Splunk or Data dog) helps us to query for error patterns, filter based on specific fields and search within the log files. We can also group the log files, query the data, sort the log files based on criteria and visualize the metrics in the dashboard.

Prerequisites for the Logging and Monitoring Framework

- A centralized folder for logs should be identified. The Security information and event management (SIEM) tools and log analytics tools can analyze the logs and generate alerts in real time.
- The security policies for the log files should be defined. The audit logs should be encrypted to maintain the data integrity and compliance needs.
- The log retention policies should be defined at the organization level.

We have depicted various steps of the logging and monitoring framework in Figure 13.4.

In the "define" phase, we set up a logging and monitoring framework to identify the data and event sources that need logging and monitoring. The application events (such as application errors or application debugging information), API call events, traffic flow and system events are logged. Monitoring is setup for security events (such as login, password change and others), configuration change events and data access events. We use logging framework, such as Log4j or AWS CloudWatch, for logging.

Once the data sources are identified, in the "ingest" phase, we enable the real-time logging and monitoring for the events of interest. We monitor the errors, traffic flow, security events, access events, performance and send the logs to the centralized folder. Application performance monitoring tools are used for monitoring.

After all the logs are ingested, we use log analytics tools to analyze the logs in the "analyze & visualize" phase. The log analysis is presented in a centralized dashboard. Operators can also write SQL-like queries on logs to filter, sort and group the log events. We can configure the alarms to notify the operators in case of any breach in the configured thresholds.

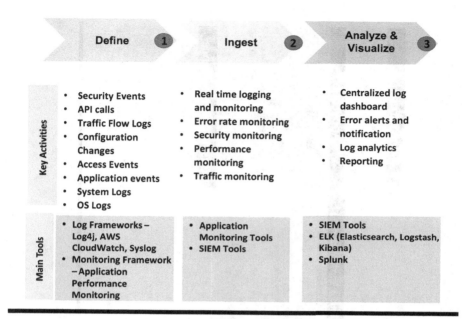

Figure 13.4 Logging and monitoring framework.

Monitoring

We monitor the crucial metrics related to infrastructure, application and business KPIs. The infrastructure-related KPIs are CPU utilization, memory utilization, disk utilization, network usage and others. On the application front, we monitor the metrics such as response time, error rate and availability.

To proactively respond to the issues, we set the threshold for each of the KPIs. For instance when we set the threshold of 90% disk utilization for 2 minutes, the monitoring system notifies the system administrator if any of the disk utilization exceeds 90% for more than 2 minutes.

Monitoring the end-to-end performance is a prominent use case. The application monitoring software provides the service map and response times for all calls across application layers.

We have depicted a log and monitoring setup in Figure 13.5. The cloud resources and on-premise resources are monitored by various logging and monitoring tools. The logging and monitoring are done across three main categories—infrastructure metrics (resource utilization such as CPU/memory utilization, storage utilization, disk metrics and such), application metrics (such as availability, response time, error rate, healthiness of dependent 3rd party services, throughput, traffic rate and such) and business metrics (such as conversion rate, average order value, success rate, error rate).

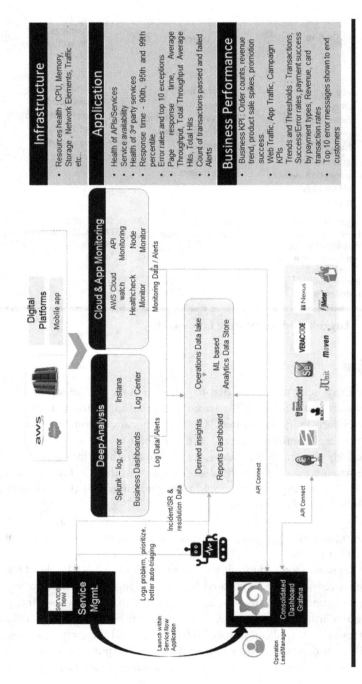

Figure 13.5   Sample log and monitoring setup.

We do the deep analysis of the logs using tools such as Splunk and build the business dashboards. Cloud-native tools such as Amazon CloudWatch logs the events in the cloud. The insights derived from the deep analysis and the monitoring systems are used in building the operational data lake and report dashboard.

We also ingest the incident data and the incident resolution data into the data lake to build the ML-based analytics data store. We can visualize the log details in the Graphana dashboard.

Table 13.3 provides the common monitoring scenarios for a digital platform.

Table 13.3 Monitoring Scenarios

Category	Monitoring Metrics	Brief Details
Availability	Platform/service/application/API/dependent 3rd party service availability	Monitor the availability of the entire end-to-end platform and the individual layer-wise services and components.
	Platform/service/application throughput	Monitor the total number of transactions that are handled.
	Mobile app/service availability	Monitor the overall uptime of the application.
Service Level Agreement (SLA)	Application/Service SLA	Monitor the pre-defined SLAs related to performance, availability of the application, service and other components.
Functionality	Application functionality	Validate the critical application functionality, such as authentication, form submission, search and checkout, using synthetic monitors.
Error	JavaScript errors	
	HTTP Errors	Monitor non-HTTP 200 error codes.
	Mobile app crash	
Performance	Page response time	Monitor time to first byte, server response time, page load time.
	API response time	Monitor overall API response time.
	Dependent 3rd party service response time	
Infrastructure	CPU metrics	Monitor average utilization.
	Memory metrics	
	Network metrics	

Security Information and Event Management (SIEM)

Monitoring the security events for potential security and vulnerabilities is crucial to improve the security posture of the platform. The organization can respond to the security events quickly. The security event management tools are used for monitoring the security events. The tool ingests the log data from various sources, such as traffic logs, application logs and data access logs, into a central repository as depicted in Figure 13.6. The security event management tool continuously monitors the traffic for threat patterns and alerts the administrator when a vulnerability is found.

We have depicted the key features of SIEM in Figure 13.6. The SIEM platform manages the security data and monitors the security events in an enterprise. The security data management is used for audit and compliance purposes and the SIEM tool analyzes and correlates the security events for detecting the potential threats and alerting the system administrators.

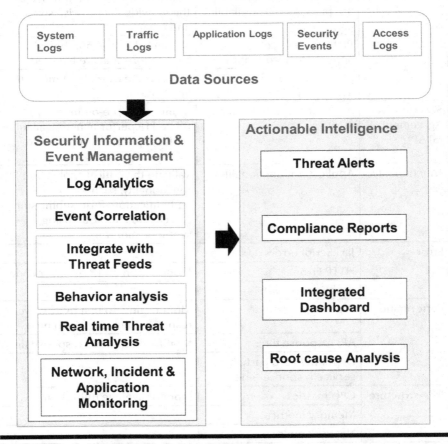

Figure 13.6 Security information and event management features.

The security data is ingested from various sources such as system logs, application logs, traffic logs, access logs and other security events. The SIEM tool performs various analysis of the collected log data and event data. The SIEM tool analysis includes security event correlation with internal and external threat signatures. Modern SIEM tools also perform the behavior analysis in real time to identify network anomalies and data exfiltration attempts. Using the log data from various sources, the SIEM tool can monitor the application, network and incidents.

We can generate actionable intelligence from the SIEM tool. Based on the analysis of the integrated log data, we can get the real-time threat alerts and an integrated dashboard of log data. We can also generate compliance reports based on the audit log information and perform root cause analysis of the incidents.

Change Management

The digital operations of an enterprise requires change management processes to efficiently track the operational changes. An enterprise change management framework defines the processes for requesting, approving, implementing and reporting the operational changes.

The enterprise change management software helps us to create a maintenance window for the configuration and operational changes. We can run the automated jobs to carry out the configuration and operational changes during that maintenance window.

Configuration Management

The application and infrastructure configurations change over a period of time to accommodate the enhancements and compliance requirements. A configuration management framework baselines the configurations and records the configuration changes over a period of time. The organization can release products and services based on approved standards. For instance the organization can mandate the developers to use an approved machine image that is hardened to meet the organization security policies. The development team can use the approved machine image to build the products and services. The configuration management software tracks the changes to the machine in real time and alerts the administrators if there are any unapproved changes.

Digital Operations Best Practices

To efficiently run the digital operations, we should define the processes, tools, standard operating procedures and checklists. The digital operation tools and processes ensure operational readiness of the operations team to efficiently manage the operations thereby improving the operational posture.

The digital operations best practices also reduce the incident response time, ensure HA, enhance the SLAs, enable the operations teams to use the past learnings and best practices and create a knowledge base for user training. In this section we detail operational best practices such as runbooks, operational scenario testing.

Runbooks

Runbooks document the detailed steps of an operational activity. The runbooks specify the prerequisites, execution steps, checklist, approvals required, activity owner, timelines, dependencies and validation steps. Runbooks provide a repeatable and consistent way to execute a complex engagement such as migration, solution troubleshooting, platform setup and configuration of platforms. The operations team continuously validates the activities in the runbook and updates them wherever required.

We have provided a sample runbook for application migration in the Appendix.

Operational Scenario Testing

The operational scenario testing defines the baseline test cases for validating specific scenarios. We identify the detailed testing steps, accountable stakeholders and alternate scenarios. We also refer to the operational runbook for specific scenario details.

We prepare for the operational scenario testing by identifying the key test cases and the required stakeholders. We also identify the timeslots for the testing. We seek the necessary approvals from all teams for testing the scenarios. During the testing we record the key metrics such as response times, resource utilization (such as CPU utilization and memory utilization), error rates, fail over times, SLAs and others. Post testing, we document the findings and report the findings to the stakeholders. We also update the operational playbook wherever required. We also use learnings from the testing to improve the future testing scenarios.

Disaster Recovery Scenario Testing

We have discussed DR scenario as an example. As part of DR drill, we need to carry out the DR related test cases to validate the resiliency of the design. We have given sample test cases for post migration scenario testing in Table 13.4.

We can create the operational scenario test cases for other common scenarios such as data migration, environment setup, application hosting, application migration, server upgrade, server patching and such.

Table 13.4 Post Migration Test Scenarios

Scenario Name	Brief Details	Testing Steps	Alternate Scenario
Server Resiliency Testing	Purpose: Test the resiliency of the server. A web server instance is stopped to test the failover of the service.	• The operations team intentionally stops one of the web server instances in the cluster. • The operations team checks the failover of the stopped instance. • The operations team monitors the availability, response time and the error rate of the web server cluster endpoint.	Test the resiliency of dependent services such as file system, storage services and database service.
Application backup testing	Purpose: Test the backup and restore of an n-tier application. The n-tier application is restored from the backup according to the RPO.	• The operations team redeploys an n-tier application from the backup according to the RPO and RTO. • The operations team validates all the restoration steps in the playbook. • The application functionality is tested post restoration.	Test the license usage for the backup server. Test the associated network components, IP/ endpoint changes after application restoration. Test the restoration of database service.
Network Failure testing	Purpose: Test the network component restoration time. The connectivity between two data centers is broken. The connectivity is reestablished within the RTO.	• The operations team simulate the network connectivity failure between two data centers. • The behavior and response times of the application is tested.	Validate the firewall rules and configuration. Validate the impact of IP changes.

(Continued)

Table 13.4 (Continued)

Scenario Name	Brief Details	Testing Steps	Alternate Scenario
		• The operations team restores the network connectivity between two data centers. • The network restoration time and the related playbook is validated.	
Dependency Impact testing	Purpose: Test the impact of application dependency failure. One of the application dependencies is stopped and the application behavior is tested.	• The operations team stops one of the application dependencies such as database or webservice. • Test the monitoring system's notification. • The operations team validates the application behavior, application response time and error handling. • Restore the dependency within the RPO.	
Application rollback testing	Purpose: Test the rollback procedure during the application deployment failure.	The operations team validates the rollback procedure.	

Appendix

Application Migration Runbook

We have provided a sample application runbook for the application migration from one data center to another data center or from primary data center to the cloud.

The migration scenario includes migration of the web application, its database and associated network and security components to the new data center or to the cloud.

The three primary sections of the application migration runbook are pre-migration activities, migration activities and post migration activities. We execute preparatory activities such as seeking approvals, security checks, reviews and other checks. In the migration activities we include the core migration tasks such as data migration, server migration, connectivity setup on new environment, application smoke testing and others. Post migration we mainly perform the validation of application, data, connectivity, security, performance, integration and monitor the resource utilization. The runbook also captures the owner contact details, schedule and timeslots for various phases.

Pre-Migration Phase

The pre-migration activities of the migration playbook are detailed in Table 13.5. We can capture additional details, such as start time, end time and dependency, as required.

Core Migration Phase

The core migration activities are depicted in Table 13.6. The data migration, application migration and migration of all dependent components are captured in this section.

Post-Migration Phase

Post migration, we mainly validate the end-to-end connectivity and validate if all monitoring and logging jobs are running as expected. We have detailed the post migration activities in Table 13.7.

Summary

In this chapter we discussed the best practices of digital operations including the patch management, logging and monitoring, business continuity, configuration

Table 13.5 Pre-Migration Activities

#	Pre-Migration Activity	Brief Details	Owner
1	Confirm the migration scope	Get buy-in about the migration scope from all stakeholders.	Migration lead
2	Confirm participation from all owners	Get confirmation about scope and timelines from owners from migration team, operations team, testing team, security team and networking team.	Migration lead
3	Finalize the migration date and timeslots	Get approvals from all teams about the migration date and timeslots.	Migration lead
4	Finalize the migration plan	Confirm the migration waves and scope for each wave.	Migration lead
5	Impact analysis and contingency plan	Review the migration impact and contingency plan for downtime handling from all stakeholders.	Migration lead
6	Outage notification	Send notification about the outage window to all stakeholders.	Migration lead
7	Setup the data migration scripts	Configure the data migration scripts to migrate data from source server to target server.	Migration team
8	Verify the servers	Verify the security and specification of the source and target servers.	Infrastructure team
9	Verify the connectivity	Test the connectivity between source and target servers.	Network team
10	Create service accounts in target environment	Create the service accounts in the target environment with sufficient privileges.	Infrastructure team
11	Impact analysis and contingency plan	Review the migration impact and contingency plan for downtime handling from all stakeholders.	Migration lead
12	Define rollback plan	Detail the activities required to rollback a failed migration.	All teams
13	Execute the InfoSec security review of the target server	Review the security posture of the target environment based on the InfoSec standards of the organization.	Security team
14	Go/No-Go decision	Stakeholders to decide the go/no-go based on the decision checklist.	All stakeholders

Table 13.5 (Continued)

#	Pre-Migration Activity	Brief Details	Owner
15	Change requests	Raise the change requests to implement the migration changes.	Migration lead

Table 13.6 Core Migration Activities

#	Migration Activity	Brief Details	Owner
1	Data migration	Perform data migration using the scripts. Validate the migrated data.	Database administrator
2	Server migration	Migrate server images to the target environment.	Infrastructure team
3	Shutdown the source systems	Shutdown the servers in the source environment.	Infrastructure team
4	Import of data	Import the data into the target environment.	DBA
5	Launch target servers	Launch all the servers in the target environment.	Infrastructure team
6	Reconfigure target server	Get new IP for target servers.	Infrastructure team
7	Reconfigure server settings	Create the SSL certificates. Configure the DNS records.	Infrastructure team
8	Reconfigure network settings	Configure the proxy, NAT rules, whitelisting rules, firewall rules and other required network settings.	Network team
9	Reconfigure security settings	Enable the authentication, authorization rules and define the permissions.	Security team
10	Test connectivity	Validate the connectivity to check for any access or performance issues.	Network team
11	Application smoke testing	Test the core functionality and do basic performance testing.	Testing team
12	Logging and monitoring	Enable logging for the application and infrastructure resources. Enable end-to-end monitoring. Enable SIEM tools and traffic monitoring tools. Enable threat detection tools.	Operations team

(Continued)

Table 13.6 (Continued)

#	Migration Activity	Brief Details	Owner
13	Enable backup jobs	Enable data backup jobs.	Infrastructure team
14	[Optional] Rollback migration	If the application migration fails, perform the rollback activities.	Infrastructure team
15	Handover to the support team	Once the migration is completed, handover the application to the support team.	Infrastructure team

Table 13.7 Post Migration Activities

#	Post Migration Activity	Brief Details	Owner
1	Monitor application performance	Monitor the application response times, error rate of the application.	Operations team
2	Monitor infrastructure resource performance	Monitor the key infrastructure resource metrics such as CPU utilization, memory utilization, storage utilization and others.	Operations team
3	Verify logs	Check if all the required application data, traffic data and monitoring data is logged in the log files.	Operations team
4	Validate the backup	Restore the instance from backup to validate the backup.	Operations team
5	Monitor security events	Continuously monitor for any security events.	Operations team
6	Validate disaster recovery	Validate disaster recovery process steps.	Operations team
7	Update the documentation	Document the process steps and learnings from the migration exercise.	Operations team

management and change management. The key attributes of patch management process are centralized management, automated provisioning and deployment, consolidated view of compliance, prioritization, testability, testability and minimal downtime. The main steps involved in the patch management process are patch acquisition, compliance scanning, patch deployment, monitoring and reporting. HA design require multi-instance and multi-zone servers, health check monitoring, automated instance failure handling and data synchronization. The DR process includes steps such as define (defining RPO and RTO and data backup processes), test (DR drills, failover testing), monitor (performance monitoring, error monitoring) and failback (failback testing). The main phases in the logging and monitoring process are define, ingest and analyze. SIEM tool ingests the log data from various sources, such as traffic logs, application logs and data access logs, into a central repository and monitors the traffic for threat patterns. The main digital operations best practices use runbooks for operational issues and operational scenario testing. Runbooks document the detailed steps of an operational activity. The operational scenario testing defines the baseline test cases for validating specific scenarios.

Chapter 14

Automation through DevSecOps

Introduction

DevSecOps is a set of practices, culture, tools and processes that uses automation to frequently and securely deliver business value. DevSecOps helps organizations to delivery business value quickly, iteratively, securely, reliably and consistently. DevSecOps impacts the organizational culture, processes and tools; we have depicted the elements in each of the categories in Figure 14.1.

DevSecOps brings in changes to the organizational culture (such as collaboration among teams) and operational culture (such as maximizing automation). Existing processes related to product delivery, configuration management and testing are also improved by adoption of DevSecOps practices. DevSecOps practices use many tools, such as a centralized code repository, continuous integration (CI), continuous delivery and monitoring and logging tools, that help us to automate and optimize the processes.

DevSecOps enables business objectives through an iterative and incremental release of features. The main phases of DevSecOps processes is depicted in Figure 14.2.

DevSecOps integrates the development, operations and security practices of an organization. DevSecOps enforces the security of the pipeline, security in the pipeline and security through the pipeline. Various business units within the organization are interested in releasing the products and services quicker in a secured way. As depicted in Figure 14.3, the DevSecOps processes enable organizations to release the deliverable with higher quality, enhanced security, stability with repeatable processes

DOI: 10.1201/9781003390893-19

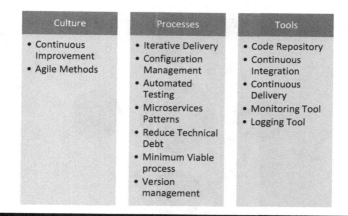

Figure 14.1   Impact of DevSecOps.

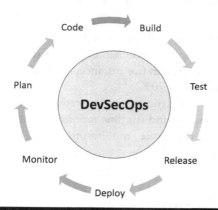

Figure 14.2   DevSecOps stages.

and increased business agility to improve the time to market and hence organizations can innovate faster.

Adopting DevSecOps practices helps organizations to effectively collaborate across various teams. The automation practices in the DevSecOps helps in the rapid and high-quality deliverables. Organizations can improve the speed and scale of their time to market. Organizations can increase their speed of innovation and grow quickly at scale by adopting the DevSecOps processes. DevSecOps enables organizations to achieve their business objectives (such as quicker time to market, faster innovation, faster product enhancements) by enforcing security policies and managing risk.

DevSecOps brings in the necessary prescriptive, preventive and detective security guardrails into the release management process thereby improving the overall security posture. DevSecOps processes can be designed to enforce the security prescriptions

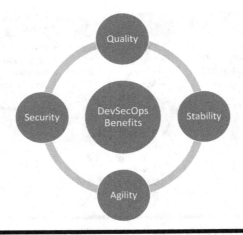

Figure 14.3   Advantages of DevSecOps processes.

(for instance, allow the code deployment only after security reviews), preventive guardrails (for instance, stop the code deployment if the unit test coverage is less than 90%) and detective guardrails (for instance, notify the administrator if the code quality percentage drops below 70%).

We include the static validation (such as static code analysis), dynamic validation (such as security testing) and runtime monitoring (such as threat monitoring, response monitoring, performance monitoring, auditing, logging) as part of DevSecOps processes.

DevSecOps Concepts

In this section we discuss the key success factors and tenets of DevSecOps. DevSecOps administrators and organizations can leverage the best practices detailed in the key success factors and DevSecOps tenets to build a robust DevSecOps practice.

Key Success Factors for DevSecOps

Implementing a robust DevSecOps practice involves building/using various tools and implementing the processes. Given below are the main success factors for building a robust DevSecOps.

Tool Integration

The DevSecOps pipeline needs various tools for build, test and deployment. For static code analysis and security testing, we can integrate Static Application Security

Testing (SAST) (for static analysis) and Dynamic Application Security Testing (DAST) tools (for dynamic analysis).

The DevSecOps administrator needs to identify the appropriate tool, integrate them with the main pipeline and secure the pipeline stages.

Process Definition

The DevSecOps administrator has to define the well-defined processes for each of the pipeline stages to achieve the business objective. For instance, the build stage of the DevSecOps pipeline should include the code review and approval steps to ensure that code is built only after appropriate reviews.

As part of agile delivery model, the team should define a minimum viable product (MVP) with just enough features needed for the product adoption. The team should perform smaller releases frequently. The failures should be automatically rolled back.

Skill Set Development

The organization has to train the DevSecOps engineers to develop the required skills in managing the DevSecOps tools. DevSecOps administrators should document the DevSecOps processes and standard operating procedures (SOP) to help the DevSecOps engineers. The organization should develop cross-functional teams who work independently to develop and own a specific service.

Security Policy Implementation

DevSecOps administrators should implement the security policies to ensure compliance to the organizational security policies. DevSecOps administrators should plug the security gaps if the underlying tools used in the pipeline lacks the required security controls for improving the overall security posture. For instance, if the chosen build tool lacks user authentication feature, DevSecOps administrator should add an additional authentication layer to secure the build stage in the pipeline.

Centralized Monitoring

The end-to-end DevSecOps pipeline should be visible through a centralized dashboard. DevSecOps enables administrators to centrally enforce uniform standards and governance. The entire team finalizes the KPIs and metrics such as time to market, code coverage percentage and build success percentage. Business stakeholders, program managers and DevSecOps engineers should be able to visualize the pipeline progress, the overall health of the project and the KPIs and metrics. The errors (such as build failures) and pipeline stages that breach the metric threshold (such as code coverage less than 90%) should trigger notifications to the appropriate stakeholders.

The deployment job should be monitored and in case of deployment failure the deployment should be automatically rolled back.

Automation

Automation is the prime tenet of DevSecOps. The DevSecOps pipeline steps are automated to enable faster release cycles and improved quality. We integrate tools and scripts to automate the core release management activities like building, testing, deployment and others.

Process automation drives the main benefits of DevSecOps processes. The core processes, such as testing, code quality checks and deployment, are automated. An example of deployment process automation is given below.

The developer checks in/commits the code to the master branch of the code repository. The deployment pipeline monitors the changes to the source code repository and the code commit triggers the static code analysis. Post the successful static code analysis, the pipeline automatically invokes the unit test stage where the code is automatically unit tested. If the overall test coverage is more than 90%, the deployment pipeline automatically builds and deploys the code to the development environment.

In the above example the complete build-test-deploy cycle is automated by the deployment pipeline. Users are notified only when there are errors in any of the stages.

Cost Control

DevSecOps administrators should choose the tools and servers to minimize the overall cost of the pipeline. DevSecOps administrators can leverage the open-source tools and on-demand public cloud resources to minimize the overall cost.

Pipeline Execution Time

The overall pipeline execution time (starting from build till deployment) should be kept minimum to minimize the disruption and to enable frequent enhancements and bug fixes. Automating the pipeline stages reduces the overall pipeline execution time.

Minimal Downtime

The DevSecOps processes should not disrupt the existing live environments and should cause minimal downtime. One of the best practices to ensure minimal downtime is to use blue-green deployment models where the updated version is deployed to the "green" environment with the "blue" environment running the current version of the code and serving the live traffic. Initially we can send a smaller percentage of the traffic (say 5%) traffic to the "green" environment and majority of the traffic is handled by the "blue" environment. We monitor the metrics (such as accuracy, performance) of the "green" environment and Once the users are satisfied with the performance and functionality of the "green" environment, we can deploy the updated code to "blue" environment.

Version Management

All the DevSecOps components, such as code, infrastructure, configuration and documentation, should be version controlled and should be treated like code.

Table 14.1 summarizes the key value differences that DevSecOps practices can bring to the organization.

DevSecOps Tenets

In this section we discuss the main tenets of DevSecOps such as integrated development, cross function collaboration, CI and others.

Integrated Development

The integrated development practice involves providing a collaborative and integrated environment for developers and project managers for development, code version

Table 14.1 DevSecOps Value Benefits

Category	Without DevSecOps	With DevSecOps
Infrastructure provisioning	Manual process taking days	Automated that can be done in minutes.
Application Deployment	Manual process taking hours Potential security risks	Secured and automated continuous delivery pipeline that can be completed in minutes.
Security	Ad-hoc security	Centralized and uniform security policies integrated into the pipeline
Monitoring	Non-centralized	Centralized and consolidated monitoring across all applications and across the environment.
Operational processes	Inconsistent processes for different platforms	Standard, consistent and automated processes.

control and project management. Tools such as GitHub and AWS CodeCommit serve as robust code version control systems; integrated development environment (IDE) such as AWS Cloud9, Eclipse and IntelliJ provide a seamless code development platform; and tools such as Atlassian Jira can be used for project planning.

Cross Function Collaboration and Communication

Various project teams, such as the development team, security team, operations team and testing team within the organization, can collaborate as one team using the DevSecOps processes.

Continuous Testing

We conduct unit testing, functional testing, security testing and performance testing in iterations. We test early and often with fail fast philosophy. The continuous testing discovers the defects early and reduces the overall risk.

Continuous Integration (CI)

CI is the set of processes and tools that are used to improve the overall delivery quality and optimize the delivery timelines. CI is focused on the code commit, build and unit testing as depicted in Figure 14.4.

As part of CI, we define the overall pipeline. The developer checks in the code and merges the code to the common source control system (such as GitLab). Once the code is checked in, the pipeline automatically triggers code quality checks, code unit testing and other automated checks.

CI enables developers across various teams to simultaneously develop the code and work in parallel. Once each of the developers complete unit testing, they merge the code into the common code source control system that is unit tested automatically through the pipeline.

Developers can rapidly release the feature requests and enhancements using CI. Continuous delivery process is responsible for packaging and building the artefacts that can be deployed across environments. The packaged artefacts are later deployed to deployment servers to carry out additional testing such as performance testing and security testing.

Continuous Monitoring

This practice helps identify issues or bottlenecks in the end-to-end pipeline and helps make the pipeline effective. We carry out various automated monitoring practices such as server health check monitoring, application monitoring, performance monitoring, security monitoring, availability monitoring and such.

Iterative Release

As part of the agile delivery model, we deliver the features in various iterations.

Modular Development

The code components are developed as loosely coupled, reusable, independent modules.

Continuous Deployment

Continuous deployment (CD) is the set of processes and tools to rapidly release the enhancements incrementally thereby improving the software delivery. CD automatically deploys the changes to the pre-production environments and also securely deploys to the production environment. CD improves the overall reliability of the pipeline. CD improves the bug fix time and reduces the overall risk and increases the deployment frequency.

Common steps in CD are depicted in Figure 14.4

CD automates the creation and deployment of build artefacts post CI process. As depicted in Figure 14.4, the CI integrates the code committed by various developers through code merging. Code merging triggers an automatic code build to run the pre-configured activities such as code reviews, unit tests and others. Continuous delivery automates the reliable delivery and release of the code artefacts to various environments.

We define the CD steps in Figure 14.4. Only the developers with appropriate access can do the code commit after the necessary approvals. Each phase in the pipeline has inbuilt security best practices.

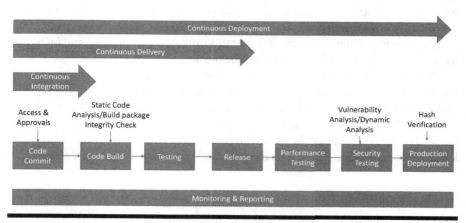

Figure 14.4 Continuous deployment steps.

For instance, the code commit stage needs appropriate access permissions and approvals for the developers to complete the code commit. We execute SAST in the code build stage to identify any code-level vulnerabilities. We also do the integrity check for the build packages to ensure the build integrity. During the security testing stage, we can do DAST to uncover the vulnerabilities (such as SQL injection vulnerabilities, cross-site scripting vulnerabilities and others). We can secure the production deployment through hash verification. We also include additional organization specific security processes in the pipeline.

We monitor all the stages of the pipeline and report the metrics (such as time taken for completion, error codes and such). When we automate the software delivery process, we can do frequent deployments enabling incremental business value with each deployment. Automation in CD also improves the delivery quality and the change management process and reduces security vulnerabilities.

CI and continuous delivery and continuous deployment (CD) enables organizations to scale the development and release management process. The CI/CD processes also automate the release management activities and improves the overall security posture.

Infrastructure as Code (IaC)

By treating the infrastructure as code, we can create standard and repeatable constructs to quickly provision the infrastructure across various environments. Infrastructure as code templates act as single source of truth for the infrastructure and are managed in version control systems like Github. When the IaC templates are in source control systems, we can plug them into the DevSecOps pipeline to automatically create the environments. IaC supplements the infrastructure management and leverages software management best practices to manage the IaC artefacts. We can replicate the infrastructure across various environments (production and non-production) using IaC.

The DevSecOps pipeline spans across various stages of release management. The pipeline comprises of infrastructure, application and data components and integrates with many workloads. We manage the pipeline also as a code.

We secure the DevSecOps pipeline through preventive and detective security controls. As part of preventive security control, we restrict who can run the pipeline and the environments in which they can run the pipeline. As part of detective controls of the pipeline, we monitor the logged in users, users who committed the code, the users who ran build and deploy jobs, the users whose code commit failed the build jobs, the code coverage percentage, the static and dynamic testing report and such.

Microservices Architecture

Legacy applications that were developed in a monolith architecture style where a small change impacts the entire application need greater time for testing and deployment. Modern applications need frequent enhancements and hence frequent changes. To drive the smaller changes frequently, the granular business functionality is created into microservices.

Microservices are logical units of functionality that are independently scalable and implement single responsibility principle (performs single functionality). Unlike monoliths, microservices can be developed in different programming languages that are best suited for the use case. Well-defined API contracts are used between microservices for communication.

Microservices are developed by leaner teams (often called two-pizza teams) that can independently take decisions. Individual team owns the microservices end to end from planning, design, development, security testing, operations, bug fixing, documentation and other activities of the microservice.

The development life cycle (build, integrate, test, deploy and monitor) of microservice happens frequently leading to faster deployments. We have discussed more about microservices in chapter 5.

Configuration Management

The configuration management system manages the configurations for all environments. For instance, we use source control system to manage the code and configuration for various environments where the code will be deployed. Artefact repository manages the deployable code artefacts for various environments.

Observability (Monitoring and Logging)

We deploy tools to measure and monitor the key metrics. We continuously monitor the metrics that impact the customer experience and system performance. We log the application events and metrics, security events, infrastructure metrics (such as CPU utilization, memory utilization) and perform the proactive alerting.

We can setup auto remediation processes for alerts with known remediation steps. For instance, when the alerting system detects a server-down scenario, the auto remediation process can restart the server using the startup scripts.

DevSecOps Tools

We have given the common tools used for DevSecOps in Table 14.2.

DevSecOps Metrics

We have depicted the main metrics in the DevSecOps pipeline in Figure 14.5. The key metrics for the overall DevSecOps process are time to market (the total time taken for releasing a product to market since its inception), total cost of the ownership and security.

Table 14.2 DevSecOps Tools

Category	Tools
Build tool	Maven, AWS CodeBuild, Gradle, Jenkins
Source control system	GitLab, SVN
Continuous integration	Atlassian Bamboo, AWS CodePipleines, BitBucket Pipelines, Jenkins, CircleCI, GitLab
Continuous delivery	Shippable, Jenkins
Container platform	Docker
Logging and monitoring	New Relic, Datadog, Splunk, Sysdig, Amazon CloudWatch, SumoLogic, Nagios
Infrastructure as Code	Terraform, Chef, Puppet, AWS CloudFormation
Application performance monitoring	AppDynamics, Dynatrace, New Relic
Configuration management	Puppet, Chef, Ansible
Load testing automation	Apache JMeter, SmartBear, Qmetry, LoadRunner
Mobile app quality profile	SonarLint, SwiftLink, Android Kotlin, SonarQube, OWASP Dependency Check
Code quality	SonarQube, FindBugs, Checkstyle, JSLint
Code coverage	Clover
Security tools	Burp Suite, AppScan
Mobile app distribution	AppCenter, Playstore alpha/beta, TestFlight
Artifact repository	AppCenter, JFrog

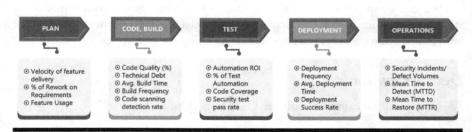

Figure 14.5 DevSecOps metrics.

At each of the Software Development Life Cycle (SDLC) phases, we mainly measure the velocity of feature delivery (the speed with which the team can deliver the planed features) and requirements rework percentage during planning phase.

During code build, we monitor the code quality (using variables such as code complexity, coupling, security, code duplicacy, code portability and such), build frequency (how often the code is built), average build time and code scanning detection rate (rate of defect detection from code scanning). During test phase, the main metrics are percentage of test automation (total percentage of tests automated), code coverage (percentage of source code covered by the test cases) and security test pass rate.

The main metrics during the deployment phase are deployment frequency (number of deployments per day), average deployment time and deployment success rate. The main metrics during the operations phase are percentage of security incidents, mean time to detect (the amount of time a deployment issue existed before it is detected) and mean time to restore (the average amount of time needed to recover from the failure).

A case study of Migration to DevSecOps

Organizations who are yet to adopt the robust DevSecOps processes would most likely be using disintegrated processes and inconsistent security policies. Moving to the DevSecOps setup enables such organizations to ensure centralized and uniform operational processes and implement consistent security policies.

In this section, we detail a case study of migrating from existing release management and deployment processes into a cloud-native DevSecOps setup.

Current State of Release Management

The code release management is handled on-premise in the current setup. Multiple tools, security policies and processes are used in the existing release management process. Due to the absence of a standardized code merge and branching process, developers often overwrite each other's code resulting in integration issues and build failures. The build engineer has to manually perform the build leading to delays. As there is no automated testing process, the testing team has to manually deploy the code to the server and carry out functional testing. The project manager does not have visibility into the overall health of the project (such as build failures, code quality metrics, code coverage metrics etc.). Code promotion to production is done manually.

As a result of non-standardized processes and lack of automation, it takes five to seven days to deploy the tested code to production even though there is a minor code change. Lack of automation has also impacted the productivity of the various teams.

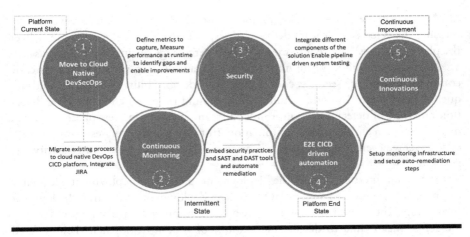

Figure 14.6   DevSecOps migration design.

Migration Design

We have depicted the migration design for existing release management process to the cloud-native DevSecOps as depicted in Figure 14.6.

The initial step is to setup the DevSecOps processes to automate the build, deployment and code quality activities. We can implement the DevSecOps at on-premise environment or on the cloud. The cloud setup is preferred as it offers native integration with DevSecOps tools and optimizes the overall cost.

Once the DevSecOps processes are implemented, we setup the continuous monitoring tools to monitor the metrics and KPIs in real time. The metrics help us to take remediation steps quickly.

We implement uniform and centralized security policies across the DevSecOps pipeline. We also integrate with SAST tools such as SonarQube for static code analysis and DAST tools such as OWASP ZAP to identify the security vulnerabilities in the module.

We enable the event-driven architecture for the entire pipeline wherein the process steps are automated and are driven by events of interest. For instance, a code check-in event triggers the code build and a code build completion event triggers the code deployment process in the pipeline.

The DevSecOps provides quicker feedback loops that help us to validate the security and testing processes and continuously improve the processes. We can also setup auto-remediation steps to automatically mitigate the common issues with known resolution steps (such as server outage requiring server restart).

DevSecOps Implementation Case study

In this section we discuss the implementation of on-premise and cloud-based DevSecOps to address the current challenges.

Automation and process optimization are key goals that are factored in while setting up the on-premise or cloud-native DevSecOps.

On-premise-based DevSecOps

We have depicted the on-premise DevSecOps in Figure 14.7. In order to automate the release management processes, we have selected the best-of-breed tools in the DevSecOps pipeline as depicted in the Figure 14.7.

In the "Plan and Develop" stage, we plan the user stories, features and backlog in Jira. The Java-based code is developed in Eclipse IDE and Apache Junit is used for local unit testing. Once the code is locally unit tested, it is checked into centralized Bitbucket repository. We create various branches in Bitbucket to manage the code deployments. Production code is managed in Master branch; trunk branch manages the development code and hot-fix branch is used for managing the production hotfixes.

In the "Integrate and Test" stage, we setup an event-driven automation in the pipeline. As soon as the code is checked into the Bitbucket dev branch, Jenkins CI triggers the build pipeline. The build pipeline pulls the code, uses Apache Maven for building the code, Junit for unit testing the code, Selenium for functional testing and SonarQube for code quality analysis. All the pipeline activities are automated. The bugs detected during the pipeline are logged in Jira for tracking and resolution.

In the "Deploy" stage, we package the code artefacts that successfully complete the code quality analysis and testing and store the package in the JFrog artefact

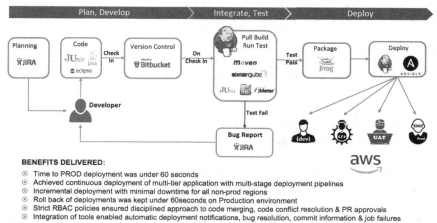

Figure 14.7   On-premise DevSecOps setup.

repository. Jenkins deploy job pulls the code artefacts from the JFrog artefact repository and deploys to various environments.

Cloud-Based DevSecOps

A cloud-native DevSecOps provides more optimal operational resiliency, better security and lower cost when compared to the on-premise DevSecOps. Cloud-based DevSecOps also has the advantage of providing pre-built and integrated services that would be easier to implement. We have depicted the AWS cloud based DevSecOps in Figure 14.8.

We can use Jira to plan and develop user stories and manage the bugs. The cloud-native tools offer better traceability and management. AWS CodePipelines are integrated with the native tools for managing the end-to-end deployment. Developer checks in the code to AWS CodeCommit for code version control, branching and merging to create a structured code base. We integrate developer security tools (such as WhiteSource), code review tools (such as SonarQube) and unit testing tools (such as Apache JMeter) with the pipeline. The pipeline is also integrated with Selenium—a functional testing tool for automating the functional testing.

The CI pipeline automatically builds the code, performs additional code quality checks using code quality tools and vulnerability assessment tools. Post successful code quality check, the pipeline prepares the artefact and publishes the artefact to the AWS CodeArtifact. The build failures and test failures are logged to Jira.

Continuous delivery (CD) is implemented using AWS CodePipelines that pulls the artefact from the AWS CodeArtifact and deploys the artefact to the Dev, QA, staging and production virtual machines. We continuously monitor the deployment using Amazon CloudWatch.

DevSecOps Benefits

Given below are the key benefits from the DevSecOps setup:

- Time to production deployment was improved.
- Achieved CD of multitier application with multistage deployment pipelines.
- Incremental deployment with minimal downtime for all non-production environments.
- Rollback of deployments was error free on production environment.
- Strict role-based access control (RBAC) policies ensured disciplined approach to code merging, code conflict resolution and PR approvals.
- Integration of tools enabled automatic deployment notifications, bug resolution, commit information and job failures.

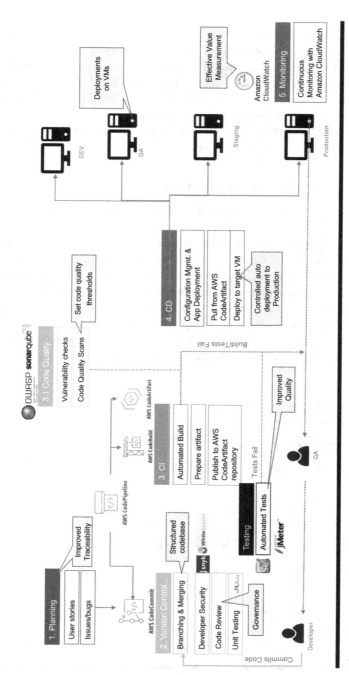

Figure 14.8 DevSecOps setup on cloud.

AIOps

We are living in an era where most of the tasks, processes and day-to-day activities are getting increasingly automated by machines. Automation brings in productivity, convenience, time savings, cost savings that allow humans to invest their time and energy in more valuable and complex tasks. Machine-led automation is revolutionizing the way we live, communicate, work and do business. AI-led systems are becoming ubiquitous, impacting modern human civilization in numerous forms and re-defining the daily tasks in our lives.

AIOps—Usage of AI in DevSecOps

We can leverage AI methods in many of the DevSecOps phases. We have depicted the DevSecOps phases where AI can be enabled in Figure 14.9.

In the "plan" stage, the AI services can be leveraged to create shift left design. The structured activities, such as scheduling and dependency resolution, can be automated and can be "shifted left" to self-service models. We can also build auto-remediation tools to automatically take corrective actions using the known remediation methods. Machine learning models can be used to build auto-triaging of tickets by assigning the tickets to appropriate resolution groups based on the ticket metadata. We can also build ticket resolution bots to handle the tickets that have structured problem statement with well-defined solution steps (such as granting access, restarting server,

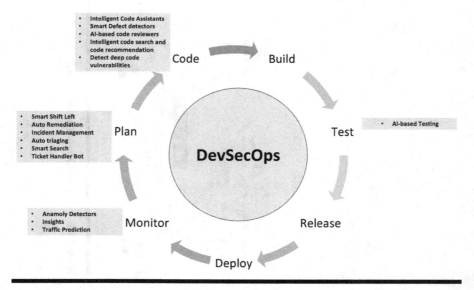

Figure 14.9   AIOps.

running a job, answering a query etc.). We can also AI-enable the search functionality to provide contextual and personalized results.

The "code" stage of the DevSecOps has many AI-enablement opportunities. AI-based code assistants can help developers in many activities such as code completion, co-piloting and recommending a piece of code based on natural language description and others. Developers can also leverage Artificial Intelligence (AI)-based intelligent code search tools and code recommendation tools to apply proven coding patterns. AI-based deep code reviewers can detect vulnerabilities and defects.

In the "test" stage we can adopt AI-based testing methods to identify the deep vulnerabilities in the application. In the "monitor" stage, we setup the real-time monitoring infrastructure to monitor the KPIs and metrics for application, infrastructure resources, network and others. We log the related monitoring metrics into a centralized logging platform. We can then use AI-based methods to detect anomalies from the metrics in real time. For instance, AI method can detect anomalous network-related patterns such as sudden spike in requests from a foreign territory or sudden spike in requests to malicious sites. We can also predict traffic and resource utilization using AI methods.

Case Study 14.1 GitLab-Based DevSecOps

We have detailed a DevSecOps setup using GitLab, a popular DevOps tool, in this section. Various stages of the DevSecOps is depicted in Figure 14.10.

During the planning stage, we use JIRA for project management activities such as user-story management, task creation, assigning and tracking tasks, project planning, issue tracking and others. We use tools such as Eclipse for code build and unit testing.

For managing the source code we create the GitLab repository and create the branches. As a general best practice, we use feature branch for user story and feature development; dev branch for development; release branch for stable releases; master branch for production code; and hotfix branch for hotfixes.

The GibLab pipeline provides a build to release pipeline using various tools. The GitLab pipeline.yml file serves as package manager for managing the dependencies, such as Maven and NPM, to build and compile. We use tools such as SonarQube for code quality checks, Selenium for functional testing and DAST tools such as OWASP ZAP to identify security vulnerabilities. Once the artifacts are successful built, and signed artefacts are uploaded to the artefact repository (such as JFrog

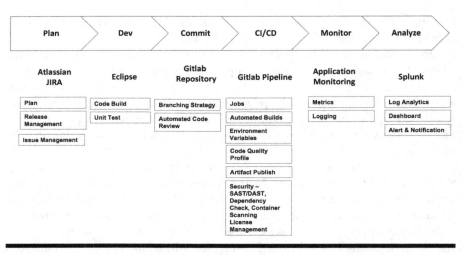

Figure 14.10 GitLab-based DevSecOps.

artefact repository). Dependency scanner tools identify external dependencies. License management process compiles all the licenses used in the build.

Once the artefacts are deployed, we monitor the KPIs and metrics related to performance and availability of the application. We use log analytics tools, such as Splunk or SumoLogic, to monitor the logs in a dashboard and get real-time alerts and notifications.

Case Study 14.2 Testing Automation Using DevSecOps

Various testing activities can be automated using the DevSecOps pipeline. We have depicted the testing scenarios that can be automated in Figure 14.11.

The testing for various applications, such as web application, mobile application, APIs and microservices, can be automated through the validation step in the DevSecOps pipeline. The driver scripts or plugins for testing tools, such as Selenium and Appium, can be built as part of the automation framework to execute various tests (such as functional testing, regression testing, web-based testing, data driven testing etc.). The test results are logged and the identified defects are created in defect management tool.

REST API and microservice testing can be automated using frameworks such as Rest Assured and Postman. The API responses are validated using automation tools.

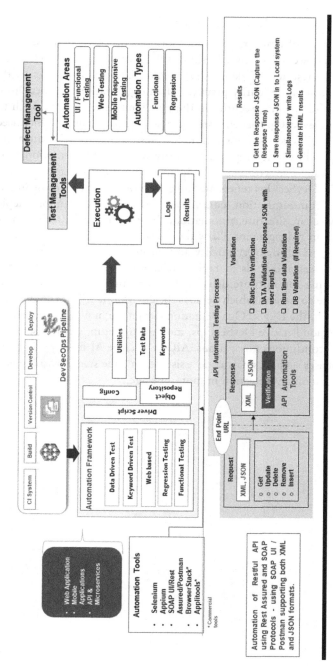

Figure 14.11 Testing automation using DevOps.

Summary

DevSecOps is a set of practices, culture, tools and processes that uses automation to frequently and securely deliver business value. The main DevSecOps stages are plan, code, build, test, release, deploy and monitor. DevSecOps integrates the development, operations and security practices of an organization. DevSecOps enforces the security of the pipeline, security in the pipeline and security through the pipeline. The main DevSecOps benefits are increased security, stability, increased agility and high quality. The key success factors for DevSecOps are tool integration, process definition, skill set development, security policy implementation, centralized monitoring, automation, cost control, pipeline execution time and minimal downtime. The main DevSecOps tenets are integrated development, cross function collaboration and communication, continuous integration, continuous deployment, IaC, microservices architecture, automation, observability (monitoring and logging) and configuration management. CI is the set of processes and tools that are used to improve the overall delivery quality and optimize the delivery timeline. CD is the set of processes and tools to rapidly release the enhancements incrementally thereby improving the software delivery. Infrastructure as code (IaC) treats infrastructure as code constructs which deploys the environment from configuration file. The main steps in the DevSecOps migration design are moving the existing process to on-premise/cloud-native DevSecOps, monitoring setup, security setup, automation setup and continuous innovations. AIOps leverage AI methods in many of the DevSecOps phases such as smart code assistants in code stage, auto remediation in plan phase and anomaly detection in monitor stage.

DIGITAL TRANSFORMATION CASE STUDIES

VI

Chapter 15

Digital Transformation Case Studies

Introduction

Organizations embark the digital transformation journey to reimagine the user experience, business processes and migrate to the latest technologies to get a competitive edge. The digital transformation involves various activities such as user experience redesign, data/content migration, cloud migration, re-building the services and others.

The digital transformation case studies provide insight into the practical scenarios of digital transformation journeys. The main types of digital transformation case studies can be categorized into four categories—strategy (business model)-centric actions, customer-centric actions, organizational-centric actions and technology-centric actions [1].

Strategy (business model)-centric actions are related to the disruptions of the industry that create new business models or redefine the current business models and redefine the value proposition. Customer-centric actions result in redesigning a customer-first user experience with an outside-in approach while engaging the customers by blending the physical and virtual experiences. Organizational-centric Actions involve the organizational changes such as fostering digital culture, understanding critical success factors of digital transformation and organizational focus. Technology-centric actions focuses on technological changes such as systems integration, analytics-driven insights and cross-platform development [1].

DOI: 10.1201/9781003390893-21

In this chapter, we discuss in detail a case study each on customer-centric action and technology-centric action. The first case study of hybrid cloud implementation of an e-commerce platform is a technology-centric action where the company used cloud to increase its business agility and reduce cost. The second case study on digital transformation of a utility's portal is a customer-centric case study.

We have detailed the case study using the four core elements (strategy and vision, people and culture, digital transformation technology and capabilities and process and governance) of the digital transformation we discussed in Chapter 1.

Case Study 15.1 Hybrid Cloud Journey of an e-Commerce Platform

The purpose of this case study is to lay out the details of the cloud migration solution of an e-commerce platform. The case study outlines a cloud-based, cost-effective, scalable and high performing solution.

XYZ e-commerce is a leading e-commerce player in the country and wants to accelerate the innovation and engage effectively with its customers digitally. The user base of XYZ e-commerce has doubled since last year and the users are increasingly finding it hard to access the platform. During the holiday seasons the platform faces performance issues and availability issues. XYZ e-commerce platform was built 15 years back and runs on Java-based server technologies running on WebSphere application server. XYZ e-commerce wants to leverage cloud to innovate faster and reduce cost.

The current customer base of XYZ e-commerce is at 10K users with about 1,000 concurrent users during peak traffic. The performance of the platform drops to 20 seconds for each page response time. The engineering team has identified the root cause for the performance issue to the underlying infrastructure not able to scale to the peak demands.

Due to these reasons XYZ e-commerce organization has decided to embark on the digital transformation initiative. The major technology decision is to migrate to public cloud to leverage the elastic scalability and reduce the cost.

We will now examine various elements of this digital transformation journey.

Strategy and Vision

The long-term vision of the XYZ e-commerce is to become the most customer friendly e-commerce platform. To achieve the long-term vision, the organization defined the goals, cloud technologies and value chain impact as depicted in Figure 15.1.

The primary goal that XYZ e-commerce wants to achieve is a cloud-first design to leverage the native features of the cloud. XYZ e-commerce wants to rearchitect

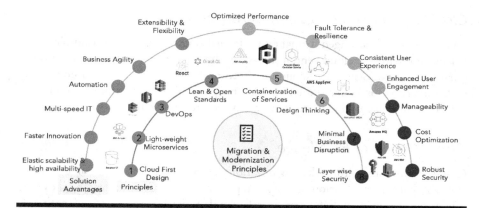

Figure 15.1   Strategy and vision of XYZ e-commerce.

the current monolith platform into light-weight microservices and use DevOps for seamless release management. The company also wants to move away from proprietary APIs to open standards. To enable on-demand scalability the company is planning to containerize the microservices. To provide engaging and inspiring user experience, the company is planning to use design thinking methodology. The company wants to minimize business disruption during the cloud migration journey. To provide defense in depth security for the overall platform, layer-wise security and principle of least privilege are planned to be used.

The main impact areas on the value chain envisioned from the digital transformation are elastic scalability and high availability to cater to peak traffic. The company wants to be agile and innovate faster by rolling out the new products and services to its customer on the cloud. Using cloud and containers, the company wants to improve the scalability and optimize the overall performance of the platform. Using the multi-node cluster, the company wants to improve the resilience and the company plans to provide the enhanced and consistent user experience through design thinking. The company plans to leverage the on-demand cloud resources to optimize the overall cost.

As XYZ e-commerce has chosen to use AWS cloud platform, the main cloud-native technologies are chosen. AWS services such as Amazon S3, AWS Fargate, AWS CodePipeline, AWS Amplify, Amazon API Gateway, Amazon RDS, Amazon MQ, AWS KMS and AWS WAF are planned to be used. We have detailed the technologies in a separate section.

People and Culture

The XYZ e-commerce planned the cloud migration in iterations. To enable the seamless cloud journey, the organization brought in the below given programs and culture changes to enable the people.

Cloud Fluency Trainings and Certifications

XYZ e-commerce arranged formal and informal trainings on cloud technologies in partnership with the cloud vendor. Based on the roles, people were given option to pursue various tracks such as cloud architecture, cloud development, cloud security or Cloud DevOps tracks. Post trainings, people took up certification exams that helped them to gain good understanding in their respective tracks.

Cloud Center of Excellence

Cloud champions within the organization setup the cloud center of excellence (CCoE) that formed the cloud innovation power house. CCoE was leading the cloud migration roadmap, defined the overall cloud migration solution and evaluated various cloud technologies that best fit the requirements. The subject matter experts (SMEs) at CCoE also helped the migration teams when they encountered complex issues.

Collaboration Platform

XYZ e-commerce developed a knowledge management platform where employees can share the knowledge articles and learnings. CCoE authored the documents that covered standards, best practices, technology evaluation and detailed design documents. The migration teams also contributed the learnings and best practices of the cloud journey.

Innovation Hackathons

The company scheduled innovation hackathons to solicit innovative ideas from the community. The innovation hackathons used design thinking concepts to build a minimum viable product (MVP) from the ideas. Employees formed smaller teams (usually a two-pizza team structure consisting of about 8–10 members) and worked on implementing their ideas. The mentors from the CCoE helped them in evaluating the design and helped them to scale the idea. The innovation hackathons were a huge success as XYZ e-commerce was able to use many of the products, such as migration accelerator, employee chatbots and database migrator, in the actual migration to automate the efforts.

Digital Transformation Technology and Capabilities

CCoE evaluated various technologies that are best aligned with the defined strategy and vision. We have given the list of evaluated technologies and the final recommendation in Table 15.1.

Table 15.1 Technology Evaluation

On-Premise Component	Cloud-Native Options	Recommendation	Rationale for Recommendation
Web components based on Java Servlets with Stateful Authentication	Containerized microservices, AWS Lambda, AWS Elastic Beanstalk, Hosted Microservices, Rehosting/lift and shift Java Servlets, AWS AppSync, IaaS model	Serverless Amazon ECS containers with AWS Fargate. AWS AppSync with stateless model	Aligned with cloud-first design, containerization principles. Pay-as-you-go model provided the optimal cost.
Java Server pages	React, Angular, JSP, AWS Amplify, AWS AppSync	React with AWS Amplify	Aligned with open standards principle. Cloud-native libraries improved the overall developer productivity.
IBM WebSphere Application Server	Amazon ECS with AWS Fargate, IBM WebSphere Server running on Amazon EC2, AWS Lambda	Amazon ECS with AWS Fargate	Designed for failure, evolutionary design, fault tolerance, serverless containers manageable, high scalability, high performance.
Jenkins with Maven	AWS CodeBuild, AWS CodeDeploy, AWS CodeCommit, Jenkins, Git Pipeline	AWS CodeBuild, AWS CodeDeploy, AWS CodeCommit	Aligned with cloud-first design.
Nagios monitoring	Amazon CloudWatch Amazon OpenSearch, Nagios	Amazon CloudWatch+ Amazon OpenSearch + Kibana, log monitoring, automated notification	Aligned with cloud-first design. Automated monitoring and notification.

(Continued)

Table 15.1 (Continued)

On-Premise Component	Cloud-Native Options	Recommendation	Rationale for Recommendation
Oracle Database	Amazon RDS, Amazon DynamoDB	Amazon RDS	Aligned with cloud-first design. Managed database that provides inbuilt backup feature.
Traditional HTTP/HTTPS/ SOAP	REST, GraphQL, HTTPS	REST, GraphQL, HTTPS	Lightweight, fast and interactive response model.

Process and Governance

As part of process and governance the XYZ organization used planning, building and optimizing to ensure minimal risk and smooth migration. We have defined various activities of the process and governance activity

Planning

The initial step in the planning process was to thoroughly understand the current state, potential challenges, the aspirations of the organization and the concerns as part of the requirements discovery phase. The key outcome of the requirements discovery phase is documented in Figure 15.2.

In understanding the context, we identified the key current state components such as on-premise infrastructure, legacy technologies and others. The key challenges with the current infrastructure were lack of agility, slow performance, high infrastructure cost and high maintenance cost. Defining the context helps us to identify the solution components and the migration roadmap to address the challenges. We also identify the aspirations and migration concerns as part of the future goals. XYZ e-commerce aspires to innovate faster on cloud and wants to leverage the cloud-native features to provide elastic scalability, high availability and resilience. XYZ e-commerce wants to build fault tolerant systems and improve manageability of the overall infrastructure. The potential challenges in the cloud migration are lack of the in-house cloud skills and the security on cloud. The key challenge is to execute the cloud migration without any business disruption.

Having understood all the dimensions of the cloud migration, we now define the cloud migration methodology to address the migration concerns. We have depicted the cloud migration roadmap in Figure 15.3.

The first step of the migration methodology is to analyze and understand the requirements. We have discussed the elements of requirements discovery such as

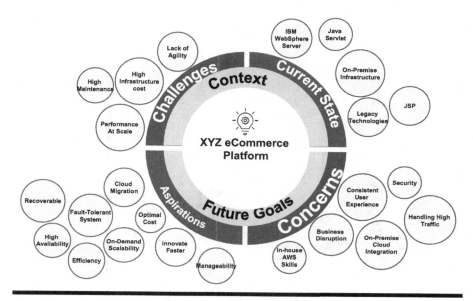

Figure 15.2   Requirements discovery outcome.

challenges, aspirations and current state in Figure 15.2. The second step is to lay out the migration principles which we had depicted in Figure 15.1 as part of strategy and vision phase. The CCoE defines the guidelines, principles and patterns as part of migration and modernization principles. The CCoE team compares and evaluates the technologies to select the best of breed products and technologies that are needed for the migration. Once the technology stack is identified, CCoE defines various architecture views such as solution architecture, integration view, infrastructure view, security view and others. Finally, we define the migration plan and cutover plan. We have detailed the migration phases in Figure 15.4.

One of the core planning activities is to identity the potential risks and define a mitigation plan for each of them. We have defined the risk mitigation options for XYZ e-commerce in Table 15.2.

Building

In the building stage, we carry out the migration in iterations as depicted in Figure 15.4.

To minimize the risk and business disruption, XYZ e-commerce planned a three-phase migration. The initial phase was to assess the readiness. During the assessment phase the CCoE team assess the existing technology ecosystem and elaborated the requirements. CCoE then came up with the application rationalization plan where they identified the applications that can be consolidated, the applications that

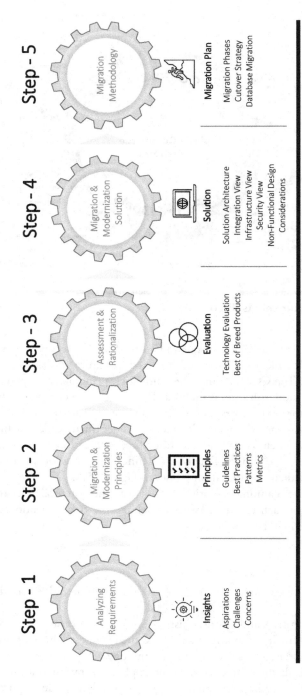

Figure 15.3 Cloud migration methodology.

Table 15.2   Risk Mitigation Options

Risk	Mitigation Options
Developers lacks sufficient AWS skills leading to productivity issues and impacts the migration timelines.	Developers will be trained on AWS services. Along with formal training, self-learning will be encouraged.
Big bang migration leading to business disruption or possible loss of data.	Phased migration strategy consisting of iterative migration sprints will be adopted. We can do a pilot migration to evaluate the migration strategy. A thorough migration testing is done after each migration sprint.
Potential performance issues with on-premise integration with billing, payments and rewards platform.	Conduct a proof of concept (PoC) to validate the performance and scalability of the chosen integration methodology.

need to retired and the applications that need to be moved to the cloud. For the applications that are planned for the cloud migration, the CCoE team identified the cloud-native technologies as defined in Table 15.1.

In phase 2, XYZ e-commerce used iterative migration strategy to minimize the migration risk. Each migration sprint involved the architecture and design stage that designed the solution components for that specific sprint. The initial foundation sprint sets up the AWS environment and the core services such as relational database service, network component and security components. We also define the migration test plan for all the sprints. The core capabilities are implemented in capability sprints in iterations; web page development, GraphQL-based microservices and data migration happen in sprints. After each migration sprint, migration testing is done to ensure the completeness of the migration and data integrity.

In the management phase, we monitor the defined metrics and key performance indicators (key performance indicators) and continuously improve the solution.

Optimizing

As part of continuous optimization, we monitor the key metrics such as availability, performance and user traffic to ensure that the migrated solution is performing as expected. We also continuously migrate the solution in phases to the cloud and optimize the infrastructure cost using the pay-as-you-go model in the cloud. Using the cloud-native features, we also offer new digital products and solutions, such as serverless functions, containers and cloud-managed services, to leverage the full benefit of the cloud.

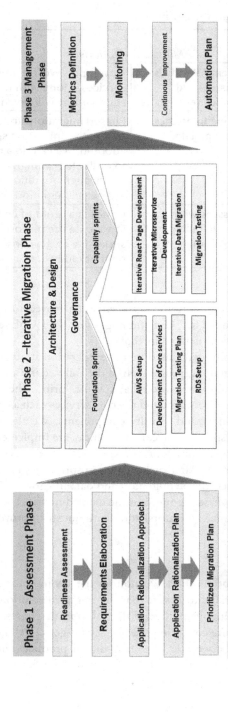

Figure 15.4 Migration phases.

Case Study 15.2 Digital Transformation of a Utilities Portal

The case study is the digital transformation of a legacy portal platform to modern web platform to cater to B2C consumers. The utilities portal offered end users to view and pay their utility bills and understand the maintenance schedules. The application provided other features such as registration, content authoring functionality, profile management, search and such. The utilities portal was built using legacy technology using IBM WebSphere Portal 6.1 (WPS) that used heavy SOAP-based webservices and WSRP calls for integration. The utilities portal solution offered a traditional user interface (UI) based on Java Server Pages (JSPs). Due to the heavy integrations the end users faced frequent performance issues.

The organization wanted to reimagine the solution to make it more customer-centric by providing the customer-first UI design, user-friendly information architecture, easier information search capability and other intuitive features.

As part of the strategy and vision we had summarized the key solution tenets along with trends in the digital platforms. For complex enterprise platforms, we had tracked the trends along various dimensions such as architecture shift, technology shift, integration shift and others and marked the recommended tenets for the solution. We have depicted the main solution tenets that will be used for modernizing the solution.

The primary focus is on optimizing the customer journey. This includes the intuitive information architecture and using domain-driven model for the solution. We also identified the key technology design patterns that are to be used for the modernized solution. As depicted in Figure 15.5, we have defined the layered microservices, standards-based open source software, API-first design, platform as service (PaaS), distributed database, featured-based delivery and DevOps as the guiding principles while defining the solution.

People and Culture

The main culture-related change for this large transformation program is to have a collaborative environment across all the team members. We have detailed the best practices of the collaboration culture in this section.

As part of agile methodology and collaboration, we use the demos and proof-of-value (PoV) exercise to collaborate frequently with customers and business stakeholders. We have detailed these concepts in the next section.

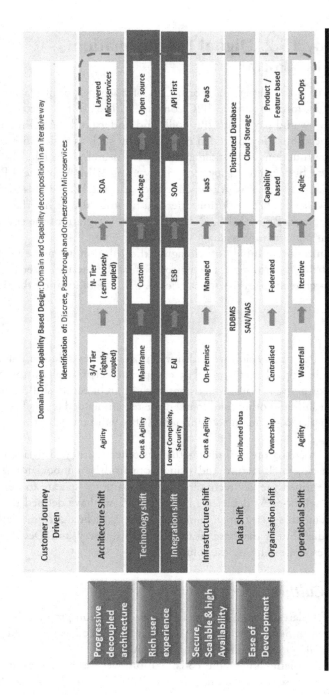

Figure 15.5 Digital transformation principles for modern platform.

Collaboration across Various teams

As this was a large project there has to be an effective collaboration multiple teams such as requirements elaboration team (BAs), cloud team/infra team, security team (Okta), testing team etc.

Given below are the best practices we followed to ensure a smooth execution:

- We clearly defined the roles and responsibilities and Single Point of Contact (SPOC) for each of the tracks.
- For any complex troubleshooting sessions, we involve track leads for faster debugging.
- We establish open communication channel so that any person can contact the SPOC of other track for support to speed up the delivery.
- The project plan clearly defined the timelines and dependencies for each of the tracks.
- Conduct an all-hands meet with all leads from all tracks twice daily. We conduct a 30-minute standup meeting during the start of the day and at the end of the day.
- The program manager was centrally managing the schedule, open risks and dependencies for each of the tracks.

Demos

We carried out the frequent demos of the in-progress application to proactively seek the feedback from the end users. Additionally, we had carried out the business user acceptance testing (UAT) for each of the monthly releases to ensure that there are no major gaps at the end of the project.

Proof of Value and Proof of Concepts

We carried out the following proof of concepts (PoCs) that helped us to assess the design feasibility:

- Mobile-first experience design using Drupal and ReactJS
- Cloud integration over the Internet vs. secured connectivity
- Okta integration with the ReactJs and Spring Boot application
- Blue/Green Deployment for high availability

Digital Transformation Technologies and Capabilities

We deliberated on various technology choices for the solution. We have listed the technology choices and the selected technology along with the rationale for selection in Table 15.3

Table 15.3   Technology Choices for Modernizing Utilities Portal

Technology Choice	Selected Technology	Rationale for Selection
UI Framework— Angular vs. React	ReactJS	Angular is a full-fledged UI framework whereas React can complement the Drupal technology. Additionally, React has powerful UI libraries that are needed for the application
On-premise vs. cloud hosting	AWS Cloud hosting	Cost optimization. On-demand provisioning. Elastic scalability.
Cloud platform— AWS vs. Azure	AWS	RDS service Better support for open-source tools and software. Amazon OpenSearch supports both Redis and Memcached.
REST-based microservices vs. SOAP-based web services	REST-based microservice	Stateless model. Decoupled architecture. Good performance.

Process and Governance

We have defined the detailed activities in planning and governance phase here.

Planning

We detail the existing challenges and digital transformation principles and define the capability roadmap in the planning phase.

Understanding Current Challenges

Table 15.4 lists the main challenges in the existing application.

Digital Transformation Principles

After analyzing the existing challenges, we defined the principles for the digital transformation exercise as shown in Figure 15.6.

In Figure 15.6 we have covered the guiding principles categorized into various categories such as governance and value, customer experience, technology and innovation and organizational transformation.

Table 15.4 Current Challenges with Utilities Portal

Challenge	Description
Technology complexity	• Too many products added to the overall technology complexity. • Too many integrations involved.
Performance and availability issues	• Too many integrations are also causing performance and availability issues for the website. • Certain inefficiencies in the front-end code as well as poor performance of back-end services.
Productivity issues	• The inherent complexity of the portal is resulting into greater time to implement. • Missing common, reusable component and frameworks. • Too many products leading to different teams thus creating coordination issues.
High maintenance cost	• High software licensing and support costs. • High development, testing and skill cost involved.
High infrastructure cost	• Current portal platforms are comparatively heavyweight product requiring high server configurations. • Missing a single, modern product offering combining functionalities in overall digital space. • Dedicated infrastructure required for both IBM- and .Net-based stack.

To align with the overall strategy, we define the key digital transformation principles. To provide customer-centric experience, we need to provide omni-channel-enabled self-service and consistent experience for all customers. On the technology front, we define the key principles as stateless design, APIfication, microservices-based APIs, process automation, DevOps-based business agility, multi-tenancy, containerization and using open standards for integration.

Roadmap Definition

We defined a three-year roadmap for modernizing the legacy utilities portal. The high-level details of the roadmap are given below:

In the first year, we migrate the critical functionality like registration, login and static and key integrations along with data migration, cloud transition, complete DevOps, basic self-service and basic analytics. In the second year, we implement the collaboration features with basic automation and develop mobile apps. In the third year, we build business self-service, social media integration and advanced analytics.

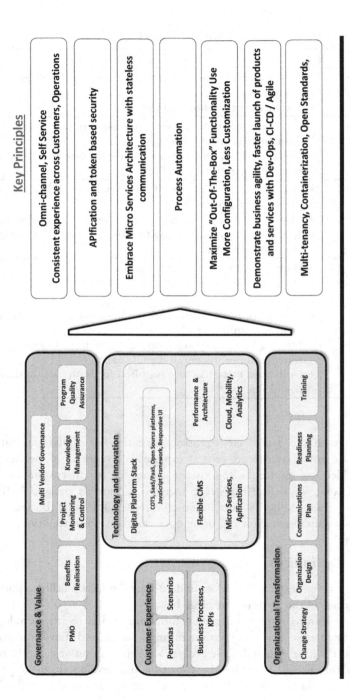

Figure 15.6 High-level solution layers.

Building

In this section, we detail the various solution components. We have detailed the solution layers and non-functional requirements (NFR) design considerations and the rollout strategy in this phase.

Solution Architecture of the Modern Utility's Portal

We have detailed the new solution that we had proposed as part of the digital transformation in this section. The new solution implements the digital transformation principles detailed in Figure 15.5.

Application Layers

We have depicted the high-level layers of the new solution in Figure 15.7. Each of the layers has distinct responsibility (single responsibility principle) and the components in each of the layers are designed based on modular and extensible principle.

Components across the layers are loosely coupled so that it will be flexible to switch and extend the technologies and products in the future.

High-Level Solution

We have depicted the high-level solution in Figure 15.7.

The overall solution consists of the below given layers.

System of Interaction

In this layer we used Drupal with ReactJS. For static marketing content we used the native Drupal CMS for managing the content. We used React blocks for dynamic content. The combination of Drupal and ReactJS provides best of both the worlds. Drupal provides in-built CMS features such as content authoring, multi-lingual content, taxonomy, search, archival, versioning and such. ReactJS provides the light-weight yet powerful UI framework.

Systems of Differentiation

The React framework gets the dynamic data through Spring Boot-based microservices. The granular microservices are modeled based on the view requirements. The Sprint Boot framework is also responsible for managing the Okta-based tokens, request validation, security filtering, logging, caching and others.

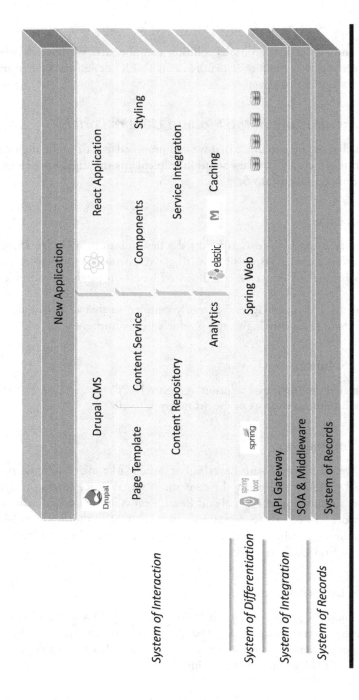

Figure 15.7 High-level solution of the modern utility's portal.

Systems of Integration

We used the API gateway to get the data from the backend systems.

System of Record

The core capabilities are fulfilled by the enterprise systems. The customer profile information, billing information, reporting systems are part of this category.

Progressive Decoupled Architecture

We used the separation of concerns, layered architecture and single responsibility principles so that we have a progressive decoupled architecture. The key responsibilities for each of the major presentation components is shown in Figure 15.8.

Progressive decoupling allows us to continue leveraging Drupal's rendering system while simultaneously using ReactJS-based JavaScript framework to power client-side interactivity and potentially a richer user experience.

We can balance the demands of content editors and site builders. For content editors and site assemblers, progressive decoupling allows for contextualized interfaces, content workflow, site preview, and other features to remain usable and integrated with Drupal as a whole. For front-end developers, dedicating a portion of the page to a JavaScript framework enables them to pursue their own velocity while keeping site assemblers unblocked.

We used Spring Boot for developing the microservices. We created granular APIs as per the needs of the UI and adopted the "Backend for frontend" pattern. We design layered architecture with each layer handling the distinct concern as depicted in Figure 15.9

We used Okta-based security tokens for authentication and Single Sign on (SSO).

Non-Functional Requirements Design Considerations

Given below are the architecture considerations for fulfilling the NFR.

Modular, Light-weight, Responsive Architecture

The main principles of modular and light weight architecture are as follows:
- Leverage smaller JSON payloads to reduce size and number of network calls
- Leverage-client-side processing capabilities leading to less stress on server

Performance

We used multi-layer caching to achieve the high performance. Memcached framework is used for caching backend data and Varnish used as reverse proxy for caching CMS HTML pages. We have used Amazon CloudFront CDN for caching static assets.

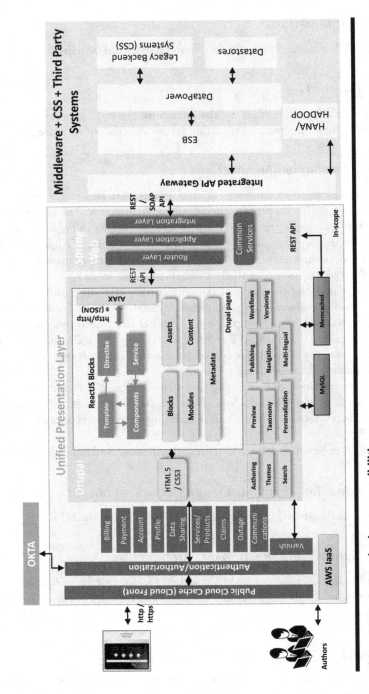

Figure 15.8 Layer-wise key responsibilities.

High Availability

We can achieve high availability of AWS cloud by designing a multi-availability zone solution for the production environment. Amazon Route 53 DNS allows to automatically failover to the disaster recovery (DR) site in case of disaster. Elastic Load Balancer to distribute the traffic across the fleet of servers and to balance the load.

Auto Scaling

We use Kubernetes auto adjustment feature to increase the pods in case of heavy load based on CPU and memory thresholds.

Security Architecture

We used Okta's Oauth 2.0-based authentication to implement the stateless token-based architecture. We have depicted the interaction of the Okta-based flow in Figure 15.10.

Rollout Strategy

In this section, we have detailed the rollout strategy.

Deployment Design

The solution was hosted in different regions to ensure high availability, high resilience and disaster recovery. The Non-Production (Dev, QA, SIT, and Pre-Production) and Production environments was hosted in a single virtual private cloud and will be isolated at the subnet level. For connecting the datacenter to AWS cloud we used AWS Direct connect that provides a dedicated link between the AWS and the datacenter.

Blue-Green Deployment Model

For deploying microservices to production environment, we used blue-green deployment model. We maintained two identical environments—blue and green in the production. Only the green instance will be serving the live Internet traffic. During deployment we route the traffic to the blue instance and deploy the updated code to green and then switch the Internet traffic to green. After this we will deploy the code to the blue environment.

Dual State Rollout Plan with Initial Co-Existence

As the new digitally transformed platform has to co-exist with the legacy platform for some time, we designed for iterative rollout strategy. We have depicted the co-existence model in Figure 15.11.

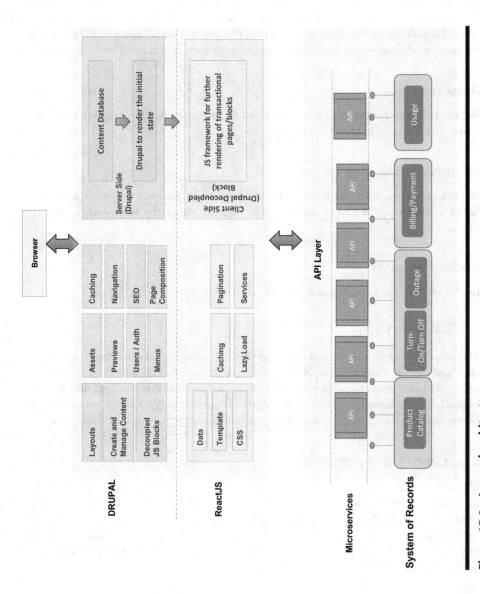

Figure 15.9 Layered architecture.

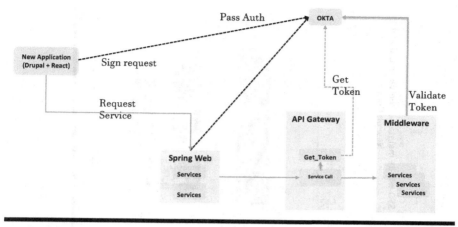

Figure 15.10   Okta security design.

We use the SSO to seamlessly login to legacy platform and the new solution. We incrementally add the features to the new platform as per the roadmap. Till the complete migration is done, we redirect the user to the old legacy platform.

Optimizing

In this section, we discuss various optimization activities such as user experience optimization. We also detail the cost optimizations and automation benefits from the solution.

Reimagining User Experience

As the principal focus of the modernization is to build a customer-centric platform, we came up with the below given list of improvements as part of digital transformation. These improvements are done iteratively with each release.

Information Architecture

- Keep the main menu structure simple and consistent across layouts making sure it's intuitive and easy to use.
- Group menu navigation based on users' needs and mental model.
- Organize content into relevant groups/categorize to increase findability.

Layout

- Ensure consistent layout with proper same/similar content categorization for findability.

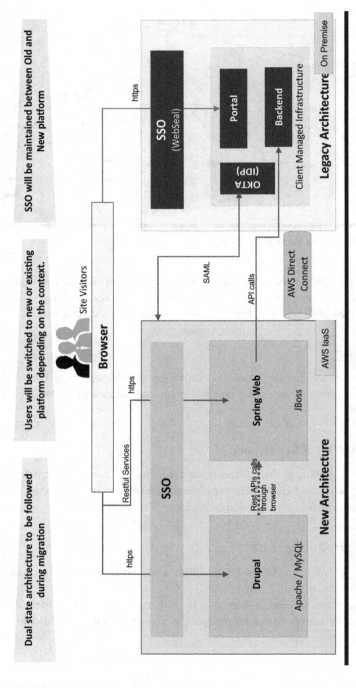

Figure 15.11 Coexistence plan of the new platform with the legacy platform.

■ While keeping the layout simple, we also need to make sure different elements are easily identifiable such as primary buttons, secondary action items and similarly non-mandatory options.

Mobility

■ Ensure that when the platform is used across devices and platforms it gives a similar experience.
■ Include mobile apps and wherever possible make it easy for customers to continue with their actions across platforms (ability to pick up where they left in one platform to the other without going through all the steps).

Content

■ Provide customized content, based on user's product and website usage patterns.
■ Ensure error messages are easy to understand and display solution to the problem.
■ Include new and useful information (recommendation, getting started, help, etc.) upfront.
■ Ensure context-based, relevant information is displayed at the appropriate places.
■ Provide task-based information (tools, offers) wherever possible.
■ Provide information about key policies on the homepage.

Navigation

■ Ensure navigation is consistent across pages and layouts making users navigate easily.
■ Reduce the current heavy navigation dependency on breadcrumbs by removing multi-level breadcrumbs where possible.
■ Match the navigation flow with the user mental model.

Total Cost of Ownership (TCO) and Business Benefits

We have listed the business benefits and TCO of the program. We optimized the platform to provide these benefits iteratively with each iteration.

Core Business Benefits

We have articulated the key business benefits in Table 15.5.

Table 15.5   Business Benefits of the New Solution

Business Benefit	Brief Details	How the New Solution Helped in Achieving the Business Benefit
Better customer self-service	How easily the customer can get customer data/services without speaking/ interacting with utility call centers	Intuitive information architecture to find the relevant information quickly. Search as the key information discovery tool.
Customer services through different delivery channels (mobile/voice/social media)	Billing/alerts/customer data available easily through multiple/safe channels	Responsive design and mobile-specific views provided omni-channel experience. CSS 3 media queries.
Better maintenance service requests	How easily the customer can get preventive/corrective service requests done by the utilities	Proactive communication module alerted on preventive maintenance. A scheduling module provided details of all the upcoming maintenance activities.
Providing new services (renewables/distributed generation)	How easily new services can be incorporated with existing customer facing channels	The new platform was integrated with all business departments and provided a single-stop-shop solution for metering and billing.
Proactive communication/ alerts from utility to customers	Payment/outage alerts	Proactive communication module alerted on preventive maintenance. The notification module that sends out the notification in various channels such as e-mail, pager etc.
Success metrics and monitoring	Customer satisfaction level, reduction in service calls, no. of customers retained/lost	Leveraged the analytics tool to measure the metrics.

Table 15.6   DevOps Benefits

Category	Process	Metrics	Before DevOps	After DevOps
Quality	Code Quality	% improvements in quality of code	< 60%	> 80%
	Unit testing	Time taken for execution and to publish results to the DEV team	> 1 hour	< 10mins
	Regression testing	Time taken for execution and to publish results to the DEV team	> 22 hours	< 7 hours
Traceability	Dashboard	% coverage of Results/Reports	Nil	> 90%
	E-mail notification	% results covered in the mail notification	Nil	100%

DevOps Business Benefits

We implemented the agile delivery model along with Jenkins-based DevOps. Table 15.6 provides the business benefits from this transformation.

Agile Delivery Business Benefits

We adopted the agile delivery methodology where the solution was delivered in sprints. Table 15.7 details the benefits of adopting the agile methodology.

Cloud Transformation Business Benefits

We implemented the below given business benefits iteratively:

- Dynamic and scalable provisioning, efficient environment management, reduced time to market and reduced TCO and usage of right sized servers.
- With cloud environments we can commission virtual machines on demand thereby drastically reducing the provisioning time.
- Faster and on-demand provisioning of resources reduces idle time and results in faster life cycles for application development and decreases time to market
- Consolidates the multiple channels for requesting environments by various projects, thereby optimizing server and application efficiency as well as infuses efficiency in managing this virtualized/cloud-based platform.
- Environment-sharing capability due to virtualization improves resource utilization and reduce the cost of hardware and software licensing expenses.

Table 15.7 Agile Methodology Benefits

Metrics	Values
Improved productivity – Continuous Integration/ Continuous Delivery (CI/CD)	• ~68% reduction in execution time of regression test suite (CI/CD vs. Manual Execution). • ~50% reduction in development Operations manual deployment (automated code quality check, unit testing, build and deployment)
Time to market–agile methodology adoption	• Improvement in release cycle time from 4 months to 2 months. • ~15% improvement in service response time.
Schedule adherence—agile methodology adoption	• 100%
Defect density	• 3 Consecutive releases with zero UAT defects.

Automation measures

We implemented the below given automation features as part of digital transformation iteratively:

- Automated code review with SonarQube at developer level and as part of the DevOps.
- Automated deployment with Jenkins for automated release management and deployment.
- Automated scalability through Kubernetes cluster using auto scalar configuration.
- Automated alerts and notification through Amazon CloudWatch.
- Automated Kubernetes pod monitoring through Prometheus.
- Automated performance and health check monitoring.
- Automated daily data sync jobs and batch jobs.
- Automated log monitoring through Splunk.

Summary

We looked at the hybrid cloud journey of XYZ e-commerce platform as the technology-centric case study. The strategy of the digital transformation was to use cloud-native features, lightweight microservices, design thinking and layer-wise security to enhance security and optimize cost. The people and culture aspects involved cloud training, establishing CCoE, collaboration platform, innovation hackathons. The digital transformation technologies mainly involved the cloud-native services such as containers, DevOps tools, open standards–based GraphQL. During the planning phase we understand the current state, challenges and aspirations after which we define the roadmap methodology. We also come up with a risk mitigation plan during planning phase. During building stage, we migrate in iterations. The optimizing phase involved metrics-based monitoring and continuous improvement.

We have detailed Digital Transformation of a Utilities portal as an example of customer-centric action. The key solution tenets such as layered microservices, open source, API-first design and DevOps were defined as part of the strategy and vision phase. Modern UI frameworks such as ReactJS and REST-based microservices are chosen as part of digital transformation technologies and capabilities. In the process and governance track, we understand the current challenges and define the digital transformation principles and roadmap during planning phase, we define the solution views and rollout strategy in the building phase and lay out the business benefits and cost benefits in the optimizing phase.

Reference

1. Loonam, J., et al. (2018). "Towards digital transformation: lessons learned from traditional organizations." *Strategic Change* 27(2), 101–109.

Chapter 16

Digital Transformation of Intranet Platforms

Introduction

Traditional Intranet platforms catered to the employees of an organization. The Intranet platforms provided policy documents, self-service tools and other resources. The traditional Intranet platforms lacked employee engagement features such as personalization, search, mobile enablement and others. The expectation of the current generation of employees are shaped by the popular social media platforms and e-commerce platforms.

Modern experience platforms offer personalized, engaging experience to the users with many features such as mobile apps, intuitive information discovery and such. Enterprises embark on journey of digital transformation from traditional web platforms (such as Intranet) into experience platforms.

In this chapter, we discuss various factors that go into a digital transformation of traditional web platforms into modern experience platforms.

Digital Transformation Exercise

In this section, we discuss various factors that go into the digital transformation of traditional Intranet platforms into personalized employee experience platforms.

DOI: 10.1201/9781003390893-22

Drivers

Let us understand the employee-related, technology-related and business-related drivers for the digital transformation.

Employee Drivers

Employees who use the Intranet platform want to achieve higher productivity and expect tools to help them work at flexible hours from anywhere. Employees also expect the self-service tools to be available through mobile apps and the experience of the platform to be engaging. Personalization of information (based on their department), intuitive search for faster information discovery are other major expectations from employees. Achieving work-life balance and enhanced collaboration are key expectations from the employees.

Technology Drivers

The pervasiveness of mobile apps has compelled the organizations to deliver mobile apps for engaging the employees. The chatbots and virtual assistants and other Artificial Intelligence (AI)-based technologies have redefined the information discovery, self-service and customer service. Cloud-based desktop-as-service (DaaS) and Virtual Desktop Interface (VDI) technologies have made the desktop procurement and provisioning processes efficient.

We have depicted the evolution of technologies shaping the employee experience in Figure 16.1.

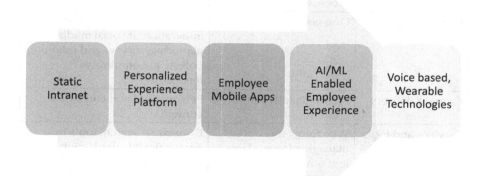

Figure 16.1   Evolution of technologies related to employee experience.

Business Drivers

Enterprises need to engage the employees to improve the employee satisfaction and employee productivity. High employee satisfaction attract talent and help in retaining existing talent. Organizations also strive to be agile and responsive to the market dynamics and as a result wants to create lean, agile and simplified processes. Organizations also plan to lower the infrastructure cost and maintenance cost for the underlying technologies.

Reimagining Opportunities Traditional Intranet Platforms

Based on the drivers, Table 16.1 provides the reimagining opportunities for an employee experience platform.

Table 16.1   Reimagining Opportunities for an Employee Experience Platform

Criteria	Traditional Intranet Platform	Reimagining Opportunity for Employee Experience Platform
Delivery channel	Mainly web platform accessed on desktops	Web and mobile platform mainly accessed from mobile devices.
User experience	Mainly static content	Personalized content, employee-centric experience, expectation of experience similar to that of popular social media platforms.
Employee processes	Complex, time-consuming multi-step processes,	Automated, simplified processes with auto-approval.
Communication	One-way	Multi-way communication, integration of social media platforms, surveys and opinion polls to get employees' feedback.
Content delivery	Predominantly static content	Personalized and contextual content.
Services and tools	Web forms for managing leave, claims and others.	Contextual search, tools to enable flexible work, mobile apps, chatbots and virtual assistants.
Information discovery	Time-consuming information discovery	Smart and personalized search, analytics driven recommendations.

Transforming the Employee Experience

The digital transformation exercise involves multiple elements such as process, technology, governance and others. In this section we discuss the key elements involved in the digital transformation of traditional Intranet platforms to modern employee experience platforms.

We have identified the four key elements of employee experience in Figure 16.2. Employee journey (various phases of employee engagement) optimization, Technology optimization, process optimization and Governance are four dimensions required for transforming traditional websites into modern digital platforms.

As part of employee journey optimization, we identify the current steps, the challenges in various stages of employee journey within an organization such as employee onboarding, employee orientation, employee learning and training and employee engagement.

Technology optimization involves using modern digital technologies to enable and support digital transformation. We personalize the employee experience based on the employee role, skill set, preferences and other factors. We provide self-service portals and mobile apps to enable employees to complete their tasks quickly and improve their productivity. Usability and accessibility of the platform is enhanced to engage the employees.

Existing processes are optimized to improve the overall employee experience. Process simplification, process automation are the most effective methods to optimize the process. For instance a multi-step approval process is simplified and can be made as an automated self-approval process to complete the process quickly. Design thinking methodology is adopted to identify the friction points in the existing processes. Forums, social media channels, chatbots, centralized knowledge base and similar methods are used to foster the communication and collaboration across the employees.

We define the governance for the processes through metrics and monitoring. Feedback tools and analytics tools are used to monitor the metrics related to employee satisfaction, employee engagement and the findings are used to continuously improve the engagement models.

In subsequent sections, we discuss the elements of employee experience transformation in detail.

Employee Experience Journey Optimization

The 360-degree digital transformation of employee experience should optimize all the phases of the employee journey within an organization and it should optimize the experience at all touchpoints.

We have depicted the key activities and the experience enhancements at each phase of the employee journey in Figure 16.3. The first step of the employee journey is employee onboarding during which the employee interviews, screening and

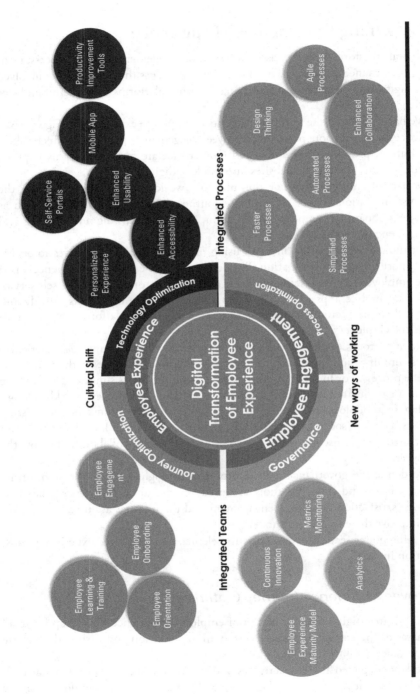

Figure 16.2 Elements of digital transformation of employee experience.

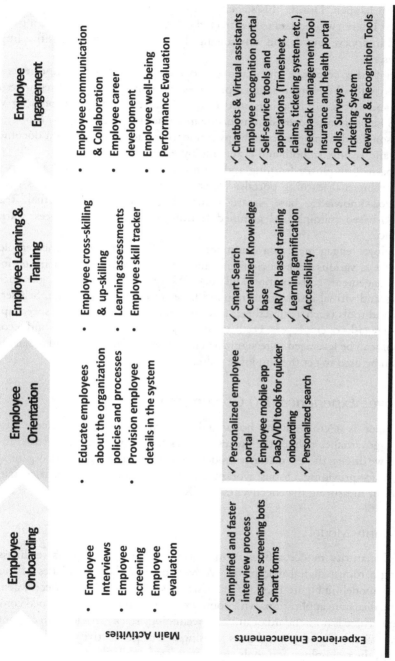

Figure 16.3 Experience enhancements in employee journey.

evaluation happen. During this stage, we can use the resume screening tools and simplified interview processes to fast-track the interview process. Completing all the required interview rounds and announcing the results faster has a positive impact on the user.

During the employee orientation, the human resources team orients the employee with all the organizational processes and policies. Required resources like laptops and access will be provisioned to the employee. During this phase, a VDI or DaaS helps in faster provisioning of the machines to the employees. Mobile app and personalized employee portal helps employees to access the relevant documents quickly and ensures smooth and faster employee orientation.

As part of employee learning and training, employees cross-skill and up-skill using the internal learning portals. We can enable employees with tools such as centralized knowledge base, smart search, Augmented Reality/Virtual Reality (AR/VR)-based training and gamified learning to improve employees' learning experience.

Employee engagement is a continuous stage where we can enhance employee experience at various stages such as communication, career development, performance management, collaboration and such. We can leverage technologies such as chatbots and virtual assistants to respond faster to employees' queries. Self-service portals and tools (such as timesheet, ticketing system and others) can speed up the day-to-day tasks of employees. Feedback management tool and rewards and recognition tools can be leveraged to recognizing employees. Polls, surveys and social media tools can be used to get the employee pulse.

Employee Experience (EX) Governance

Governance is a cross-cutting horizontal concern across various phases of EX. Broadly, governance defines the processes, roles and responsibilities for EX. In this section, we discuss the EX maturity model that defines various stages of organization readiness for providing a robust workplace. We also define the key metrics that can be used for measuring the effectiveness of EX.

EX Maturity Model

The EX maturity model defines various stages of an organization's readiness for building a robust digital workplace. We have defined the four phases of the EX maturity model (in Figure 16.4). In the basic EX stage, the technology ecosystem has multiple disparate applications with complex business processes and siloed communication. There is no standard or uniform technology stack. This leads to continuous context switching among employees, causing loss of productivity. In the integrated EX stage, the technology and tools are standardized, while the service and functions are consolidated.

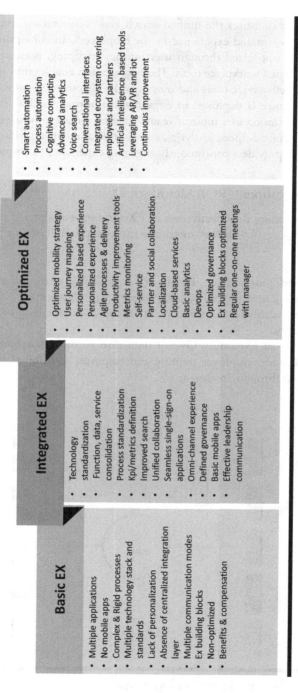

Smart EX

- Smart automation
- Process automation
- Cognitive computing
- Advanced analytics
- Voice search
- Conversational interfaces
- Integrated ecosystem covering employees and partners
- Artificial intelligence based tools
- Leveraging AR/VR and iot
- Continuous improvement

Optimized EX

- Optimized mobility strategy
- User journey mapping
- Personalized based experience
- Personalized experience
- Agile processes & delivery
- Productivity improvement tools
- Metrics monitoring
- Self-service
- Partner and social collaboration
- Localization
- Cloud-based services
- Basic analytics
- Devops
- Optimized governance
- Ex building blocks optimized
- Regular one-on-one meetings with manager

Integrated EX

- Technology standardization
- Function, data, service consolidation
- Process standardization
- Kpi/metrics definition
- Improved search
- Unified collaboration
- Seamless single-sign-on applications
- Omni-channel experience
- Defined governance
- Basic mobile apps
- Effective leadership communication

Basic EX

- Multiple applications
- No mobile apps
- Complex & Rigid processes
- Multiple technology stack and standards
- Lack of personalization
- Absence of centralized integration layer
- Multiple communication modes
- Ex building blocks
- Non-optimized
- Benefits & compensation

Figure 16.4   Employee experience Maturity model.

The organization uses the unified search and collaboration strategy to provide a holistic and integrated experience to the employees. In the optimized EX stage, the EX will be optimized through user journey mapping, persona definition and personalized digital workplace tools. The organization enables multiple productivity improvement self-service tools and monitors the effectiveness continuously. A well-defined governance is deployed to engage and improve the EX. In the smart EX stage, the organization uses innovative and state-of-the-art technologies, such as cognitive computing, advanced analytics, voice search and conversational interfaces like AI, AR/VR, to provide a continuously engaging experience to employees.

Return of Investment (ROI) Metrics of EX

We need to measure the effectiveness of EX through well-defined metrics. We have depicted in Figure 16.5 the key metrics to measure the ROI of an effective employee experience.

- Increased productivity: Employees completing more tasks with increased quality is a measure of increased employee productivity.
- Higher inclusivity: Greater diversity of the workforce is an indicator of higher inclusivity.
- Overall cost reduction: Overall reduction in the infrastructure, application maintenance, employee training and employee attrition-related costs can be achieved through an elegant EX.

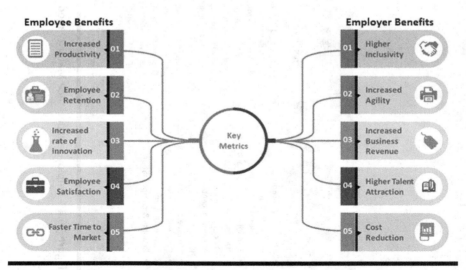

Figure 16.5   Key metrics for Employee experience.

- Increased business revenue: If the organization provides self-service and analytics tools to employees, they will use it to cross-sell and up-sell the products, thus improving the business revenue.
- Faster time to market: Agile delivery models and productivity improvement tools help in accelerating the time to market for products and services.
- Rate of innovation: The shared knowledge hub, innovative culture and autonomy accelerate the rate of employee innovation.
- Improved customer satisfaction: Engaged employees with right set of tools and quicker access to relevant information lead to improved customer satisfaction.
- Increased organization agility and flexibility: Productivity improvement tools help employees to be more responsive to implement organizational and business changes.
- Higher talent attraction: Brand image and efficient interview processes help in talent attraction.
- Higher employee retention: Improved employee engagement increases the employee retention rate.
- Improved employee satisfaction: Employee-friendly policies, personalization and flexibility improves the overall employee satisfaction.
- Business process time: The time taken for employee-related business processes is measured by this metric.
- Time to productivity: The time taken by a new joiner to be fully productive is measured by this metric.
- Adoption of the digital workplace: The percentage of knowledge workers who are using digital workplace tools is measured by this metric.
- Automation percentage: This determines the number of rules-driven processes that are automated.
- Utilization of knowledge base: This comprises various metrics such as the percentage of incidents avoided and articles shared to understand the effectiveness of the knowledge base and search efficiency.
- Employee engagement score: Understand the overall employee engagement through the employee engagement survey.

Technology Optimization

We have defined the four prioritized stages to transform the existing platform into a smart digital workplace and derive maximum business value, and find a quicker time to market (in Figure 16.6). We can start using the facelift method, where we reskin the existing platform with the new experience and provide a gateway for existing enterprise applications. This is a low-hanging-fruit as we can quickly reuse the as-is processes. In the second step, we evaluate various commercial tools and cloud platforms to select the most appropriate one to define the next generation of EX. We can identify the quick wins that can be implemented using the selected tools.

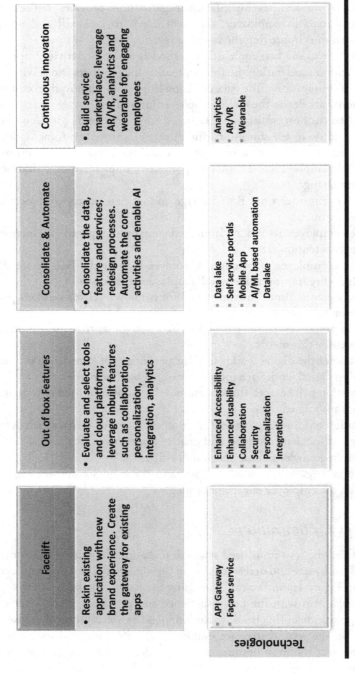

Figure 16.6   Stages for transforming the Intranet to employee experience platform.

We then leverage the inbuilt features of the selected platform, such as collaboration, security, personalization, integration and analytics, to enable modern EX features. We can derive maximum business value in a quick time using out-of-the-box features. In the next level, we consolidate data, features and services to maximize the information value for the employees. We also automate the core activities, redesign processes and enable AI for building smart digital workplaces. The next step in the journey is that of continuous innovation wherein we build a service marketplace in our platform and leverage cutting edge technologies such, as AI, AR/VR, wearables etc., to actively engage with employees.

Process Optimization

In this section, we define the process optimization best practices and improvement guidelines of EX.

Reduce the cognitive load on employees: The EX platform should provide intuitive information architecture, personalization, contextual information and smart search to reduce the overall cognitive load on the employees. Employees should be able to find the relevant information quickly.

Enterprise social media: Enable corporate social media platforms where employees can voice their opinions, connect and share.

Optimizing information value: Organizations should be able to maximize the information value for the employees by providing relevant, timely and reliable information. The information should be usable and actionable for the employees. As majority of employees' time is spent in finding relevant information [1], the organization must make it easier for employees to find what they're looking for that is spread across multiple systems. This includes providing intuitive information architecture, smart search, personalized content delivery, personalized recommendations, metadata tagging etc.

Optimal user experience: The user experience for the digital workplace should provide a holistic and a "single-stop-shop" experience. Provide a simplified and minimalist user interface that is easy to navigate and easy to find. Organizations should use rapid and iterative design principles to continuously improve the user experience.

Unified security: Enable a single employee identity across all applications. This helps the employee to get consistent access across all applications.

Analytics: Organizations can use the employee surveys and feedback, and analyze the employee voice to identify and address the gaps. Based on the employee journey mapping, we can identify the popular touchpoints and optimize the employee journey.

Omni-channel assistants: The EX platform should provide chatbots and virtual assistants to employees on all channels.

Data-driven decision-making: EX platforms should provide tools such as calculators to help employees make informed and data-driven decisions.

Gamification: The concept of gamification can be used to align, encourage employees for achieving the organization goals. Gamification can be used for features such as leader boards, sales dashboards, health initiatives, employee wellness goals, collaboration features and others.

Idea hub: Employees should be able to contribute to the organization's knowledge base through blogs, articles, how to documents and such. The idea hub acts as an innovative tool to promote innovation and knowledge sharing culture amongst employees. We could also use the idea hub to brainstorm various initiatives and internal campaigns, and for innovating process improvements. By harnessing the collective intelligence of its employees, an organization can innovate faster and be more agile.

Employee safety, health and wellbeing: EX platforms should provide tools to promote and encourage the overall wellbeing of the employees.

Insights and analytics: EX platforms should understand the employee behavior and provide vital insights to the employees and management. In essence, cognitive digital workplaces that analyze the employee data to recommend the tools needed for better work quality.

Removal of barriers: The organization should proactively remove all the barriers that restrict employee productivity. Employees will be better engaged and motivated, with their productivity improving, given that there are no barriers.

Rewards and recognition: The organization should be able to recognize and reward its employees, and celebrate their contribution, participation and achievements. Build a culture of appreciation and recognition. Reward employees to recognize the organization values.

Less complexity and simplicity: The organization should simplify the business processes so that employees' productivity is not impacted.

Tools and technologies: Provide tools, technologies and processes to enable employees to work from anywhere anytime. Make the work enjoyable again by introducing policies such as BYOD (Bring Your Own Device), on-the-job learning and training opportunities.

Articulation of organization goals: Articulate and communicate the organizations goals and vision clearly and define the quantifiable metrics for each employee to fulfil them. More than half of the employees feel that communication of core values improves the positive relationship with managers [2].

Collaborative culture: Define, design, build and adopt a collaborative culture across the organization. Encourage regular one-on-one discussions between the manager and employee. The manager could provide regular feedback, appreciation, track progress, identify growth opportunities, define mutually agreed future goals and increase their trust with their reportees. Regular one-on-one meetings also act as open communication mechanism for employees where they can voice their concerns and policy questions. Employees who had regular one-on-one meetings reported positive EX.

Team bonding: Encourage team building and professional bonding among employees. For instance, an employee with a best friend at work performs better. Investing in team development improves the overall organization efficiency.

On-the-job learning: Enabling employees for on-the-job learning as professional growth acts as a key motivating factor and improves the employee performance. Incentivizing the learning, training and growth ultimately leads to a positive EX [2].

Work-life balance: Organizations should design policies to provide the right work-life balance for their employees. This includes predictable paid time offs, paid vacation, flexible work hours, leaves to take care of family commitments and such. Employees with predictable time offs have lower turnover rate [3].

Innovative culture: Foster a culture of creativity and encourage employees to innovate and take risks. When employees are more creative and share innovative ideas, the team performs better.

Continuous monitoring: Define a continuous result-oriented metrics-based employee progress monitoring mechanism. Establish regular 360-degree feedback channels and articulate quantifiable goals for each of the employee and track them.

Ways of working: Define "ways of working," providing common terms, processes, tools, standards and protocols for each job role. Managers should clearly articulate the responsibilities for each role. Also address and remove all the barriers that come in the way of working. This includes language barriers, complex processes, multi-level approvals and such.

Digital workplace ecosystem: The digital workplace should be leveraged for suppliers, partners, vendors, contractors and partners wherein all the participants can contribute, share knowledge and get involved in the seamless process.

Career mobility: Providing newer roles and job responsibilities help employees to widen their skills and improves engagement, productivity and teamwork.

EX Measurement and Improvement

EX can be measured with five dimensions—belonging (a feeling of being part of team), purpose (understanding the importance of one's work), achievement (sense of accomplishment of the completed work), happiness (a general pleasant feeling in the work environment) and vigor (energy, excitement and enthusiasm at work). As per the research [4], employee-friendly practices such as building organizational trust, work relationships, meaningful work, recognition feedback and growth, empowerment and work-life balance heavily influence the EX dimensions. These dimensions ultimately impact the work performance and employee retention.

As per the research [4], the below given practices are needed to create effective EXs:

Personalization: An employee should be able to personalize the workspace as per his/her needs. The organization should be able to provide personalized learning, training and development opportunities at work. The organization should also provide the personalized tools and information to the employee based on his or her needs and goals through the digital workplace.

Transparency: Employees seek to understand the contribution of their work to the organization goals. The organization should also be proactive and open in its policies and communications.

Simplicity: Organizations should remove barriers and non-value adding processes to ease the EX. Organizations should provide easy and relevant information access and simplify processes for its employees.

Authenticity: The EX should be part of the organization culture and value system. Organizations should implement employee-friendly practices.

Responsiveness: Employees should provide and seek feedback about their performance from the organizations. Organizations can use the employee voice to understand the concerns and warning signs, and proactively act upon them to improve the productivity, performance and the overall EX.

Summary

The key drivers for the digital transformation of the Intranet platforms are employee-related, business-related and technology-related. The main employee-related drivers are higher productivity, personalization, intuitive search, work-life balance and enhanced collaboration. The main technology-related drivers are mobile app enablement, enabling employees with chatbot and virtual assistants and providing VDIs for employees. The main business drivers are improving the employee satisfaction and employee productivity. Employee journey (various phases of employee engagement) optimization, Technology optimization, process optimization and Governance are four dimensions required for transforming traditional websites into modern digital platforms. Employee journey optimization includes optimizing the experience during journey stages such as employee onboarding, employee orientation, employee learning and training and employee engagement. EX maturity model defines various stages of an organization's readiness for building a robust digital workplace; EX maturity model consists of stages such as basic EX, integrated EX, optimized EX and smart EX. The key metrics to measure employee experience are higher inclusivity, increased agility, increased business revenue, higher talent attraction, cost reduction, increased productivity, employee retention, increased rate of innovation, employee satisfaction and faster time to market. The main four stages for transforming the Intranet as an employee experience platform are facelift, leveraging out-of-the-box features, consolidate and automate and continuous innovation.

References

1. Findwise. (2012). Enterprise Search and Findability Survey 2012. Retrieved July 15, 2014, from www.findwise.com/blog/theenterprise-search-and-findability-report2 012-is-ready/
2. PRWeb. (February 21, 2018). PRWeb. www.prweb.com/releases/2018/02/prweb1 5229205.htm
3. Making Time Off Predictable and Required. (October 1, 2009). Harvard Business Review. https://hbr.org/2009/10/making-time-off-predictable-and-required
4. Lesser, E., Mertens, J., Barrientos, M. P., & Singer, M. (2016). *Designing Employee Experience: How a Unifying Approach Can Enhance Engagement and Productivity.* IBM Institute for Business Value.

Appendix A – Digital Transformation Playbook

In this appendix we map the key phases, activities, outcome and tools/frameworks that can be used in each of the phases of a digital transformation exercise. Enterprises can use it as a reference document and as a checklist for their digital transformation exercise.

Phase	Activity	Outcome	Tools/Frameworks/ Mechanisms
Strategy & Vision	Identification of business process changes (such as reimagining of inventory management, supply chain automation and such)	Quantification of business outcome	Process simplification, Digitization, Design Thinking
	Identification of key areas of optimization (such as faster time to market, cost optimization, maintenance optimization and such)	Definition of success metrics	Design Thinking

Phase	Activity	Outcome	Tools/Frameworks/ Mechanisms
	Business process transformation	Improved business processes, agile processes, nimble processes, Prioritized business capabilities for transformation	Design Thinking, Agile delivery model, Business process assessment
	Identification of core customer engagement areas (such as engaging mobile apps, hyper-personalization)	Customer engagement metrics	User-centric design, Self service, Automation, Virtual assistants, Digital Persona, AI-driven Search, customer feedback and survey tools
	Identification of areas for automation (such as automated query resolution, infrastructure provision automation and such)	Definition of Automation metrics	Process Automation, Robotic Process Automation (RPA)
	Identification of core business metrics that need to be improved (such as customer lifetime value, order value, ticket resolution time, customer satisfaction index, productivity improvement and such)	Definition of Key business metrics	Analytics tools for tracking metrics, Real time monitoring tools, Smart recommendation tools, Personalization
	Identification of new revenue streams and monetization opportunities (such as data as a service)	New product and service areas,	Digital marketplace, API marketplace,

Phase	Activity	Outcome	Tools/Frameworks/ Mechanisms
	Organization structure changes to align to the digital transformation	Revised organization structure	
	Acceleration of innovation	Competitive advantage	Fail-fast learn fast
	Gathering deeper insights on customer experience	Improved ways to engage customer.	User journey mapping, User analytics tools, prototyping tools, co-innovation with customer
	Digital maturity assessment	Faster digital transformation	Capability mapping, Gap assessment,
People & Culture	Train people on new processes and technologies	People with new skillset, improved learnability	Training and learning workshops, Self-learning tools, skill-gap assessment
	Create a centralized knowledge base to harness collective intelligence	Improved user productivity, empowered users	Collaboration tools, productivity tracking tools, AI-based search tools.
	Culture re-alignment	Improved collaboration, faster experimentation, customer focus.	Ways of working,
	Redefined agile culture	Agile mindset	Agile workshops
Technology	Identification of right-fit technology	Improved automation, improved productivity, faster innovation	Production evaluation, Technology assessment, Proof of concept (PoC)
	Identification of ways to optimize compute resources	Improved scalability, Reduced cost, flexible integrations	Cloud computing, Open source tools

Phase	Activity	Outcome	Tools/Frameworks/ Mechanisms
	Identification of ways to automate using technology	Improved automation, improved productivity,	Artificial Intelligence, Machine Learning
	Identification of technologies for improved customer engagement	Improved customer engagement	Virtual assistants, digital personas, conversational interfaces, Mobile Apps, AR/VR platforms
	Migration to modern technology stack	Reduced technical debt, Reduced cost, improved scalability	Automated migration tools, Pilot migration
Governance	Identification of ways to improve monitoring	Real time monitoring and notification	Monitoring tools, Analytics tools
	Identification of ways to improve the project management	Faster delivery, faster time to market	Agile delivery model
	Defining roadmap for digital transformation	Quicker realization of business values	Agile deliver model
	Change Management	Faster change handling	Incident management tools
	Operation digitization	Automated operations, improved productivity, faster response times	Robotic process automation, AI/ML models
	Process digitization	Optimized processes	Low code no code tools, Citizen development tools, Business process management tools

Index

Printed in the United States
by Baker & Taylor Publisher Services